Footsteps of Faith

Old Testament, Volume 1

Revised Edition

God Calls Us

by

Bernice Claire Jordan

BCM International, Inc.

237 Fairfield Avenue, Upper Darby, PA 19082-2299

798 Main Street East, Hamilton, Ontario L8M 1L4 Canada

39a Swiss Road, Weston-super-Mare, N. Somerset BS23 3AY England

Footsteps of Faith is BCM's primary Bible teaching curriculum for children's Bible Clubs. This unique series has been revised for teaching God's Word in other settings, such as Sunday school, children's church, Christian schools and home schooling.

Revision Committee

Revised by Pamela Rowntree
Edited by Donna Culver
David and Lois Haas
Richard Winters
Patricia Black

Cover design:
Bert VandenBos
Book design and layout:
Bert VandenBos and Elinor Fischer

Original title: *Genesis*

ISBN 0-86508-027-5

CONTENTS

God Calls Us
Course Overview

No.	Title	Theme God Calls Us...	Scripture	Verse
1	God Creates the World	By His Works	Gen. 1:1-25	Rev. 4:11
2	God Creates Man	By His Love	Gen. 1:26-2:25	Gen. 2:7
3	Adam & Eve Disobey God	By His Mercy	Gen. 2:16,17; 3:1-24	Rom. 5:19
4	Cain & Abel Bring Sacrifices	Through the Sacrifice of the Lord Jesus	Gen. 4:1-16	Rom. 5:8
5	Enoch Goes to Heaven	By His Word	Gen. 4:16-26; 5:1-32	Rom. 10:17
6	God Destroys the World by a Flood	To Safety in Jesus	Gen. 5:1-9:19	John 10:9a
7	God Confuses the Language	To Obey Him	Gen 9:1-19; 11:1-9	Acts 5:29b
8	God Calls Abraham	To Serve Him	Gen. 11:10:12:9	Gen.12:2
9	Abraham & Lot Choose	To Make Right Choices	Gen. 13; 17:1-8; 18, 19	Josh. 24:15
10-1	Ishmael and Isaac Are Born	To Trust Him	Gen. 15:18-21	Prov. 3:5
10-2	God Provides a Sacrifice		Gen. 22:1-14	
11-1	Jacob and Esau Are Born	To Learn His Ways	Gen. 23:1-25:28	Gal. 6:7
11-2	Jacob & Esau Reap What They Sow		Gen. 25-27	
12-1	Jacob Leaves Home	To Make Us Like Jesus	Gen. 28-30	Phil. 1:6
12-2	Jacob Becomes Israel, a Prince		Gen. 31:1-33:16	
13	Joseph Obeys His Father	To Do His Will	Gen. 35, 37	Psa. 40:8
14-1	Joseph Suffers Unjustly	To Suffer for Him	Gen. 39, 40	Psa. 46:1
14-2	Joseph Is Promoted to the Palace		Gen. 41:1-45	
15	Joseph Forgives His Brothers	To Forgive Others	Gen. 41:46-50:26	Eph. 4:32

INTRODUCTION

Footsteps of Faith is an eight-volume Bible teaching curriculum that covers the Bible in basically chronological order. Its overall aim is to help children respond to the love of God in Christ and learn to walk in the footsteps of faith and obedience.

Each volume is complete in itself and centered around a theme that is carried through every lesson in that volume to provide for consistent learning as well as continual review and application of truth.

The course is non-graded and undated, written for teaching children ages 6-12, but adaptable to different age groups and many teaching situations. It has been used effectively in Bible Clubs, children's church programs, vacation Bible schools and Sunday school classes, as well as in Christian schools and home school classes.

The series...

- shows God at work in the world. The Old Testament points ahead to Christ's coming, revealing man's fall into sin, God's promise of a Savior and His program for accomplishing this. The New Testament records the actual fulfillment of God's program in the birth of Christ, His life, death and resurrection, the birth of the Church, the establishing of a missionary program and the yet-to-be-fulfilled promise of Christ's return!
- teaches Bible doctrine and history along with the principles of Christian living.
- emphasizes Scripture memorization and provides Bible study helps which are coordinated with the lessons and may be used as work sheets or take-home devotionals.
- is both evangelistic and Christian-growth oriented, clearly presenting the plan of salvation and emphasizing practical Christian living.

The lessons...

- emphasize specific Bible truths.
- include practical, hands-on application of those truths for both Christian and non-Christian children.
- are structured with a teaching aim designed to help the teacher present the Bible truth and encourage the children to relate and apply that truth to their daily lives.

A unique review system...

- is built into each volume and visualizes the main theme of that course and the complementary lesson themes.
- relates the lessons logically to each other and to the central theme of the course.
- provides a framework for remembering biblical truth so that the children can apply it in their daily lives.
- enables the teacher to review and reinforce previous lessons and memory verses quickly, regularly and in an interesting way.
- stimulates the children to *see*, *hear*, *verbalize* and *do*, thus involving them in the learning process.

Correlated visual aids enhance learning.

- Full-color flannelgraph figures focus attention and encourage children to visualize scenes as you tell the Bible story.
- Correlated flannel backgrounds provide a scenic backdrop for the figures. (Available from

BCM Distribution Center in black and white, with instructions for coloring.)

- The *Bible Verses Visualized* packet furnishes colorful visuals for teaching every Bible verse in the course.
- Memory verse tokens and token holders (adapted from the review charts) are a convenient way for children to collect all the verses.
- Suggested optional activities, methods and visuals provide the teacher with a wealth of ideas for teaching children with widely differing needs.

God Calls Us, volume one of the *Footsteps of Faith* series, covers the book of Genesis. It aims to help children know and trust the Genesis record of the creation, of the entrance of sin, of God's dealing with man's sin and of how God works with and provides for those who follow His call.

The course answers two basic questions: "How does God call us?" and "Why does God call us?" The lessons illustrate the truth of the lesson theme through the Bible content. The course clearly presents the plan of salvation and emphasizes practical teaching that shows children how to respond to the truth in their daily lives.

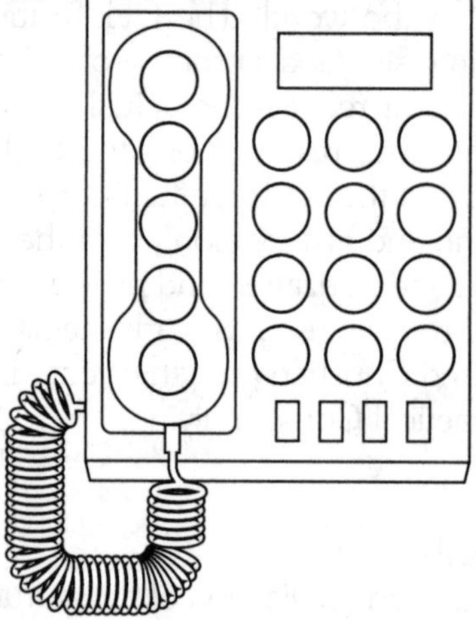

This volume's review system is a flannelgraph Telephone Review Chart and circle symbols on which are printed lesson themes and corresponding memory verse references. Using these the teacher can visually coordinate individual lessons with the overall theme "God Calls Us" and involve students in an enjoyable review of Bible facts and truths as well as Bible memory verses.

Understand Your Children

Today's children are different from previous generations. Growing up in a fast-paced, "instant-everything" society, accessing the world through computers and the internet, they are bright, eager to learn and well informed. They...

- receive much of their information in "sound bytes" (capsulized reports).
- are accustomed to seeing most problems solved within a 30- or 60-minute time slot in a television schedule.
- consequently, have short attention spans.
- expect great variety in all they see and hear.
- can be impatient with sitting still, being quiet or waiting.

Children learn in many different ways:

- some by *seeing* what they're learning;
- others by *talking* about it;

- still others by *moving* or *doing*—being actively involved or making things;
- some process information globally—by seeing "the big picture";
- others are analytic thinkers and want all the details.

Remember these things when preparing to teach. Try a variety of the teaching methods and options suggested in the text, even if they do not all appeal to you. They will help you incorporate variety in methods and visuals and capsulize important points in "sound bytes" the children can see and hear over and over. You will soon know which are most effective with your class members.

Many of today's children come from stable homes where parents are working hard to prepare them for the future. Many others come from broken families or from homes where parents have no time to spend with them or listen to them. Most of them...

- are exposed by the media to too much too early.
- are being conditioned to accept materialism, deteriorating moral standards and a secular world view as the norm. Unless they are taught the eternal Word of God, how are they to know otherwise?
- are assaulted by violence in the media; some, in their homes and neighborhoods.
- feel a deep need for someone to love them, to care about them, to give them a reason to hope.

What a privilege—and what a sobering responsibility—to take to them the wonderful news that God loves them, that He has provided salvation for them and that He has a plan for their lives! There is hope in Him!

For *GOD never changes*! His truth is timeless! The experiences of Adam and Eve, Cain and Abel, Noah, Abraham and Lot, Jacob and Esau and Joseph are not that much different from experiences of people today. God's eternal Word is a guidebook for living a life that pleases God in any age. Knowing Him and walking in the footsteps of faith and obedience provide security and stability in an uncertain world.

Because we know God and His Word, we can demonstrate God's love to them; we can lead them to that secure place in HIM in the midst of their insecure world. So take time to get to know your students and understand their needs.

Prepare Yourself to Be God's channel

You, the teacher, are the living link between God's truth and the children in your class. You channel Christ's love to them. You teach them God's Word so that they may understand His truth and receive Christ as Savior, then follow Him in loving obedience. You model how to practice in daily life the truth they are learning. And you are their guide to discovering truth for themselves and attaining their greatest potential for God.

- Submit yourself to God that you may be a Spirit-empowered teacher.
- Expect God to speak to you personally as you study your lesson each week, then to guide you as you prepare to teach.
- Realize that you are a tool in God's hands. As you depend on Him, He will work through you and in the hearts of the children to draw them to Himself.
- Enjoy your class! Be enthusiastic, enter into activities with the children so they see you not only as teacher but as a friend.
- Encourage the children to bring their Bibles and plan ways for them to use them every week. Teach them how to find passages in Scripture. Frequently have them follow along in their Bibles as you teach the lesson. As you instruct boys and girls to love and respect God's Word, show them how to use it correctly and inspire them to obey it, you give them an invaluable gift that will go with them throughout life. (If some don't have Bibles, look for

a place to get them inexpensively—a Bible society or an organization that distributes free ones.)

- REVIEW, REVIEW, REVIEW! Some studies show that people need to hear new information up to 75 times to learn it.
- Avoid using many questions that can be answered with a simple yes or no.
- Use the open-ended questions suggested in the lesson or others you devise yourself to involve the children in the learning process and find out what they have or have not learned. Then you will have the opportunity to correct faulty understanding and they will learn more because they are thinking and interacting.
- Avoid calling on students who find it difficult or embarrassing to read aloud or answer questions publicly. Find other ways to involve them until they feel safe enough to interact.

Remember that your effectiveness in class often depends upon the relationship that you have established with students outside of class.

- Find ways to spend time with students—before and after class— by attending some of their school or neighborhood activities, and visiting at least some of their homes.
- Learn their names and show a real interest in them.
- Listen when they talk about their families, their friends and their struggles. Listening shows the child that you care and helps you learn how to apply Scripture effectively.
- Notice individual's strengths and affirm them regularly.
- Compliment those you see practicing what they're learning.
- Seek to discern the spiritual progress of individual students and help them to grow in Christlikeness.
- Don't be afraid to be explicit when dealing with the issues that surround them. They are exposed to life experiences and life styles far beyond what they should be. They need to know what God has to say and how to live for Him in the midst of their life situations. Ask God to guide you and make you sensitive to their needs and His direction.
- Pray for them.
- Make the brief time they spend with you each week a happy time, a safe place—a refuge.

Prepare Your Lesson

Pray that God will speak to you through the Scripture passage, then guide you as you prepare to teach.

- Study the Scripture passage thoroughly, making notes of points that seem important to you. Look for answers to six important questions: *Who* was involved? *What* was happening? *Where* were they? *When* did it happen? *Why* did it happen? or *Why* did he say that? *How* did it happen?
- Read the printed lesson, thinking it through with your children in mind. Each part of the lesson has a specific purpose.
  The **Aim** is the statement of what you want to accomplish—with God's help—as you present the lesson.
  The **Introduction** is a plan for getting the students' attention and directing their thinking in preparation for the Bible story.
  The **Bible Content** is the Bible story and the Bible truth it illustrates and reinforces.
  The **Conclusion** is a plan for completing the lesson by showing the children how to apply the Bible truth and providing a way for them to respond to it in daily life.

Using a lesson plan keeps you on track. It helps you use your time wisely and accomplish the purpose God lays on your heart for the lesson. Follow the one in the teacher's text or use it as a pattern to write your own.

- Make simple outline notes to use as a guide when teaching. Put them in your Bible so the children will see you teaching from God's Word, not the teacher's manual.

- Sort out the figures you will need and stack them in the order you will use them. Put them in a file folder to carry to class.
- Put the flannel backgrounds on the flannelboard in the order they will be used with the last one on the bottom. Secure them to the top of the board with large clamps.
- Use sketches in the lesson as guides for placing figures on scenes. Check from the side of the board to see how they appear. Remove them (in the same order you put them there so they're ready to use again) and practice placing them as you stand at the side of the board. Check from the front to see if they are straight and in their proper places.
- Practice telling the story aloud as you put the figures in place until you can do it comfortably and without interruption. This will take some time in the beginning, but—like any skill—it will gradually become easier and less time consuming.
- When you teach, be careful to always work from the side of your board so you don't block students' view. Maintain eye contact with the children and don't turn your back on the class.

- Plan to be at your class location early. Put the room in order, set up your equipment and materials, and pray with your helper before the children arrive. Then you will have a heart free to welcome the boys and girls and listen to their chatter as they come in.
- Arrange seating so every student can see the flannelboard. Try to avoid distractions like having them looking into bright sunlight or facing a door where people come and go during class. Control the room temperature when possible, so that the children are neither too hot nor too cold. Get rid of clutter. A neat and orderly room helps children be orderly. An attractive room contributes to their enjoyment.

Manage Your Class Effectively

A well-managed classroom honors God by creating an atmosphere for learning, providing a secure refuge for students, making learning enjoyable and preventing many behavior and discipline problems. A well-managed classroom requires three elements.

A prepared teacher...

- yielded to God in mind, heart and spirit.
- ready with both lesson and program.
- knowing each student's name, characteristics, needs and interests.
- praying for each student.
- planning behavioral goals for the children.
- arriving early to prepare the room before the children arrive.

A prepared environment...

- visuals and equipment set up and in working order.
- appropriate seating arranged so all can see and hear.
- comfortable temperature and adequate lighting.
- minimal distractions (e.g., clutter, noise, activities).

Prepared students...

- knowing class rules: for example, where to put their coats, where to say their verses, how to answer or ask questions, enter and leave class or take bathroom breaks.
- aware that you expect them to obey class rules, that you appreciate good behavior and will praise them for it, and that there will be consequences for misbehavior.

The ultimate purpose of managing your class well is to create an environment in which God the Holy Spirit is able to work through the Word of God to bring about change in the childrens' lives.

Lead Your Children To Christ

Leading children to receive Jesus Christ as their Savior is a glorious privilege and an awesome responsibility. It is our deep conviction that to adequately carry out this responsibility the teacher must do four things:

- Present salvation truth frequently.
- Give students opportunities to respond to the truth.
- Speak privately with those who respond.
- Follow up on those who make a profession of faith.

In class...

- *Present salvation truth.*
  "God is holy. We are sinners, deserving punishment. We must believe the Lord Jesus Christ died for us and receive Him as Savior."
  Use the salvation ABCs:
  - ADMIT I am a sinner: I've done wrong things, displeased God (Romans 3:23).
  - BELIEVE that Jesus Christ is God, that He died on the cross for me, and that He rose again (Romans 5:8).
  - CHOOSE to receive Christ as Savior and Lord (Romans 10:9).
- *Invite the children to respond.*
  "Perhaps you have never received Christ as your Savior and would like to do that today. If so, I'd like to talk with you after class and show you how."

After class...

- *Speak with those who respond.*
  Talk individually with the children, being careful to have the door open, a helper nearby. To find out if they understand why they came, ask:
  - "Is there a special reason you came to talk to me?"
  - "Have you ever received Christ as your Savior before?"
- *Review basic facts about Christ.*
  - Who Jesus is (both God and man).
  - What Jesus did (died on the cross to take the punishment for our sins; rose again to be our living Savior) 1 Corinthians 15:3-4.
  - Why they need Jesus ("You are a sinner deserving punishment for your sins. Jesus can make you right with God and give you eternal life in heaven").
- *Review the ABCs of salvation listed above.*
  - Say, "Jesus wants to be your Savior right now. Will you receive Him?"
  - If they say yes, ask them to pray aloud. Let them use their own words, but guide them if necessary ("I admit I am a sinner. I'm sorry for my sins and want to be free from them. I believe You died for me, and I receive You as my living Savior) John 1:12.

- Be sure they base their salvation on God's Word, not on their feelings! Show them Scriptures (Romans 10:9; John 1:12; 1 John 5:11-13) that indicate salvation is by faith, believing what God says.

- *Follow up.*
  Give them a tract, such as BCM's "A Child of God," as a reminder of what they have done. Read through it with them. Then use it as a guide for Christian growth in the weeks ahead.

**Do you have suggestions or questions? need help?
want training or a catalog of available teaching materials?
Contact us at:**

BCM INTERNATIONAL, INC.
237 Fairfield Avenue, Upper Darby, PA 19082 USA
Phone: (610)352-7177 FAX (610)352-5561
E-mail: BCMIntl@compuserve.com

798 Main Street East, Hamilton, ON L8M 1L4 CANADA
Phone: (905)549-9810 FAX (905)549-7664
E-mail: mission@BCMintl.ca

39a Swiss Road, Weston-super-Mare, N. Somerset BS23 3AY, ENGLAND
Phone and FAX: 1934-413484; E-mail: BCMUK@aol.com

God Creates The World

Theme: God Calls Us — By His Works

Lesson

I

 ***BEFORE YOU BEGIN...***

Teaching that God created the heavens and the earth is a challenge today. Most of the children who come into your class are being taught that the world evolved into being, so when you teach what the Bible says, they may think you are wrong. Or they may try to accept both positions—creation in religious circles and evolution elsewhere. Often, children grow up to repudiate the Bible and church because they think that to believe the Bible they must deny sound scholarship.

Remember that evolution is an unproved theory and depends upon how data is interpreted. Evolutionists use the arrangement of fossils in sedimentary rock layers to prove progression from simple to complex organisms. Creationists use the same data to indicate a catastrophe sometime after creation.

Teach the children that accepting creation as the way the universe began does not make a person unscientific or ignorant. Patiently show them that accepting the existence of God requires accepting what God says about everything, including the origin of the universe. Help them see that creation is what God says and evolution is what man says. Then rejoice with them that "the heavens declare the glory of God and the firmament shows his handiwork" (Psalm 19:1, NKJV).

AIM:

That the children may

- Know that God created everything in the world and that His creation shows His purpose and design.
- Respond by acknowledging God as Creator and thanking Him for His wonderful works in creation.

SCRIPTURE: Genesis 1:1-25

MEMORY VERSE: Revelation 4:11

Thou art worthy, O Lord, to receive glory and honor and power; for thou hast created all things, and for thy pleasure they are and were created.

MATERIALS TO GATHER

Visual for Revelation 4:11
Backgrounds: Review Chart, Plain (solid color)
Figures: R1, 1, 2, 3, 4, 5, 6, 7, 8, 9, 10, 11, 12, 14, 21, 76
Special:

- ***For Introduction & Application:*** Real objects or pictures of things from nature.
- ***For Bible Content 1:*** A 24-inch piece of string or yarn; "trinity" circles; new word strip TRINITY (see Note below); chalkboard and chalk or newsprint and marker.
- ***For Bible Content 2:*** A 12-inch black felt or flannel circle with a white half-circle overlay; a 12-inch light blue felt or flannel circle with a darker blue overlay for water and a green overlay for grass (see Sketch 3).
- ***For Response Activity:*** "Dear God" Prayer handouts.
- ***For Options:*** Additional materials for any options you choose to use.
- ***Note:*** *To make "trinity" circles,* see Sketch 2. Cut two 8-inch circles from flannel. Print GOD on one circle; divide the second circle into three parts; print *God the Father* on one section, *God the Son* on the second and *God the Holy Spirit* on the third; cut the sections apart.
  To make new word strips throughout the course, print the word (in this case TRINITY) on a construction paper strip. Then use sand paper to roughen the back enough to adhere to your board.
  To make "Dear God" Prayer handouts, use a copy machine to duplicate pattern R-2 found on page 157.

REVIEW CHART

Display the Review Chart on the flannelboard. Add R1 (By His Works) when called for in the lesson.

The Bible is a very special book. Can anyone tell me why this is so? *(Encourage children to answer your questions when they can.)* It is special because it is God's written message to us—many words written into a book we call God's Word. It tells us who God is and all about God's Son, the Lord Jesus Christ. It also tells us God's plan for the world and for us.

The Bible has two main parts: the Old Testament, which contains 39 books (or sections), and the New Testament, which has 27 books (sections)—66 books (sections) altogether. Each of these books is divided into chapters and verses so that we can find the part we want to read. *(As you talk about this, have the children locate the Old and New Testaments in their Bibles. Use Genesis to show them the chapter and verse divisions.)* ▲#1

We are going to study the first book of the Bible, which is also the first book of the Old Testament. It is called Genesis. Does anyone know what the word *genesis* means? It means "beginnings," and that

is exactly what Genesis talks about. It tells of the beginning of the world and all life—how God made our earth and everything in it. It tells about the first family, the first temptation, the first sin. It also tells us why we have more than one language.

Genesis tells us about different people God called to follow Him and obey Him. We will learn what happened to those who followed Him and to those who didn't. We will learn why God made us and that He loves us and cares very much about us. We will also learn that He wants to speak to us today.

We may think of God as far away in heaven and wonder how can He speak to us. When you want to talk to someone across the street or far away, how do you do it? Yes, by using a telephone. The telephone is a wonderful means of communication. It is used by two people, the one who calls and the other who answers.

We will learn that God calls us. He does not use a telephone, but we will use this telephone *(show the Telephone Review Chart)* to remind us that God is calling us in a special way. He is trying to get our attention so He can show us His love, His plan and the right way to live.

God speaks to us through the Bible. In our Bible lessons we will be looking for answers to two questions: "How does God call us?" and "Why does God call us?"

Today and for the next few weeks we will be finding answers to the first question, "How does God call us?" We want to learn how God communicates with us today. Here is the first answer to this question: God calls us by His works *(place R1, By His Works, on Review Chart).* God calls us—or seeks to get our attention—by the wonderful things He has made in our world. He wants us to be reminded of who He is and all He has made. Today we'll learn how God made these "works" and why He made them.

▲ Option#1:

Prepare simple visuals for teaching this section. Make flashcards or word strips showing the two divisions and the number of books in each.
Or print the books of the Bible on the face of paper plates.
Or purchase a books of the Bible teaching visual from your local Bible bookstore.

♥ MEMORY VERSE

Use the visual from Bible Verses Visualized *to teach Revelation 4:11 as Part 3 of the Bible Content.*

BIBLE LESSON OUTLINE

God Creates the World

■ Introduction

A wonderful design

■ Bible Content

1. God made everything in the beginning.
2. God worked for six days.
3. God created all things for a purpose.
   Memory verse presentation

■ Conclusion

Summary

Application

Acknowledging God as creator of all things.

Response Activity

Giving God credit for all He has created and thanking Him for it.

BIBLE LESSON

■ Introduction

A wonderful design

Use real objects, or pictures of objects, from nature.

Did you ever see a beautiful flower, a sunset, or a sky full of stars, and wonder how they got to be so pretty? *(Allow students to examine and identify the pictures or objects. Comment on each design and how unique it is.)* Did it happen by accident or did someone have a plan for putting the pieces together? ▲#2

▲ Option#2:

Some children learn best by doing. Others find it hard to sit still in class. Use the following activity to help them.

Give the children paper and markers or crayons. Have each one draw some favorite thing from nature. Take time to share each one and comment on its design and uniqueness.

Perhaps you have learned in school that all the things around us and all life came into being by the process called evolution. Evolution assumes there is no God and that the universe began by chance or accident. It says that all living things began with one cell that multiplied and changed until all forms of life appeared on the earth.

It's important for us to understand that there is no scientific way to determine how life began because no one saw it happen and we cannot reproduce it (or make it happen again). Even though evolution is taught as if it were a fact, it has not and never can be proved. It is still an unproved theory used by some people to explain how life began. ▲#3

▲ Option#3:

Prepare definition word cards to help children remember the difference between fact and theory.

Fact = something that can be proved to be true.
Theory = something that appears to be true but can't be proved.

Use when teaching or reviewing because many of your children learn best when they see what they are hearing.

There is another theory—the creation theory. Creation assumes there is a God and that He brought the universe into being. There is no scientific way to prove this theory, either, but God (who was there) has told us in His Word, the Bible, that He created the world, how He created the world and why He did it. We are going to learn what God says about the beginning of all things.

The Bible tells us that all the beautiful things we see are the result of God's work. Sometimes we simply call the things God made His "works"—just as a painting or a statue is sometimes called a "work of art." God made all these wonderful things so that each time we look at them we will be reminded of Him and how great and marvelous He is (Psalm 19:1).

Open your Bibles to the book of Genesis, chapter one, verse one, and we'll read the verse together. *(Or ask a child or a helper to read the verse aloud.)* This verse tells us how the earth and the heavens came into being. Which word tells us what God did? That's right, the word *create*. ▲#4

▲ Option#4:

Definition word card:
Create = make something new, sometimes out of nothing.

Create is a special word used in the Bible only of God. It means to make something original, new and different. Sometimes God creates out of nothing; sometimes He creates out of something that already exists. God "created" the heavens and the earth. He made them out of nothing in the beginning when nothing existed except Himself. *(Have class repeat Genesis 1:1 together after you. Print the verse on chalkboard or newsprint to display and refer to throughout the lesson.)* ▲#5

It is impossible for us to make—or create—something out of nothing, but it was not impossible for God because He is all-powerful. When God made our world, He began with nothing. And He created all things according to the design—or plan—He had in mind. Only God could do that!

■ Bible Content

1. God made everything in the beginning. (Genesis 1:1-2).

(Cross 1, eternity 2, world 3, GOD 14. Special: 24-inch piece of string or yarn, trinity circles, new word strip TRINITY, chalkboard and chalk or newsprint and marker.)

Genesis is called the Book of Beginnings. The very first verse says, "In the beginning God created the heavens and the earth." Before that there was nothing except God—no people, no earth, no sun or moon or stars. There was only God. He never had a beginning and will never have an ending. He always was and always will be. *(Place eternity 2.)* He made our earth and all our universe from nothing!

We will let this line stand for all the time since that "beginning"—since the world was made. *(Place string or yarn line across flannelboard; add world 3.)* We would not know anything about when or how or why all things were created if God had not told us in His Word. ▲#6

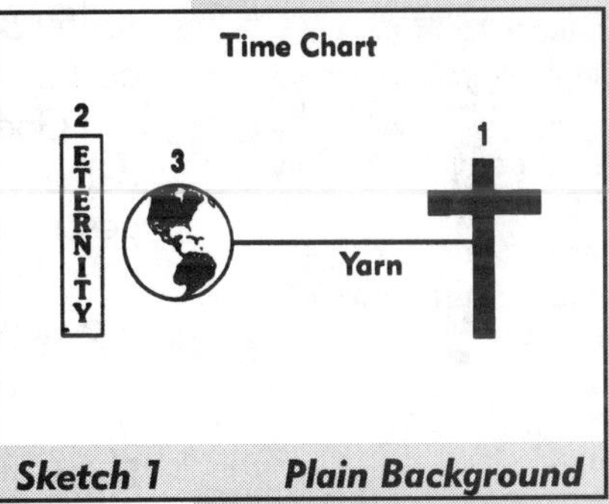

Sketch 1 **Plain Background**

It's hard for us to think how long ago that was. Ten years ago some of you had not yet been born. One hundred years ago your grandparents, and perhaps your great-grandparents, were not yet alive.

About 2000 years ago the Lord Jesus was born as a baby. We'll let this cross stand for the time He lived on earth *(add cross 1)*. People lived on the earth for thousands of years before Jesus came *(indicate line before cross)*. We live over here *(point to right side of cross)* 2000 years after Jesus came.

We date time from when Jesus came to earth. *(Draw cross on chalkboard or newsprint.)* Sometimes you see the year written with the abbreviation A.D. after it. *(Write current year date with A.D. to right of cross. Add words Anno Domini and their meaning as you talk.)* These letters, A.D., stand for two Latin words, *Anno Domini*, which mean "in the year of our Lord." The years before Jesus came are counted backward from when He lived on the earth and are written

▲ Option#5:

Use to help explain the meaning of "create" in a concrete fashion.

Place a mixing bowl and a wooden spoon on a table. Ask for a volunteer to "create" a cake for the group. Give that person specific instructions for the kind of cake he or she is to create: size, flavor, icing, etc. Then hand over the ingredients. Actually, gesture with empty hands, but give no ingredients at all. Say, "Please 'create' a cake for us." Then discuss with the class why it is impossible to do this.

Object lessons like this benefit most children, but especially those who learn best when physically involved.

▲ Option#6:

Make a "living" time line: Temporarily attach cross 1, ETERNITY 2 and world 3 to flashcards. Have two children hold a long piece of yarn or rope while others holding the flashcards take their proper places along the time line.

Note:

The word trinity comes from "tri" meaning three (*tri*angle, *tri*cycle) and "unity" meaning one. The word does not appear in the Bible, but we use it to help us understand the nature of God. When we say that God is a Trinity, we are saying what the Bible says: that God is three separate Persons while still being only one God. Another way to say it is that God is Three-in-One.

Nothing else in the universe illustrates the concept of Trinity exactly, nor can we comprehend it completely. Consequently, many teachers avoid teaching this truth to children. However, that leaves our students unprotected against the false teaching of the cults, particularly in the area of the deity of Christ and the personhood of the Holy Spirit. We must teach it through careful presentation and consistent review.

with the abbreviation B.C., which means "before Christ." *(Write 100 B.C. to left of cross and add the meaning of B.C. as you teach.)*

Verse 2 *(look at it together)* tells us that when God created the earth in the beginning, it was dark and covered with water, but "the spirit of God," or God the Holy Spirit, was there.

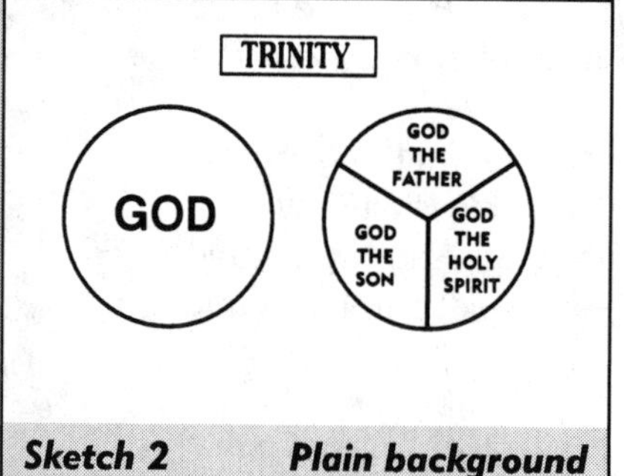

Sketch 2 **Plain background**

The Bible verse we will be learning in a few minutes tells us that the Lord (Jesus Christ), who is God the Son, created all things, so He was there too.

The Bible teaches us that our God is one God *(place the GOD circle on the board)* in three Persons—God the Father, God the Son and God the Holy Spirit. *(As you teach, place the three parts of the trinity circle on the GOD circle to illustrate how God is one God, yet three distinct persons.)* Each of them worked in creation. Together they make up the Trinity *(place word strip)*: one God in three Persons. This is a mystery— something hard to understand. Our God is a great God!

2. God worked for six days. (Genesis 1:2-25; Psalm 147:4; Revelation 4:11)

(Cloud 76, flowers 4, sun 6, moon 7, stars 5, fish 10, bird ll, rabbit 8, deer 9, lizard 12, lamb 21, two 12-inch circles and overlays; add overlays and figures as indicated in text.)

God has all power, and nothing is too hard for Him to do, but He did not do all the work of creation at once. Genesis chapter one describes six days during which God worked to change the earth that was dark and covered with water into a wonderful earth filled with growing things and living creatures.

Days of Creation:

Creation Circles

white black

Sketch 3 **Plain background**

Day 1: Find Genesis chapter one and verse three. Let's read it together. *(Do so, or ask a student or helper to read it aloud.)* What are the first three words of the verse? "And God said...." *(Have class repeat these words aloud here and for each day of creation.)*

What does this tell us God made? *(The light)* But how does it say He did it? Yes, He spoke and it was there. *(Put black circle on board and add white overlay.)*

What did God say about the light (vs. 4)? *(Encourage responses throughout.)* It was good! What did God call the light and the darkness (vs. 5)? He called the light day and the darkness night. God gave us the daylight for work and play and the darkness for sleep and rest. In hot climates of the world, night provides opportunity for cooling. Since He gave us the darkness, we don't need to be afraid of it. God said that what He made was good. This was the first day.

Day 2: Now let's look at verse six and read together the first three words *("And God said")*. This verse tells us that God made the firmament on the second day. *(Put blue circle on board and place cloud 76 in upper part.)* ▲#7

The firmament is the atmosphere or air that surrounds the earth. When God spoke, He separated the water that covered the earth into two parts—water on the earth and water in the sky. God placed the air, or atmosphere, around the earth between the two waters because He knew that the animals and people He planned to create would need air to breathe. God was preparing a place for His creatures to live. This was the second day.

Day 3: On the third day God spoke again (vs. 9). *(Read words aloud together.)* ⍓ "And God said...." He gathered together in certain places all the water on the earth to form oceans and seas and lakes. *(Place water overlay on lower part of second circle.)* Then the dry land appeared—hills and valleys and plains. *(Add grass overlay to circle.)* When God saw this, what did He think about it (vs. 10)? He saw that it was good.

Now what are the first three words of verse 11? "And God said...." *(Repeat together.)* This time, God commanded and the earth produced all kinds of plants and trees, grass, flowers, vegetables and fruit and grain—each with seeds so they could produce more. *(Add flowers 4 to circle.)* We read again that "God saw that it was good" (vs. 12). This was the third day.

Day 4: On the first day God made light. In verse 14 we read that on the fourth day He created the sun, moon and stars to be lights for the earth. *(Place sun 5, moon 6, stars 7 in sky.)* God simply spoke—*(say it together)* "And God said..."—and they appeared. We read that God created them to give light to the earth, to divide the light from the darkness and to control day and night and the change of seasons.

The Bible says that God knows all the stars by name (Psalm 147:4), even the ones we can't see! After He made them, He "saw that it was good." This was the fourth day.

Day 5: The world was now ready for living creatures. The seas were ready for fish, and the trees and grass were ready to be homes for the birds. On the fifth day, God spoke *(say the words "And God said" together)* and made all kinds of fish and water animals and every kind of bird and fowl. *(Place bird 11, fish 10 on circle.)* How God must have enjoyed looking at all the different kinds of beautiful fish and birds He had made! The Bible says that God saw they were good and that He blessed them and told them to multiply (to have many

▲ Option#7:

You may choose not to use the cloud. Though we are accustomed to seeing clouds in the sky, they probably did not appear until after the flood recorded in Genesis 6-8.

⍓ Note:

Many of us remember better if we hear ourselves repeat the words aloud. Use this teaching technique to help your children retain important truths.

baby fish or birds) so that there would be many, many more birds and fish, enough to fill the forests and the oceans. This was the fifth day.

Day 6: On the sixth day, God made all the land animals, large and small. *(Place rabbit 8, deer 9, lizard 12, and lamb 21 on circle.)* How did He do it? Yes, He spoke: "And God said...." *(Say it aloud together.)* He made the creeping things such as lizards and snails. He made all kinds of livestock, or tame animals, and all the animals that live in the wild. Chapter two, verse 19 tells us He formed them out of the ground. "And God saw it was good." This was the sixth day.

3. God created all things for a purpose. *Memory verse presentation*

(Verse visual, Revelation 4:11)

Now we have seen how God created our earth and all plants and animals. He spoke: "And God said...." *(Say it aloud together.)* How long did it take Him to do this? *(Six days)* How did God describe what He had made? The Bible says that He saw it was very good. God created a very special and beautiful world. But why did He go to all the trouble of making it?

A wonderful verse in the last book of the Bible tells us why God created all things: Revelation 4:11. *(Display verse visual.)* As we read it aloud together, see if you can find why God created everything. *(For His pleasure)*

The name "Lord" in this verse (and in all the New Testament) is another name for Jesus, the Son of God. He came into the world as a baby to show us what God is like and then to die and rise again to pay for our sins. The Lord Jesus is alive and in heaven now.

What does this verse tell us our Lord is worthy to receive? *(Glory and honor and power)* Why is He worthy to receive glory and honor and power? ⍓ Because He created all things.

⍓ Note:

Definitions: Worthy is deserving or excellent; glory is admiration or fame won by doing something important; honor is high regard or great respect; power is authority, great ability to act or influence.

And why, according to the verse, did He create all things? For His pleasure or because it made Him happy; He wanted to. Let's say those words together: Because He wanted to. It gave God pleasure to create the world. Imagine our great God wanting to create life and to make a beautiful earth!

Because He is God He already has all power. But we can give Him glory and honor by praising Him for who He is and by recognizing His right to rule over creation. *(Work on learning the verse and reviewing its meaning together.)* ▲#8

Conclusion

Summary

Aren't you glad that God has told us in the Bible where the heavens and the earth and the creatures on the earth came from? Who created them? *(God)* How did God create all things? *(By His Word and great power)* Why did God create them? *(For His pleasure; because He wanted to.)*

Application

Have you ever told God that you believe He created the world and everything in it? So many today are saying that it all happened by accident. But it couldn't be accidental; God did it on purpose. *(Show nature objects or pictures from Introduction again.)* As you see the beauty in a flower or in trees, listen to the song of the birds, watch the sun set, or play with one of your pets, remember that these are God's creation. Each time we see them, we can know that there is a God, the only true God, and that He has all power.

God also loves us. It is as if He is "speaking" to us when we look at His creation and see His design in it. It reminds us that He is always there and can do anything. Let's say our verse again and think of all the things for which we can thank God. *(Repeat memory verse together.)*

Response Activity

Ask the children to mention things God has made that they are especially thankful for. Give each one a ***"Dear God" Prayer handout*** *(see Materials to Gather). Have them silently pray the prayer to God. Encourage them to use the prayer sheet each day this week and to thank God for a different one of His works of creation every time.*

Ask them to bring one of God's "works" (a flower, leaf, etc.) for which they are thankful when they come next week. Have a "show and tell" sharing time.

HELPS FOR YOUNGER CHILDREN

Memory Verse: Shorten the verse to "Thou hast created all things,... for thy pleasure."

Bible Lesson: Omit Section 1, the Time Chart and explanation p. 5. Go directly from the Introduction to Section 2 p.6.

▲ Option#8:

Learning the verse: Use the verse to lead the children in giving three "cheers" for the creation of our wonderful world.

Teacher, say each line as you do the suggested motion (or make up your own motions); have the children repeat words and motions after you, one line at a time.

- "Revelation 4:11" *Rest hands on hips.*
- "Thou art worthy" *Raise right hand.*
- "Ohhhh Lord" *Raise left hand.*
- "to receive" *Extend right hand, palm up.*
- "glory and honor" *Extend left hand, palm up.*
- "and power" *Raise arms at elbows and make fists to show strength.*
- "for thou hast created" *Extend right arm to the side.*
- "a-l-l-l things" *Extend left arm to the side.*
- "and for thy pleasure" *Rest both hands on waist.*
- "they are and were created" *Both hands on hips, kneel on right knee.*
- "Revelation 4:11" *Stand with both hands on hips.*

Repeat twice.

God Creates Man

Theme: God Calls Us — By His Love

Lesson 2

BEFORE YOU BEGIN...

"God loves you and made you special" is a truth your boys and girls need to hear. In a culture that often mistreats children, crushes their self-worth or treats them as "throw aways," they desperately need to understand that God made them, that He loves them and that they are very special to Him.

As you teach how God created the first man and woman in His own image, be careful to communicate that they too are made in God's image. "Thus says the Lord who created you,... 'Fear not, for I have redeemed you; I have called you by your name; you are Mine' " (Isaiah 43:1, NKJV) and "I have loved you with an everlasting love" (Jeremiah 31:3).

AIM:

That the children may

- Know that God created the first man and woman in His own image and provided all they needed because He loved them.
- Respond to God by acknowledging His love for them and thanking Him for how He has made them.

SCRIPTURE: Genesis 1:26–2:25

MEMORY VERSE: Genesis 2:7

And the LORD God formed man of the dust of the ground, and breathed into his nostrils the breath of life; and man became a living soul.

MATERIALS TO GATHER

Visual for Genesis 2:7
Backgrounds: Review Chart, Plain, River
Figures: R1, R2, 4, 8, 9, 11, 14, 15, 16, 17, 18, 19, 20, 21, 25
Special:

- ***For Introduction:*** A small box of soil.
- ***For Bible Content 1:*** Creation circles from Lesson 1; body/soul/spirit circle.
- ***For Bible Content 3:*** A small bone.
- ***For Conclusion:*** Body/soul/spirit circle.
- ***For Response Activity:*** "Dear God" Letter handouts.
- ***For Options:*** Additional materials for any options you choose to use.
- ***Note:*** *To make the body/soul/spirit circle*, see Sketch 4. Cut a 12-inch circle from flannel or felt. On it draw 6-inch and 9-inch concentric circles to indicate three divisions. Carefully cut around the two inner circles so that you can handle the three parts separately.
  To make "Dear God" Letter handouts, use a copy machine to duplicate pattern R-3 found on page 157.

REVIEW CHART

Display the Review Chart with R1 in place. Have R2 ready to use when called for in this section. Use the following questions to review Lesson 1.

1. According to the Bible, who created all things? *(God)*
2. How did God create our world? *(He spoke —"And God said....")*
3. What was God's purpose in creating our world? *(He created all things for His pleasure; it made Him happy; He wanted to.)*
4. What is the Lord worthy to receive from us because He created all things? *(Glory, honor and power)*

We have already found one answer to the question, How does God call us (or seek to get our attention)? What is it? He calls us by His works. ▲#1 Today's answer to that question is, God calls us by His love. *(Place R2 on the Chart.)*

Review Token:

▲ Option#1:

"Show and Tell" time. Encourage the children to show the object from nature they have brought and tell why they're thankful for it.

♥ MEMORY VERSE

Use the visual from Bible Verses Visualized *to teach Genesis 2:7 as part of Bible Content 1. (See Bible Lesson Outline.)*

BIBLE LESSON OUTLINE

God Creates Man

Introduction

Where do we come from?

Bible Content

1. God makes the first man, Adam.
   Memory verse presentation
2. God makes Adam special.
   a. In His image
   b. Body/soul/spirit
3. God makes a home for Adam.
4. God makes a wife for Adam.
5. God blesses Adam and Eve.
6. God rests on the seventh day.

Conclusion

Summary

Application

Seeing God's love in creation and in how He has made us.

Response Activity

Signing a special "Dear God" letter to express thanks for God's love in creation.

Thanking God for His love.

BIBLE LESSON

Introduction

Where do we come from?

(Verse visual for Genesis 2:7; a small box of soil.)

Did you ever wonder where you came from or why you are here on this earth? People have asked these questions for hundreds of years. As we discussed last week, some say that all life on earth, including people, began millions of years ago with a single cell that grew and changed from one form to another until finally people appeared. They assume that there is no God and that all this happened by chance.

What did we learn about evolution last week? *(It is taught as a fact, but is really an unproved theory.)* Most science books call it the theory of evolution, but teach it as though it really happened.

What is the difference between a fact and a theory? *(A fact can be proved to be true; a theory appears to be true to some people, but cannot be proved.)* ▲#2 Why do we call evolution a theory? *(Because it cannot be proved by scientific means.)*

▲ Option#2:

Use the definition word cards for "fact" and "theory" from Lesson 1 to help children remember the difference between fact and theory.

People's ideas about where we came from and why we are here keep changing. Where can we find truthful answers that do not need to change? In God's Word, the Bible *(show your Bible)*. God's Word is truth that never changes and it gives us God's answers to these questions.

We have already discovered from the Bible that God made our world and all the life in it. We called this the creation theory. Why did we call it a theory? *(Because it cannot be proved by scientific means.)* We cannot prove the creation theory through scientific means and only God was there when it happened. But God *was* there and He tells us in His Word how He did it. Today we will learn where the human race came from.

■ Bible Content

1. God made the first man, Adam. Memory verse presentation (Genesis 2:7)

(Creation circles from Lesson 1; verse visual, Genesis 2:7.)

Let's review together the things that God made on each of the six days of creation. *(Involve students in answering. Use creation circles from Lesson 1 to review.)* ▲#3

But God was not finished yet. Even though the world was beautiful and filled with living creatures, there was no one whom God could love and who could love Him in return. Some of us have pets we love very much. They can be very loyal and seem to love us, too, but that's not the same as a loving person who talks with us and helps us and is a friend. Just so, God must have enjoyed the animals He had made, but He wanted someone to love—someone who would be something like Himself.

Today's memory verse, Genesis 2:7, tells us how God made the first human being, a man. Let's read the first half of it together. *(Display the first part of the verse visual; read it with the children.)*

"And the Lord God formed man of the dust of the ground...." What does this verse tell us about where we came from? *(Encourage children to answer.)* It tells us two things: 1) It was God who made man, and 2) God formed, or shaped, the man's body out of the soil of the earth. *(Show soil from box. Allow children to touch and feel.)* Scientists today tell us that our bodies contain many of the same minerals that are found in the earth—iron, lime, phosphorous, and more. This must be the reason why.

Now let's read the second half of the verse. *(Display the remainder of the verse visual and read it with the children.)* "... and breathed into his nostrils the breath of life, and man became a living soul." God put His own life into that human body and made it into a living, breathing person. What a miracle! Only God could do something like that! *(Memorize verse and review its meaning.)* ▲#4

▲ Option#3:

Title seven sheets of paper "Day One," "Day Two," etc. Lay the first six on a table with crayons or markers. As you review each day of creation, have a child draw on the appropriate page what God created on that day. Display completed pages.

Or have individual children choose one day ("Day One," "Day Two," etc.), tell what God created on that day and do an action or motion to represent what God made.

▲ Option#4:

Learning the verse: Antiphonal verse choir. Divide the class into three groups and assign each group part of the verse. Group 1: to "...ground,"; Group 2: to "breath of life;"; Group 3: remainder . Entire class: reference. *Procedure*: Have each group practice their part, using the visual. Then have the groups stand and face each other as they recite their parts back and forth, all joining to say the reference.

2. God made Adam special. (Genesis 1:26; 2:7)

a. In His image

Look back to Genesis 1:26. Here God said, "Let us make man in our image, after our likeness." It was as if God the Father, God the Son and God the Holy Spirit said this as they worked together. So God made the first man as He wanted every person to be, in His image, like Himself in many ways. Being made in the image of God is wonderful and tells us some important facts about man, God's special creation. ▲#5

▲ Option#5:

Print three flash cards:

1) God made me different from all other created beings.

2) God Himself made people.

3) I am special to God.

Punch holes in each card and attach string so it can be hung around a child's neck, or back each card with flannel and place on the board as you teach. Take the cards to class in an envelope on which you have printed IN GOD'S IMAGE.

1) Being created in God's image means that people are different from all other created beings. *(If using option #5, show card 1.)* The way they're made and the abilities God has given them make them superior to and separate from all other living creatures. We have all seen apes or gorillas in a zoo or on TV which appear very human. They walk upright and seem to love and care for their babies. Some have learned to get the food they want by pushing the right buttons. But they cannot talk with you, read a book, do a math problem, build a computer or figure out how to go into outer space. God made people different from animals and like himself in many ways like being able to communicate, to think of new ideas and to create new things.

2) Being created in God's image means that the first human being could not have happened by accident. If you dumped your box of building blocks on the floor and waited, would they build themselves into a house or a fort? Of course not. You must build the blocks into whatever you want. God made the first man, Adam. *(Show card 2.)* People could not possibly have evolved accidentally from animals.

3) Being created in God's image also means that every person is of great value and very special to God. *(Show card 3.)* People in the world look different, have different ideas, speak different languages and even have different-colored skin, but every single person is special to God. Human life is worth more than any other thing on earth. This means that you are very special to God and that He loves you very much. *(Read together from cards what it means to be made in God's image.)*

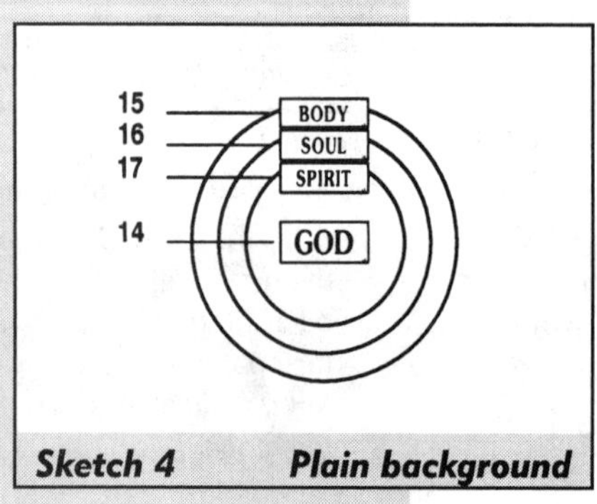

Sketch 4 **Plain background**

b. Body, soul, spirit

(Word strips: GOD 14, body 15, soul 16, spirit 17; body/soul/spirit circle.)

We learn from our memory verse that God made the first man (and every person since) with body, soul and spirit. Understanding this helps us appreciate how wonderfully God has made us. ⌂

Your body is the "house" you live in, a very wonderful house that can do many things. *(Place outer circle on board; add 15.)* Isn't it great to be able to run and play? ▲#6 To enjoy eating, or seeing beautiful sights with your eyes or making things with your hands? Our bodies breathe for us and digest our food and grow without our even thinking about it. What a wonderful creation!

Your soul and spirit make up the "real you" that lives inside your body. Your soul *(place middle circle inside outer one; add 16)* is the part of you that can think and reason, love other people and feel joy or sadness, communicate with others and make choices. Each of us has a unique personality that makes us different from everyone else. Think about the people you know. ▲#7

Some really like to study and are careful about details. Others are more fun-loving. Some have a good imagination. Others are good at making and fixing things. It's all part of the way God made us.

Your spirit is the part of you that makes you aware of God and able to know and love God. *(Add center of circle and 17.)* Your spirit is where God can live within you. *(Add 14 to center.)* Having a spirit— being able to know and love God— is the greatest reason why people are superior to the rest of creation.

The body gets sick. Someday it will get old and die. But the soul and spirit never die! The Bible teaches that when a person dies his soul and spirit leave his body, but live on forever, either with God in heaven or separated from God in hell.

God created the first person as a grown man, for there was no one to take care of a little baby. God made him with a body, a soul and a spirit and called him Adam. Everything Adam did was right and good, for he was sinless in the beginning. Sin had not yet come to the earth.

3. God made a home for Adam. (Genesis 2:15,19)

(GOD 14, Adam 18, tree 20, flowers 4, rabbit 8, deer 9, bird 11, lamb 21, Eve 19, small bone.)

God placed Adam in a garden called Eden. *(Place 14 and 18 on board; add 20 and 4 as you teach.)* This first home was very beautiful. It was filled with flowers and fruit trees, and a river flowed through it. When Adam was hungry, he could gather fruit from the trees and food from the plants that grew all around him.

The animals were there, too, and they were not afraid of each other *(add 8, 9, 11, 21)*. In that garden everything was good and pure and lovely. Adam's work was to take care of the garden and to be in charge of all the plants and animals. God brought all the animals to Adam so he could give them names.

4. God made a wife for Adam. (Genesis 2:18,21-22)

In all the beautiful world that God had made, Adam was the only

Note:

God gives to every human being a body, a soul and a spirit (1 Thessalonians 5:23). The soul and spirit will exist forever, but not necessarily with God. God the Holy Spirit comes to live within an individual the moment that person trusts Christ as Savior from sin. Thus, God's life takes up residence within the person's spirit, making it alive with God's life and fit for heaven, one day to live with Him forever.

If an individual chooses not to come to God for forgiveness through Christ, his soul and spirit will still exist forever, but separated from God in a place called hell, which was prepared for Satan and his angels (2 Thessalonians 1:8-10; Matthew 25:41).

▲ Option#6:

Have several children demonstrate things we can do with our bodies: move, wiggle fingers, open and close eyes, throw, jump, sit.

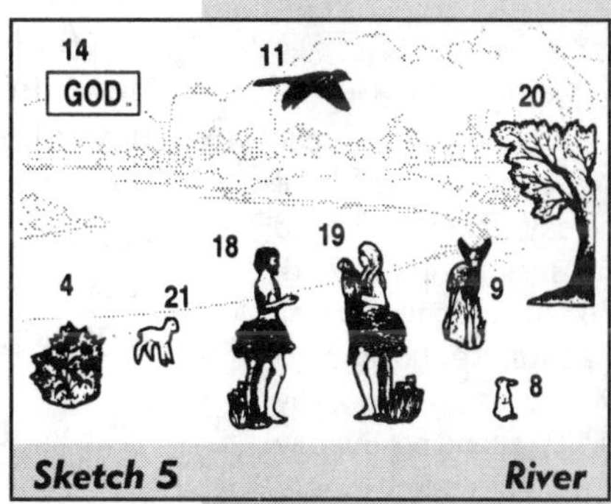

Sketch 5

▲ Option#7:

If time permits, have class members share some of these characteristics they know they have.

▲ **Option#8:**

Use the six posters the children made at the beginning of class to review the six days of creation.
Or, have the individual children who acted out the days of creation at the beginning of the lesson repeat their motions while the class tells what day that was and what God created then. Be careful to restate each time HOW God made these things.
Add man and woman to Day Six. Hold up "Day Seven" paper and ask, What should we draw on this day. *(Leave blank or print REST.)*

⍓ **Note:**

God has given us a special day, too. It is Sunday, the first day of the week. We call it the Lord's day because it is the day on which our Lord Jesus rose from the dead. It should be different from all other days. We should do all we can to make it special by faithfully attending Sunday school and church where we can read and study His Word and worship Him with others who love and serve Him, too.

living person. He was not alone, for every day God came and talked with him. God loved Adam, and Adam loved God. Because God loved Adam very much, He knew that Adam needed another human person to talk with and to love. God said, "It is not good for the man to be alone; I will make a helper suitable for him."

God caused Adam to fall into a very deep sleep. While Adam was sleeping, God removed one of his ribs and then closed the place in his body from which he had taken it. *(Show bone.)* From that rib God made a woman and brought her to Adam *(add 19)*. She, too, was made in God's image, with a body, a soul and a spirit, with the ability to know and love God. Adam must have been very pleased and happy. He named her Eve.

Here was another beginning: the first marriage and the first family. This, too, is a part of God's plan. The Bible tells us here that a man should leave his parents and live with his wife in marriage. They should be as close to each other as if they were one person. It is God's plan that a husband and wife should stay together for life and love each other even more than they love their parents or any other person.

5. God blessed Adam and Eve. (Genesis 2:8-9; 1:28-29; Psalm 8:4-8)

God blessed Adam and Eve. This means that He loved them, helped them and provided for them. As part of His plan He gave them special work to do. God told them that they were to be in charge of all His creation and to take care of it for Him. They were to be over the animals and every other created thing.

God also told them to multiply (have children) and fill up the earth. He had made Adam and Eve as grown people, but He would not make anyone else that way. Instead, He gave Adam and Eve the ability to have children born into the world and to make a home for them. Adam and Eve are sometimes called our first parents, because everyone born into the world since then has come from them.

Adam and Eve were very happy in their garden home. They were never tired or sick. They were pure and innocent because they had never known anything bad or evil. They wore no clothing and they were not ashamed, for they knew nothing of sin or shame. God would come to the garden to walk and talk with them. He loved them and they loved Him. They enjoyed one another and were very happy together.

6. God rested on the seventh day. (Genesis 1:31; 2:1-3)

For six days God had worked. ▲#8 The Bible says, "And God saw everything He had made, and, behold it was very good." Then, on the seventh day, God rested from all the work which He had done. He didn't rest because He was tired, but because His work of creation was finished. We read in God's Word, "And God blessed the seventh day and sanctified it." This means He set it apart as a special day on which He rested from His work. ⍓

Conclusion

Summary

(Body/soul/spirit circle; boy 13; word strips: GOD 14, BODY 15, SOUL 16, SPIRIT 17; Adam 18, Eve 19, heaven 25.) Let's see if we can remember all the things God did when He created the first man and woman. ▲#9 *(Place 14, 18, 19 on board. Encourage children to list what God did; add body/soul/spirit circle and 15, 16, 17 as answers are given).* How great and wise and powerful is our God!

Sketch 6 **Plain background**

What had God done for Adam and Eve even before He made them? *(Prepared a home in the Garden and provided everything they needed.)* What work did God give Adam and Eve to do? *(Be in charge of God's creation and take care of it for God.)* Why did God do all this? He wanted someone to love; He came to the Garden to walk and talk with them.

▲ Option#9:

As the children respond, write their answers on chalkboard or newsprint so all can see them.

Application

Have you ever thought about God's loving you? *(Add 13.)* Does it seem unlikely that God who is so great could single you out of all the people on earth and actually love and care about you? Well, this is what our lesson is telling you today. God made the world for you to enjoy. He made you and gave you special abilities to develop and use in your lifetime. He loves you and promises to care for you all through your life. He has provided a place in heaven for you to live with Him forever *(add heaven 25)*. Wouldn't you agree that God loves you?

Sometimes you might question whether God loves you, expecially when things don't go the way you want them. And you may wonder why He made you the way He did. But the Bible says God loves you and that you are special to Him (John 3:16).

Response Activity

*Distribute the **"Dear God" Letter handouts** (see Materials to Gather). Go over the four sentences briefly and give the children opportunity to sign their names to indicate they agree with what the letter says. Lead them in a closing prayer.*

HELPS FOR YOUNGER CHILDREN

Memory Verse: Shorten Genesis 2:7 to "And the LORD God formed man of the dust of the ground...", but explain the truth of the entire verse. Use the box of soil visual aid here to help the children understand what God did.

Adam and Eve Disobey God

Theme: God Calls Us — By His Mercy

Lesson

3

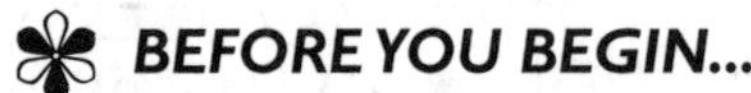

BEFORE YOU BEGIN...

Has a child ever said to you, "How did all the badness get into the world?" Children certainly know about goodness and badness, about right and wrong, about obedience and disobedience. But most do not know that God—in his love—set the standard for right and wrong, and that He has communicated that standard to us in His Word. They do not always understand that disobeying God's commands is sin and that there are consequences for wrongdoing.

Through this account of mankind's first disobedience help your boys and girls learn what sin is and how God deals with it—the consequences of wrongdoing and God's loving provision of salvation for those who turn to Him. "For the wages of sin is death, but the gift of God is eternal life in Christ Jesus our Lord" (Romans 6:23, NKJV).

AIM:

That the children may

- Know what sin is and how it came into the world and recognize God's mercy in dealing with it.
- Respond by acknowledging their sin and accepting God's way of forgiveness through the Lord Jesus Christ.

SCRIPTURE: Genesis 2:16,17; 3:1-24

MEMORY VERSE: Romans 5:19

For as by one man's disobedience many were made sinners, so by the obedience of one shall many be made righteous.

MATERIALS TO GATHER

Visual for Romans 5:19
Backgrounds: Review Chart, Plain, River, General Outdoor
Figures: R1-R3, 1, 3, 4, 8, 9, 11, 14, 15, 16, 17, 18, 19, 20, 21, 22, 23, 24, 25, 26, 27, 28, 29, 30, 31, 32, 33, 34, 126
Special:

- ***For Review Chart:*** New word strips SIN and MERCY.
- ***For Introduction:*** Current front pages or newspaper headlines printed on newsprint or poster board.
- ***For Bible content 1:*** Newsprint & markers or chalkboard & chalk;
- ***For Conclusion:*** Body/soul/spirit circles; cross object lesson.
- ***For Options:*** Additional materials for any options you choose to use.

Note: *To make cross object lesson*, see Sketch 10. Cut two pieces to form cross from brown flannel, felt, or construction paper roughed on the back with sand paper. Draw stones or bricks on the long upright piece to make it look like a wall and print SIN vertically on it; cut shorter piece long enough to form the crosspiece and print JESUS across it, placing S in the middle.

REVIEW CHART

Display Review Chart. Use R1 and R2 to review themes from Lessons 1 and 2. Have R3 and new word strips SIN and MERCY ready to use as indicated. Use the following questions to review Lesson 2.

1. What did God use to form the first man? *(Dust of the ground)*
2. How did God put His life into Adam? *(He breathed into his nostrils the breath of life.)*
3. How did God make the first woman? *(He formed the woman from a rib He had taken from the man.)*
4. Name the three parts that make up each person. *(Body, soul and spirit)*
5. Why did God make people? *(Because He wanted someone to love and who could love Him.)*
6. How were Adam and Eve different from people born today? *(They were created directly by God; they were adults immediately; they were not sinners when God made them.)*
7. How did God make man special, different from all other things He created? *(By creating man in His image, superior to other beings, making man of great value and worth to Himself.)*

Who can tell me the ways we have learned that God calls us or seeks to get our attention? *(Place R1 and R2 on chart as they are*

Review Token:

named.) Our next symbol *(place R3 on chart)* says that God calls us by His mercy. What is mercy? *(Place word strip MERCY on board.)* ▲#1

Mercy is what one boy had when he pinned another boy to the ground because he had hit him and then, instead of punching him back, let him up. Mercy is what a mother has when she catches her child doing something wrong and, instead of punishing him, gives him another chance. Both the boy and the mother showed mercy by not punishing someone who deserved it. So then, mercy is not punishing someone who deserves to be punished. ▲#2

Does God show mercy toward us? In order to answer this question we have to know about another word—sin. *(Place word strip SIN next to MERCY.)*

▲ Option#1:

Show pictures of these illustrations of mercy. Or, choose children before class to role play each scene and give them instructions as to what to do. Ask class to identify and explain how mercy is shown in each situation.

▲ Option#2:

Definition word card:
Mercy = not punishing one who deserves it.

♥ MEMORY VERSE

Use the visual from Bible Verses Visualized *to teach Romans 5:19.*

Our memory verse will help us understand these two words. It speaks of two men. Let's read what it says about the first one. *(Display the first half of the verse visual and have a child or the group read the words aloud. Encourage children to find answers to your questions from the verse so they see for themselves what the Scripture says.)*

What did this man do? *(Disobeyed.)* This man was the first man, Adam. What happened because Adam disobeyed? *(Many were made sinners.)*

Adam was the father of the whole human race. What was he like when God created him? *(Perfect and without sin.)* Today we will learn how Adam and his wife, Eve, turned away from God and chose to go their own way. They chose to disobey God. The Bible calls this disobedience sin. So, when Adam and Eve disobeyed, they became sinners and changed the kind of people that they had been. Because they were our first parents, everyone born into the world since then has been born a sinner, wanting to go his or her own way. ▲#3

As sinners, all of us deserve to be punished by God, but God had mercy on us. What did we say mercy is? He sent His Son, the Lord Jesus Christ, to die on the cross to take the punishment for our sins. Our verse says *(have class say it together)*, "...so by the obedience of one shall many be made righteous." *(Display the remaining portion of the visual as you read this.)*

Because Jesus was willing to die for us, when we trust Him as our Savior we can be forgiven and made righteous, or right, in God's sight. ▲#4 We will not have to be punished for our sin because Jesus was punished in our place. *(Work on learning the verse and reviewing its meaning together.)* ▲#5

▲ Option#3:

Definition word card:
Sin = choosing your own way instead of God's way.

▲ Option#4:

Definition word card:
Righteous = right in God's sight.

BIBLE LESSON OUTLINE

Adam and Eve Disobey God

Introduction

Our sinful world

Bible Content

1. God's enemy, Satan.
2. God's command to Adam.
3. Eve's temptation.
4. Adam's disobedience.
5. God punishes sin.
6. God shows His mercy.

Conclusion

Summary

Application

Understanding how God in His mercy made a way for us to come to Him.

Response Activity

Responding to God's mercy by receiving Jesus as Savior or telling the class how they trusted Christ.

▲ Option#5:

Learning the verse: Use motions correlated to visual pieces to help the children drill the verse:

"For as by..." *Bring hand to mouth as if biting into fruit;*

"...many were made sinners" *Spread arms wide, bring index fingers of both hands to corners of mouth and turn down to indicate sadness;*

"So by the..." *Stretch arms to side or make a cross with arms in front;*

"...shall many..." *Spread arms wide, bring index fingers to mouth and turn up to indicate joy.*

BIBLE LESSON

Introduction

Our sinful world

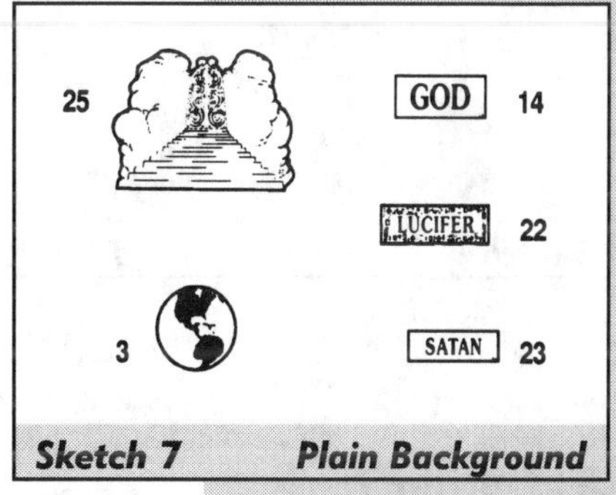

Sketch 7 **Plain Background**

Print the following newspaper headlines on newsprint or chalkboard or bring actual front pages of similar content to class. Have several children read the headlines aloud.

"Grocery Store Robbed"; "Airplane Hijacked—Hostages Taken"; "Two Found Guilty of Murder"; "Four Injured in 17 Car Pile-up"; "Unknown Disease Overtakes City—Many Hospitalized."

These are not happy headlines. Our news is full of sadness, evil, sickness and death. Why is that so? God made everything good. How then did our world get into this mess? Let's see what God's Word tells us.

Bible Content

1. God's enemy, Satan.
(Ezekiel 28:12-15; Isaiah 14:12-16; Luke 10:18; Revelation 12:9)

▲ Option#6:

Print SATAN on newsprint or chalkboard. Say, "Let's list what you know about Satan." Write children's responses and use them, while introducing this part of the lesson, as a basis for correcting wrong ideas. Have some idea starters in mind if children don't respond: e.g., "evil," "an angel," "tempted Adam and Eve."

(GOD 14, Lucifer 22, Satan 23, heaven 25, world 3; newsprint and markers or chalkboard and chalk.)

To understand Adam's disobedience *(refer to memory verse)*, we must first learn something about God's enemy, Satan. ▲#6

In heaven, where God lives *(place 25 and 14)*, there are many angels whom He created. Long before the world was created, there was a beautiful angel whose name was Lucifer *(add 22)*. The Bible tells us that he was the highest of all the angels. He was wise and beautiful. He was dressed in clothing covered with precious stones, and he was in heaven with God (Ezekiel 28:12-15).

Lucifer became proud and wanted to be greater and more important than God. He even wanted to be like God (Isaiah 14:12-16). Perhaps he wanted the angels to worship him as they worshiped God.

In heaven everything is holy, pure, good and right, like God Himself. When Lucifer decided he wanted his own way instead of God's way, God had to put him out of heaven. Rebelling against God and His way is sin, and there is no sin in heaven. When Jesus was here on earth He said that He had seen Lucifer fall from heaven (Luke 10:18). At that time his name was changed to Satan (meaning enemy; *add 23*) or the devil (meaning evil one). The Bible calls him a deceiver (Revelation 12:9). He has been God's enemy ever since. Satan becomes our enemy, too, when we choose to go God's way.

All through the Bible we learn about the war or conflict between God and Satan. When Satan saw the beautiful new world and how happy Adam and Eve were as they talked with God, he moved the conflict down to earth *(add 3)*. Satan was determined to get Adam and Eve to follow him instead of God.

Sketch 8 **River**

2. God's command to Adam. (Genesis 2:16-17; 2:9; 3:22)

(Tree 20, flowers 4, rabbit 8, deer 9, bird 11, lamb 21, Adam 18, Eve 19, GOD 14.)

There was no sin in God's beautiful new creation. *(Have 20, 4, 8, 9, 11, 21 on board ahead of time or place them now.)* No one did anything wrong and no one was sad. Adam and Eve were perfectly happy and good *(add 18 and 19)*. God *(add 14)* was very close to them and very real, even though He did not have a body as they did.

In the middle of this beautiful garden there were two special trees. One was called the Tree of Life; anyone who ate its fruit would live forever. The other was called the Tree of the Knowledge of Good and Evil. God had told Adam that they could eat as much as they wanted from any tree in the Garden except this one. *(Have the children turn to Genesis 2:16,17 in their Bibles. Then read, stopping each time at the word "thou" or "you" and having them read to the next punctuation mark.)* ▲#7

▲ Option#7:

Display a large sheet of newsprint on which you have printed Genesis 2:16,17. Have the children read together from this, following the instructions given. This will be especially helpful if they are bringing different Bible translations to class.

God said, "You are not to eat from this tree. The day you do, you will die." Adam knew only about goodness; God did not want him to know about evil.

Adam heard what God said and understood just what God meant. He would be sure that Eve understood it also. God was testing them to see if they would choose His way or their own way. *(Remove 18 and 14.)*

3. Eve's temptation. (Genesis 3:1 - 6a)

(Serpent 24, SATAN 23, word strip SIN.)

One day a serpent came to visit Eve *(add 24)*. If we would have such a visitor, we would be very frightened, but in the Garden Adam and Eve were not afraid and neither were the animals. This serpent was a very clever and sly animal. The Bible says he did not crawl on the ground as all snakes do today. We don't know exactly what he looked like.

However, when the serpent came to Eve, there was another visitor present whom Eve did not see. Satan, God's enemy, was speaking through the serpent *(add 23)*. Satan has no body of his own and he likes to use the lips and bodies of living creatures to do his work.

The serpent spoke to Eve: "Did God really say you couldn't eat from every tree in the Garden?"

Eve answered, "We may eat the fruit of the trees in the garden, but God did say, 'You must not eat fruit from the tree in the middle of the Garden, and you must not touch it, or you will die.'"

Did Eve quote God correctly? Let's check. *(Have children look again at 2:16,17 in their Bibles or on the newsprint poster to see what God said. Ask one child to read the verses aloud, or read them together.)* No, she changed what God had said by adding to it. What did she add? *(Allow response.)*

Then Satan told Eve that what God had said was not true: "You will not surely die...you will be like God, knowing good and evil." It was as if Satan said to Eve that God didn't love her and was not good to her or He would have let her eat from that tree so she could be like Him. Many years later the Lord Jesus said that Satan is a liar and the father of lies (John 8:44).

Eve listened. She began to believe Satan's lie and to doubt what God had said. She saw how good the fruit looked on the tree. She thought how nice it would be to be wise. Then she put out her hand, took the fruit, and ate it. She disobeyed God's command. That was SIN *(place word strip SIN on board)*. It was choosing her own way instead of God's way *(remove 23 and 24)*.

4. Adam's sin. (Genesis 3:6b-13)

After Eve ate the fruit, she gave some to Adam *(replace 18)*, and he ate it, too. Because the fruit was from the Tree of the Knowledge of Good and Evil, their eyes were opened to see good and also evil.

What does our memory verse tell us happened because of their choice? "By one man's disobedience many were made sinners." *(Show verse visual if necessary.)* Adam disobeyed and he became a sinner. He had known only good before. Now he knew evil from experience. Disobeying God was sin.

At once, Adam and Eve realized they were naked and they felt ashamed. They made themselves clothing out of the leaves of a fig tree. When they heard the voice of God calling to them in the early evening, they were afraid and hid themselves among the trees.

God *(replace 14)* called to Adam, "Where are you?"

Adam answered God, "When I heard You in the garden, I was afraid because I was naked, so I hid."

God said to him, "Who told you that you were naked? Have you been eating the fruit I told you not to eat?"

Because Adam was now a sinner, he began to blame Eve for his actions. When God questioned Eve about what she had done, she blamed the serpent.

▲ Option#8:

Prepare eight word cards to use on flannelgraph board or to have children hold. On four, print names of those God punished. On the other four, print brief descriptions of their punishments:

SERPENT, Cursed, Crawl on belly, Hated & feared;
SATAN, Enemy of God & believers;
EVE, Pain in childbirth, Husband in charge;
ADAM, Work hard, Thorns & weeds grow.

Have children match name cards with punishment cards from reading Scripture. Or use the matching cards as your visual when you tell this part of the story.

5. God's punishes sin. (Genesis 3:14 -19)

Because Adam and Eve had disobeyed God, God had to punish them just as He had said He would. God first punished the serpent, then Satan *(replace 24 and 23)*, and finally Adam and Eve. ▲#8

a. Serpent (vs. 14). God said to the serpent, "Because you have done this, you are cursed above all cattle and every living thing. You will crawl on your belly and eat dust all the days of your life." Today snakes or serpents move by crawling on their bellies, and are hated and feared by most people *(add 24)*.

b. Satan (vs. 15). God said to Satan, "I will put enmity between you and the woman, and between your offspring and hers." Enmity means a conflict or war between Satan and those who trust in God, and between Satan and the Lord Jesus. This battle still goes on today *(add 23)*.

c. Eve (vs. 16). God told Eve she would have much pain in giving birth to children and that her husband would be in charge of her.

d. Adam (vss. 17-19). God told Adam that because he had listened to his wife and eaten the fruit God told him not to eat, he would have to work hard all the days of his life. For the first time thorns and thistles would grow along with the fruits and vegetables so that it would be very difficult to get their food.

God had told Adam and Eve, "When you eat of the tree you will surely die." When Adam sinned by disobeying God, his sin came between him and God; he died in his spirit. This is called spiritual death or separation from God.

Both Adam and Eve had to leave the Garden because they were now sinners. Death (sickness and aging) began to work in their bodies and many years later their bodies died, too. This is called physical death. If they had not disobeyed God, they could have lived forever.

6. God shows His mercy. (Gen. 3:21-24)

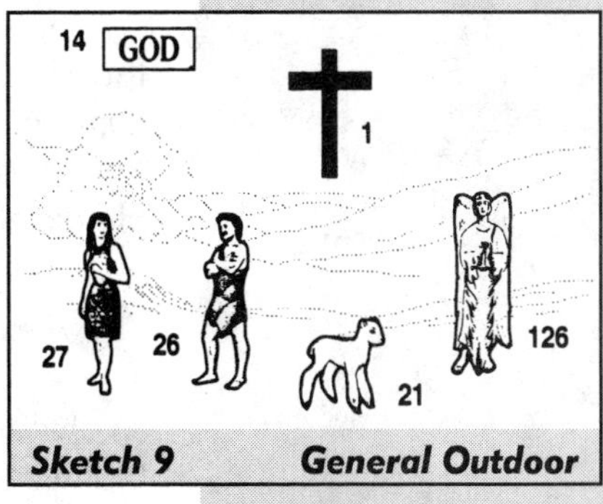

Sketch 9 **General Outdoor**

(GOD 14, Adam 26, Eve 27; add cross l, lamb 21 and angel 126 as lesson progresses.)

God didn't stop loving Adam and Eve when they chose to disobey Him *(place 14, 26, 27 on board)*. He had to punish them in order to keep His word, but He showed them His love and mercy in some special ways:

a. He made them clothes of skins (vs. 21). God made them clothes from the skins of animals. When He did this, an animal had to give up its life *(add 21)* to provide them a covering--a beautiful picture of Jesus who gave up His life to make us fit to come into God's presence.

b. He promised a Savior (vs. 15). In verse 15 we read the first promise of the coming of the Savior, the "seed [offspring] of the woman." The Savior was to come as the son of a woman from the human family of Adam and Eve. His Father would not be a man, but God himself.

This promise also says that Satan would try to defeat Jesus—he would "bruise his heel." It looked as though Satan had won a victory when Jesus was nailed to the cross *(add 1)*, but Jesus rose from the grave and showed that Satan's power was broken.

c. He protected them (vss. 22-24). Then God said, "Now the man knows both good and evil. He must not be allowed to eat the fruit of the Tree of Life and live forever." So, because God loved Adam and Eve,He sent them away from the Garden and placed cherubim (special angels) at the entrance to guard the way to the Tree of Life *(add 126)*.

■ Conclusion

Summary

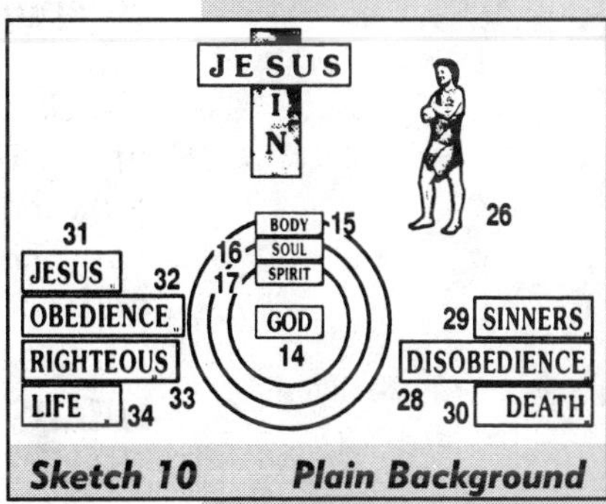

Sketch 10 **Plain Background**

(Cross object lesson; Adam 26, GOD 14, disobedience 28, sinner 29, death 30, Jesus 31, obedience 32, righteous 33, life 34; body/soul/spirit circles, and words body 15, soul 16, and spirit 17.)

Our memory verse reminds us of how sin entered the world *(display verse visual and say verse together)*. Which words in our verse describe Adam? *(Disobedience, sinners; place 26, 28, 29.)* Sin is disobeying God and His Word. What did God say would happen if Adam disobeyed? *(Adam would die; add 30)*.

Death is separation. God is holy, He cannot stand sin in His presence, so Adam's sin separated him from God. ▲#9 God could no longer live in Adam's spirit. *(Place body/soul/spirit circles on board; move 14 from the inner circle; place to the left of SIN barrier, opposite Adam.)* Sin was like a wall blocking Adam's way to God. Adam went on living, but without God in his spirit. Everyone born into

▲ Option#9:

Definition word card: Death = separation.

the world is like Adam, having an empty place in his spirit where God wants to live.

How can God live in us when we are sinners? Our verse tells us that Jesus made this possible. He, the second Man, obeyed God by dying on the cross and rising from the dead so that we could be made righteous (or right in God's sight; *add 32,33*) and have our sins forgiven. He did all this so He could give us life *(add 34).*

Application

How can we have this life? First, we must *believe* two things: 1) that we are sinners and cannot make ourselves righteous or good; we need a Savior; and 2) that the Lord Jesus Christ is the Son of God who died to pay for our sin and be our Savior.

Then we must *do* two things: 1) confess to Him that we have sinned, and 2) receive Jesus as our Savior. When we do this, God forgives our sin and the Holy Spirit comes to live within us. *(Place crosspiece across wall to form a cross, covering the S in sin with the middle S in Jesus. Move GOD back to spirit section of circles.)* He gives us everlasting life, the kind of life that can live with Him in heaven someday. Then God sees us as righteous because of what Jesus did for us.

Which side of this wall are you on? Have you obeyed God by believing Jesus died for you and asking Him to be your savior? Has He forgiven you for your sin? Do you have God's life within you? Let's thank God for sending His only Son to make a way for sinners like us, to be forgiven and made ready for heaven.

Response Activity

Give opportunity in class for those who are not sure which side of the wall they are on to trust Christ as Savior. Invite those who took that step to come after class to tell you or a helper. Encourage any who have trusted Christ as their Savior to tell the group how and when this happened in their lives.

HELPS FOR YOUNGER CHILDREN

Memory Verse: Shorten to "By the obedience of One shall many be made righteous." Reinforce the meaning of the word righteous. Teach the meaning of the first part of the verse (see p. 20).

Bible Content: Simplify the details of the punishments in Section 5 (p. 24) and God's mercy in Section 6 (p. 25).

Conclusion: Omit word strips and body/soul/spirit circles; emphasize on disobedience and obedience, the meaning of sin and forgiveness.

Cain and Abel Bring Sacrifices

Theme: God Calls Us — Through the Sacrifice of the Lord Jesus

Lesson 4

BEFORE YOU BEGIN...

Most people try to relate to God in some way. Some make it their goal to do more good deeds than bad, hoping the good will outweigh the bad when they stand before God. Some become very active in a church and attempt to live a "good" life. Still others create and worship gods of their own design.

The story of Cain and Abel tells of two men who came to God in very different ways, and how God responded to their acts of worship. Take this opportunity to help your children gain a biblical view of God and how He wants them to come to Him. Show them the only way of salvation from sin—the way God has provided through Jesus Christ our Lord. "For there is no other name under heaven given among men by which we must be saved" (Acts 4:12, NKJV).

AIM:

That the children may

- Know and understand God's reason for requiring an animal (blood) sacrifice for sin in Old Testament times.
- Respond by accepting Jesus Christ as the sacrifice for their sin and by giving thanks to God for sending Jesus to be their sacrifice.

SCRIPTURE: Genesis 4:1-16; Hebrews 11:4.

MEMORY VERSE: Romans 5:8

But God commendeth His love toward us in that while we were yet sinners, Christ died for us.

MATERIALS TO GATHER

Visual for Romans 5:8

Backgrounds: Review Chart, Plain, General Outdoor, Plain with Tree

Figures: R1-R4, 1, 14, 26, 27, 35, 36, 37B, 38, 39, 40, 41, 42, 43, 44, 45, 46, 47, 87, 108

Special:

- ***For Review Chart:*** New word strip SACRIFICE.
- ***For Introduction:*** Pictures or replicas of idols or gods from various countries.
- ***For Memory verse and Conclusion:*** Chalkboard & chalk or newsprint & markers.
- ***For Options:*** Additional materials for any options you choose to use.

Review Token:

▲ Option#1:

Definition word card: Sacrifice = giving up something I value for someone or something of greater value.

▲ Option#2:

Before class, help some children prepare to role play one or more situations containing a sacrificial act; e.g., giving up T.V. time to help a friend with homework; giving a favorite toy to a new child on the block who has none. Ask the class to tell what was sacrificed and why. Discuss what each person would gain from the sacrifice.

REVIEW CHART

Display the Review Chart. Review lesson themes and memory verses, placing R1-R3 on the chart as the themes are stated. Have R4 and word strip SACRIFICE ready to use when indicated. Use the following questions to review Lesson 3.

1. What is sin? *(Disobeying God)*
2. How did sin enter the world? *(By Adam's disobedience)*
3. Why does Adam's disobedience make us sinners today? *(Because Adam and Eve were our first parents, everyone born since them has been born a sinner.)*
4. How many people are sinners? *(All)*
5. According to the Bible, how can people be made righteous and have their sins forgiven? *(By trusting Jesus as their Savior)*
6. Describe (or act out) how Adam and Eve disobeyed God.

Today we are learning an important way God calls us: through the sacrifice of the Lord Jesus *(place R4 on Review Chart)*. The word "sacrifice" *(display word strip)* means to give up something that is of value to you for the sake of someone or something that has greater value. ▲#1 Have you ever given up some of your time for watching a favorite TV program in order to help a friend with homework? ▲#2 You made a sacrifice. Though you gave up something you wanted, you gained the satisfaction of helping someone.

Because God loves us, Jesus gave up His life—something of great value—when He died on the cross so that He might gain eternal life for all those who believe in Him. The Bible tells us this is the only way anyone can come to God. Now God is calling all people, including us, to come to Him through the sacrifice of His Son, Jesus Christ.

♥ MEMORY VERSE

Use the visual from Bible Verses Visualized *to teach Romans 5:8. Have newsprint and marker or chalkboard and chalk available.*

To begin, brainstorm with the class about how they think God shows His love today. Have some idea starters ready to trigger thinking, in case they don't respond: e.g., making our world, giving us families, giving us Jesus. Write responses on chalkboard or newsprint. Discuss briefly.

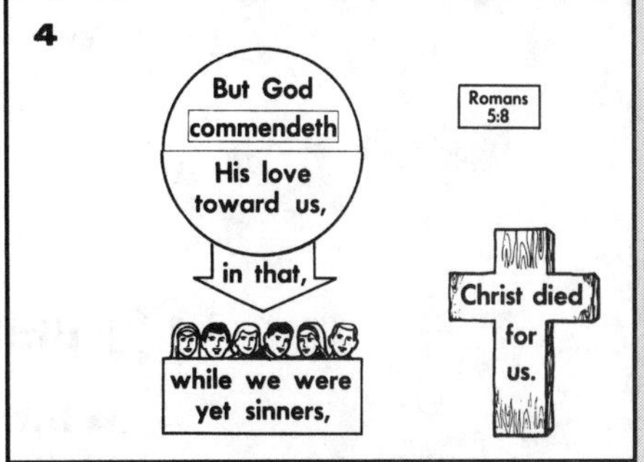

Our verse tells us something very special about God's love. *(Display verse visual and read it together.)* It says God commendeth His love to you and me. To "commend" means to show or demonstrate. How did God show His love? *(Allow response.)* The verse says that Jesus Christ, God's Son, died for us. He gave up His life, His most valuable possession, to take the punishment for our sin.

We are all described in this Bible verse. *(Ask children to find the word that describes us.)* We are all called sinners, or those who want to go their own way instead of God's way, who have disobeyed God and His Word. The Lord Jesus gave up His life for those who did not love or obey God.

How many of you can think of someone you'd be willing to die for so they could live? Why? *(Response)* It would be very difficult to give up your life for someone you love very much. Most of us would find it almost impossible to die for an enemy. But Jesus did just that. He sacrificed His life for you and me! Now God can forgive sin. And if you have trusted Jesus as your Savior, He has forgiven you for your sin. We can never doubt God's great love for us when we remember how He showed His love by sending His only Son, Jesus Christ, to be the sacrifice for our sin. *(Work with the children on memorizing the verse and reviewing its meaning.)* ▲#3

▲ Option#3:

Learning the verse: Have the class read the verse from the board. Allow different children to remove pieces of the verse visual, one at a time, and have the class or individuals repeat the verse each time a piece is removed, until the group can say it without any visual at all. Then have several children put the pieces back on the board in correct order and say the verse once more.

BIBLE LESSON OUTLINE

Cain and Abel Bring Sacrifices

■ Introduction

How do we come to God?

■ Bible Content

1. A new home.
2. The first baby.
3. Cain's and Abel's sacrifices.
4. Cain's sin.
5. Cain's punishment.

Conclusion

Summary

Application

Wrong ways and the right way to come to God.

Response Activity

Coming to God through Jesus.
Thanking God for sending Jesus to be their sacrifice.

BIBLE LESSON

Introduction

How do we come to God?

Use pictures or replicas of idols or gods from various countries.

The Bible tells us there is only one true God, the Creator of all things, but people do not always know or recognize this and so they worship many other kinds of gods. Can you think what they might be? *(Response)* Some worship gods of stone or metal or even objects in nature, such as trees, the sun and lightning. *(Show pictures or replicas of gods or idols.)* They try to please their gods by bringing them food and other gifts. They believe if they do this, they can pray to their gods and the gods will hear and answer their prayers.

The Bible also tells us that there is only one way to come to God. This is through believing that His Son, the Lord Jesus Christ, sacrificed His life on the cross to pay for our sins, and receiving Him as our Savior.

God planned for this sacrifice long ago. He taught Adam and Eve the meaning of sacrifice to prepare the way for the coming of the Lord Jesus into the world many, many years later. Today's lesson takes us back to that time.

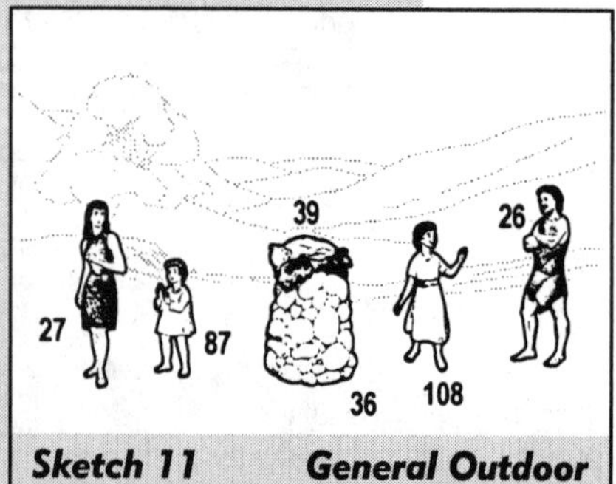

Sketch 11 **General Outdoor**

Bible Content

1. A new home. (Genesis 3:23,24)

(Adam 26, Eve 27, Cain 87, Abel 108, altar 36, offering 39.)

After Adam and Eve sinned, God put them out of the beautiful Garden *(place 26 and 27 on board)*. To keep them from going back, He placed a flaming sword that turned in every direction at the east side of the Garden. Then He sent cherubim (special angels) to guard the way to the Tree of Life so that Adam and Eve could not eat of it and live forever in their sin.

Adam and Eve had to make a new home for themselves—maybe a place under a tree or in a cave. Adam had to work very hard to get enough food for both of them to eat. Thorns and thistles and weeds now grew along with their food plants. They must have become tired and probably were often sad about what they had done. Maybe they thought about the beautiful Garden and wished that they had not disobeyed God. Perhaps they talked often about what had happened and remembered God's promise to send them someone (Jesus) who would defeat Satan and sin.

2. The first baby. (Genesis 4:1,2)

After Adam and Eve had established their new home, God gave them a baby boy. They named him Cain. Eve experienced pain when Cain was born, as God had promised mothers would, but it was worth it when she saw her baby son—the first baby ever born into the world! How happy Adam and Eve must have been as they cared for him. Sometime later God gave them another baby boy. They called him Abel. Adam and Eve watched their sons grow *(add 87 and 108)* and taught them all they knew about the animals and the land.

As they were growing up, Cain and Abel had many things to learn. Abel must have enjoyed playing with the little lambs and looking after them for his father. When he was older, he became a shepherd, looking after the flocks of sheep and leading them out to pasture. Cain liked to work in the garden, to dig in the earth and watch things grow. When he grew older he became a farmer.

▲ Option#4:

Review the meaning of the word sin, using the definition word card you made last week.

Because Adam and Eve had become sinners when they disobeyed God in the Garden (by eating the fruit God had told them not to eat), Cain and Abel were born as sinners, wanting their own way. ▲#4 Probably they argued and fought as children do today.

Perhaps, as many children do, Cain and Abel asked their father and mother to tell them a story. Then Adam may have told them about the beautiful garden home where they had once lived. Maybe Cain and Abel asked why they no longer lived there. Do you think it was hard for Adam to tell his sons how he and their mother had sinned and how God had punished them and put them out of the Garden?

Adam must have told his sons that he knew God still loved them because He had promised to someday send one who would defeat Satan and sin. And he must have explained to them that when he and Eve left the Garden, God made clothes for both of them from animal skins, and that the animals had to die in order for them to have the clothing. They might have seen their father offer an animal as a sacrifice to God for himself and his family *(add 36, 39)*.

The Bible does not tell us how Cain and Abel learned about offering sacrifices, but it does say that when they were older, they brought offerings to God. They did not have God's Word written down as we do today, so they must have heard from their father that this was the way to come to God.

3. Cain's and Abel's sacrifices. (Genesis 4:3-5; Hebrews 11:4)

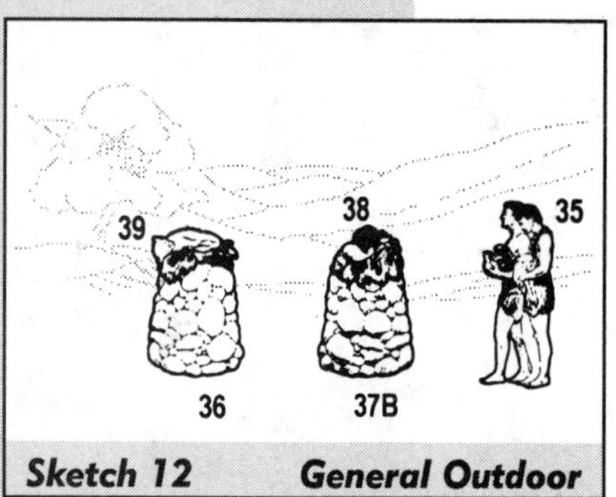

Sketch 12 **General Outdoor**

(Cain and Abel 35, altars 36, 37B, offerings 38, 39. Remove Cain and Abel 35 after offerings are placed on altars.)

One day Cain brought an offering to God. Perhaps he built an altar from stones on which to place the offering. Maybe he thought that he would like to give God the best thing he could find. He brought some of the fruits and vegetables from his farm and offered them to the Lord. Perhaps he thought that God would be especially pleased with his offering because he had raised the fruits and vegetables himself.

Abel also brought an offering to God. He went to the flock, took some lambs, killed them and offered the best parts as a sacrifice to God. ⍓

⍓ Note:

There is little to be found concerning the nature and substance of sacrifices and offerings to God prior to the instructions of the Mosaic Ceremonial Law.

Cain and Abel were brothers. They had the same parents and were brought up in the same home. Both were sinners just like their parents. Both wanted to bring offerings to God, but there was one difference. That difference was the kind of offering each brought.

What did God think of their offerings? Look in Genesis 4:4. What does it tell us? *(Wait for the children to look at the verse and answer the question.)* Yes, that God was pleased with or accepted Abel's offering. We don't know exactly how God showed His acceptance.

In the book of Hebrews (11:4) in the New Testament we learn that Abel offered to God a more acceptable sacrifice by faith. ▲#5

▲ Option#5:

Print Hebrews 11:4b and 5a on chalkboard or newsprint for all to see and think about as you discuss this truth.

Faith is believing what God says and then doing (or obeying) it. Where did Abel hear what God had said about offerings and what he should bring as a sacrifice to God? From his father, Adam. When Abel brought his offering, he did it by faith. He believed and obeyed what God had said and God was pleased.

Now look at Genesis 4:5. What does it tell us about God's response to Cain's offering? *(Wait for a child to answer.)* God was not pleased. In some way God showed that He did not accept the offering. Had Cain shown faith in God when he brought his offering? Did he bring what God had told them to bring? No. It seems as though Cain decided his fruits and vegetables were just as good an offering for God as anything else, even though he knew that God had said He wanted an animal sacrifice. God was not pleased with Cain's offering for He knew what Cain was thinking and feeling in his heart. He knew Cain did not want to do exactly as God had said he should.

Sketch 13 **Plain with Tree**

4. Cain's sin. (Genesis 4:6-8)

(Cain 46, Abel 47. Add Adam 26, Eve 27, GOD 14.)
When Cain saw that his brother's sacrifice was accepted and his own

was not, he became very angry and it showed on his face *(place 46 on board)*. God spoke lovingly to him *(add 14)* and asked why he was angry. He told Cain that if he obeyed, if he did what was right, he would be accepted. But Cain would not listen to God. He was not willing to come God's way. If he could not come to God by his own way, he would not come. But God was not willing to accept Cain's way *(remove figures)*.

Cain was jealous of Abel because God had accepted Abel's sacrifice, but refused Cain's. Instead of obeying God, he allowed his jealousy to turn to anger at God and at his brother. This anger was sin. He kept this anger inside himself instead of confessing it.

Sometimes when we disobey God and He shows us that we are wrong, it makes us irritable and we strike out at people around us. One day when Cain and Abel were out in the field, they started to argue. Before Cain knew what was happening, he killed his brother Abel. *(Place 46 and 47 on board.)*

How sad Adam and Eve must have been when they discovered this *(add 26 and 27)*! They knew that Cain had sinned because they had first sinned in the Garden by disobeying God's command. Adam and Eve experienced sorrow and saddness because of their sons. *(Remove 26, 27, and 47.)*

5. Cain's punishment. (Genesis 4:9-16; 5:4; Jude 11)

God came to Cain *(add 14)* and asked where Abel was. Cain lied, saying that he didn't know, but God knew what had happened. God told Cain that he would be punished for his sin. He would have to leave home and wander on the earth. And he would no longer be able to grow fruits and vegetables in the soil as he had been doing. So Cain left his father and mother and went far away to live and to make a home for himself and his wife.

Note:

Someone may ask, Where did Cain get his wife? Since Adam and Eve were the first parents and the entire human race came from them, Cain probably married one of his sisters or nieces (Genesis 5:4).

In verse 16 we read that Cain went out from the presence of the Lord. He tried to run away from God. He would not give up his own way, and he would not come to God for forgiveness.

Conclusion

Summary

(Altars 36, 37B, offerings 38, 39, cross 1, word strips 40-45; chalkboard and chalk or newsprint and markers.)

These two altars picture the ways that Cain and Abel tried to come to God *(place 36, 37B on board)*. What did Cain do? He brought the things that he had grown *(add 38)*. What was wrong with this? It was not the way God had said to come.

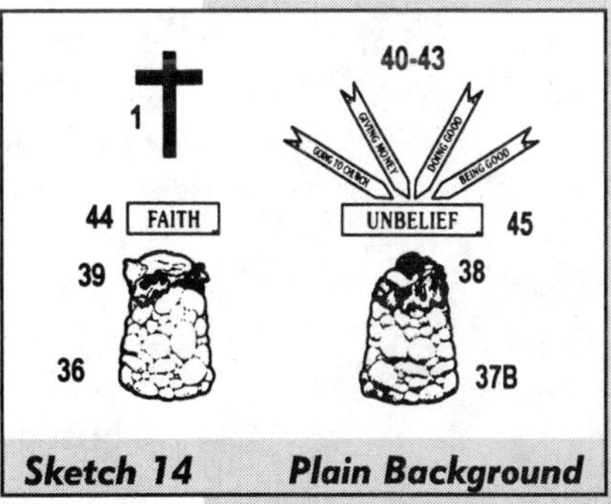

Sketch 14 Plain Background

Abel discovered the way to God and obeyed. He offered the sacrifice God asked for *(add 39)*. He killed lambs from his flock and brought the best parts as a sacrifice to God. Abel came by faith, bringing the kind of offering God required. It was pleasing to God and He accepted it.

Today we don't need to bring a lamb when we come to God. People did this to show that they believed, or had faith, in God's promise of a Savior before Jesus came and died on the cross. Jesus, God's Son, became our Sacrifice by giving up His most valuable thing—His life—to take the punishment for our sins *(add 1)*.

Application

What are some ways people today try to come to God, hoping He will accept them? *(Allow students to respond. Write responses on newsprint or chalkboard for all to see. Use idea starters below, if necessary.)* ▲#6

One way is by being good, trying to do the right thing on your own. Another way is by doing good for other people. We should be good and we should do good for others, but can we have our sins forgiven that way? No, for we can never be good enough or do enough good things to be accepted by God.

Some people try to be accepted by God by giving money or by going to church. It's good to give money to the church, and we need to go there to learn about God and to be with those who love Him, but that is not the way to come to God for forgiveness.

Which person are you like, Cain or Abel? Have you come to God through the Lord Jesus by believing He died as your sacrifice for sin? Our memory verse tells us that God sent Jesus to die for our sins because He loved us! Let's say our verse together and then thank God for His great love.

▲ Option#6:

Print on 4"x6" cards some ways people try to come to God—one way on each card. Ahead of time hand the cards to pairs of children to pantomime. Have the children do simple role plays of some ways people try to come to God. Include those cited in text.
Or, provide paper (or mural paper) and crayons for class members to illustrate these ways, as time permits.

Response Activity

Invite those who want to receive Christ as Savior to come to you after class.

Give opportunity to those who belong to the Lord Jesus to thank God for His great love and for sending Jesus to be their sacrifice. Encourage the children to pray sentence prayers of thanks either aloud or silently.

HELPS FOR YOUNGER CHILDREN

Memory Verse: Shorten verse to "... while we were yet sinners, Christ died for us." Be careful to emphasize why Christ died and rose again and that He did it because He loved us.

Enoch Goes to Heaven

Theme: God Calls Us — By His Word

Lesson

5

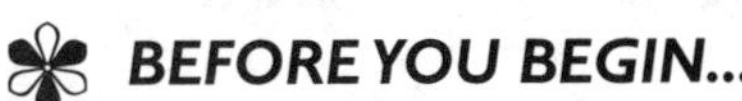

Every one of us has experienced peer pressure. We know how hard it is to be different, to do what is right and good when others laugh or make fun. It's hard for children, too. They need to know how important it is to stand for God and how they can do it when it seems that everyone else is against them.

Enoch is an outstanding example of standing for God in the face of a world that had turned its back on Him. Encourage your boys and girls to follow Enoch's example of hearing God's voice and obeying Him. Make it a priority to help them form the habit of reading and obeying God's Word daily so they can stand for God with His help. "Be strong and of good courage;... for the Lord your God is with you wherever you go" (Joshua 1:9, NKJV).

AIM:

That the children may

- Know that God speaks personally to us today through His Word, the Bible.
- Respond by learning to trust and obey God through reading and obeying His Word.

SCRIPTURE: Genesis 4:16-26; 5:1-32

MEMORY VERSE: Romans 10:17

So then faith cometh by hearing and hearing by the Word of God.

MATERIALS TO GATHER

Visual for Romans 10:17
Backgrounds: Review Chart, Plain, General Outdoor
Figures: R1-R5, 13, 14, 18, 19, 24, 26, 27, 35, 44, 45, 46, 48 (7 stick figures), 49 (6 arrows), 50, 51, 52, 53, 54, 87, 92, 93, 108, 116, 126
Special:

- ***For Introduction:*** A light-weight chair.
- ***For Conclusion:*** Chalkboard & chalk or newsprint & marker; Bible reading forms.
- ***For Options:*** Additional materials for any options you choose to use.
- ***Note:*** To make Bible reading forms, use copy machine to duplicate pattern R-4 found on page 158.

Review Token:

REVIEW CHART

Display the Review Chart. Have R1-R5 ready to use when indicated. Place figures of characters already studied on either side of the telephone (serpent 24, Adam 18, Eve 19, angel with sword 126, Cain 87, Abel 108, GOD 14). Use the following suggestion to review highlights from Lessons 1-4.

Invite the children, one at a time, to choose a character from the board and tell one or two things they have learned about that person. ▲#1

▲ Option#1:

Let volunteers choose a person from the board and act out things they have learned about him or her. Have the class guess the character.

Ask them to list R1-R4 and say the memory verses as they place the symbols on the board. Tie the character review to the Review Chart-memory verse review by asking the children to identify each character with a particular lesson and theme. (For example, Adam, Lesson 2, God Calls Us by His Love, Genesis 2:7.) Place R5 on the chart as you introduce the new theme, By His Word.

We've been learning how God spoke to people long ago by things He did. Let's list them: By His wonderful works of creation, by His love in creating people, by His mercy when Adam and Eve sinned, and by sending Jesus to be the sacrifice for sin. God still calls us, using these things to get our attention. He also speaks to us today by His Word, His written Word, the Bible *(place R5 on Review Chart)*. Our lesson and memory verse will help us understand how He does this.

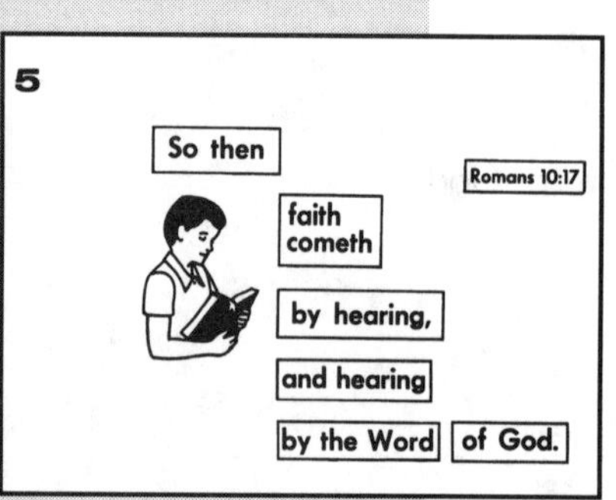

♥ MEMORY VERSE

Use FAITH 44 and the visual from Bible Verses Visualized *to teach Romans 10:17.*

What is faith? *(Place 44 on board; allow children to tell what they think it is.)* We cannot see it or feel it or smell it, but faith is one of God's greatest gifts. Faith is trusting God completely, even when we can't see or understand His ways. We need faith to receive the Lord Jesus as our Savior and to believe that He has forgiven all of our sin. Then we need faith to live a life that pleases God. But where do we find faith?

(Display verse visual and have a child or the class read it aloud.) Where does our verse tell us faith comes from? *(Encourage the children to answer your questions.)* But from hearing what? The Word of God. How do we hear the Word of God? By reading the Bible. We do not hear an actual voice coming out of the pages, but we learn what God wants us to know as we read and memorize His Word. We also hear what God wants us to know when someone (like your Bible club or Sunday school teacher or pastor) teaches us what God's Word says.

It is very important to read the Bible so your faith in God will grow strong. After you read what God has promised, you can count on Him to do that very thing for you just when you need it. *(Have the children explain the verse in their own words as you learn it together.)* ▲#2

▲ Option#2:

Learning the verse: After you have said the verse together several times, hand the parts of the visual to different children. Have them come to the board and put the pieces back in correct order. Allow a second group to do the same. Say the verse together each time. For a variation, time the groups to see who can "beat the clock."

BIBLE LESSON OUTLINE

Enoch Goes to Heaven

■ Introduction

We use faith every day

■ Bible Content

1. The human race grows.
   a. Cain's unbelief.
   b. Seth's faith.
2. God preserves His Word.
3. Enoch does not die.
4. Enoch is taken to heaven.

■ Conclusion

Summary

Application

Learning to hear God speak through the Bible.

Response Activity

Reading the Bible for themselves to know and do what God says.

BIBLE LESSON

■ Introduction

We use faith every day.

Use a light-weight chair and FAITH word strip 44.

Did you know that each one of us lives by faith every day? *(Place*

FAITH 44 on flannelboard.) We put our trust in people and things all the time without ever thinking about it. Can anyone think of some ways we do this? *(Encourage answers. If necessary, give some examples of faith as idea starters: trusting the school bus driver to get me to school safely, believing the food I eat each day will make me strong and not sick.)*

▲ Option#3:

Have a child help test the chair with you as the object lesson proceeds.

Here's a simple example of what it means to have faith in something or someone. *(Place chair in front of you before the class. Pretend you have never seen it before and have never sat in it.)* ▲#3 This looks like a good chair, solidly built. The bolts are tight, and nothing seems loose or broken. Do you think it would hold me up if I sat on it? *(As you mention the qualities of the chair, pick it up, examine it and check its parts, color and design. Demonstrate its sturdiness by thumping it lightly on the floor.)*

Yes, this seems to be a very good chair. I believe—have faith—that it will hold me if I sit on it. But is that all faith does? Just say, "I believe"? No, that's not all. What must I do to prove that I have faith in this chair? Yes, I must sit on it. *(Sit on the chair.)* When I act upon what I say I believe, I show that I really have faith. When I actually sit on the chair and it holds me, like I expected, it helps me to have faith in the chair for the future.

That tells us a little about what it's like to have faith in God. We know about Him and what He can do from what we learn in our Bible lessons and by reading our Bibles. We say we have faith in Him, that we believe what He says, because of all we know. But is that enough? No, of course not.

It's important to know what the Bible tells us about God and that He can be trusted to keep His promises. That's a little like knowing the chair is sturdy and safe and will hold me if I sit on it. But it's just as important to act on what I know—like when I sat on the chair. By faith, I must obey what God tells me to do, even though I have no proof that He will keep His promise to me. When I see that God can be trusted to keep His promises, it will be easier to obey and trust Him in faith the next time. Sometime in the future this chair will become old and weakened with use. It may not always be dependable. But God never wears out. I can always count on Him to do what He says in His Word—no matter what!

Sketch 15 General Outdoor

■ Bible Content

1. The human race grows. (Genesis 1:28)

(Adam 26, Eve 27, Cain & Abel 35)

When God created Adam and Eve and placed them in the Garden *(place 26, 27)*, He told them to multiply (have many children and grandchildren) and fill up the earth. If they had not sinned by disobeying God and choosing to go their own way, their children would have been sinless like them, and they all could have lived forever. But since Adam and Eve sinned, Cain and Abel *(add 35)* were born sinners like their parents.

Sin always separates us from God. Because of his sin of pride, Lucifer was thrown out of heaven. Because of their sin of disobedience, Adam and Eve were sent out of the Garden of Eden *(remove 26, 27)*. Later, because Cain sinned by refusing to go God's way and finally killing his brother *(remove 35)*, he was sent away from home to become a wanderer in the earth.

a. Cain's unbelief (Genesis 4:16-24).

(Cain 46, UNBELIEF 45, city 65.)

When Cain left his father and mother, he traveled east *(place 46)*. He and his wife settled in a land called Nod and began to build a city. A baby boy was born into their home. Then more babies were born until there were many people living in this city. They were all sinners like their parents. Cain and his family passed their unbelief in God down the line from father to son to grandson by example and by teaching. Cain had chosen to go his own way without God. His children and grandchildren did the same.

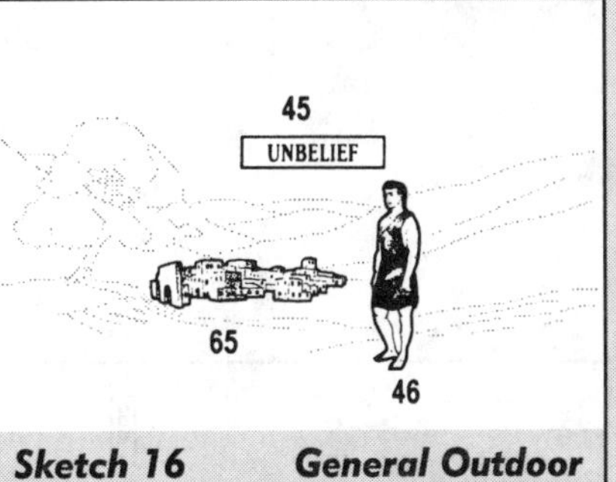

Sketch 16 **General Outdoor**

The people who came from Cain's family were very clever people and they began to do many new things. Of course, the only things they had to work with were those they made themselves. One member of Cain's family invented musical instruments and was called "the father of all who play the harp and the flute." Another man from Cain's family made the first tent as his home and became known as "the father of those who live in tents and raise livestock." Still another discovered that he could forge (or make) all kinds of tools—perhaps knives and shovels and hoes—out of bronze and iron.

The city where these people lived *(add 65)* probably grew rapidly into quite a wonderful place, but it was a city where God was left out. The people did not believe in God and did not teach their children to believe in God. Instead, they believed in themselves and what they could do. They did many good things; they also did many sinful things. One word describes Cain and all the people in his city—UNBELIEF. *(Move Cain to left of city; place UNBELIEF 45 above him.)*

Even today many people are like Cain's family. Smart and able to do great things on their own, they do not know God and, sadly, leave Him out of their lives.

b. Seth's faith (Genesis 4:15, 26).

(Add Adam 26, Eve 27, Seth 116, word strip FAITH 44.)

Adam and Eve must have been very sad after Cain killed Abel. Abel had lived by faith and obeyed God by bringing the right sacrifice. Now he was gone. They must have wondered if there would ever be anyone else who would live

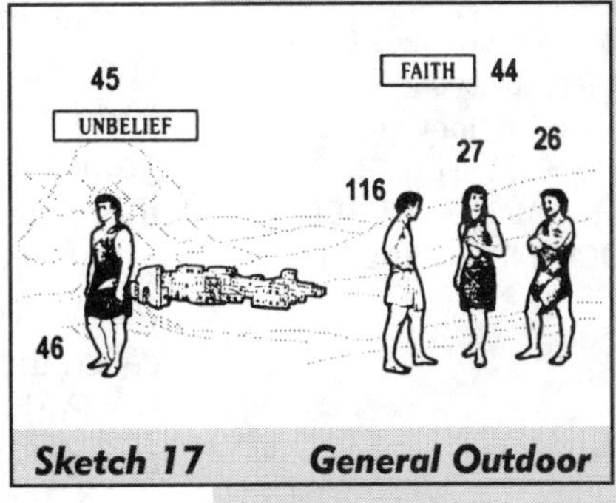

Sketch 17 **General Outdoor**

by faith in God and help their children and grandchildren to believe in and obey God.

But God knew there would be people who would believe in Him. He had a plan, and it included sending Adam and Eve another baby boy. They named him Seth. Seth believed in God and His promises and obeyed God's commands. He taught his family to believe God and obey Him. The Bible tells us that people began to call on the name of the Lord at that time.

All of Seth's family who believed what they knew of God's promise and obeyed His commands passed their faith in God down the line. They taught the things they had learned to their sons and grandsons and so on. In this way they prepared the way for the coming of the promised Savior.

2. God preserves His Word. (Genesis 5:6-25)

(Adam 26, arrow GOD'S WORD 50; add stick figures 48 and arrows 49 as indicated.)

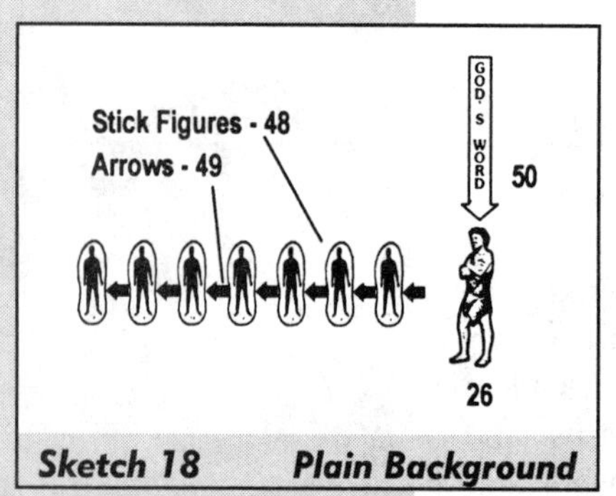

Sketch 18 **Plain Background**

Adam was 130 years old when Seth was born. That sounds strange to us, for today not many people live to be even 100 years old, and parents are much younger than that when they have babies. But Adam was probably like a young man at 130, for he lived another 800 years, until he was 930 years old!

Adam and Eve had many other sons and daughters. When they were grown, they had children and their children had children.

And all these people lived for many years. No doubt their bodies were much stronger than ours today, because the world was new and fresh, free from pollution.

Perhaps God allowed people to live a long time in those days so that His Word could be told over and over again to each new generation and in this way be preserved. The Bible was not written down then, so God used people to pass His words from one generation to another.

▲ Option#4:

Prepare flash cards for names listed below to represent generations from Adam to Methusaleh. Place Adam 26 on board. Give one flashcard to each of seven children; have them take their places in line as you discuss their person: SETH, ENOSH, KENAN, MAHALALEL, JARED, ENOCH, METHUSALEH.

Let's think about how God's Word was handed down through the years. *(See sketch and place figures on board as each generation is named.)* ▲#4 From whom did Adam hear God's Word? *(Place arrow and Adam.)* Directly from God. To whom did Adam pass it on? *(Add arrow and stick figure.)* To Cain and Abel and Seth (and his other children). Seth grew up and had a son who was Adam's grandson. *(Add arrow and second stick figure.)* And his son was Adam's great grandson. Now we can add five more arrows and figures to show us that Adam lived to tell God's Word to his great, great, great, great, great grandchildren. (Enosh, Kenan, Mahalalel, Jared, Enoch, Methusaleh) The seventh figure here stands for Methuselah who is called the oldest man who ever lived. He lived 969 years!

Perhaps as these grandchildren and their families visited Adam and sat around a campfire at night, he would tell all that he knew about the living God who had made the world and made him. He would tell them about the beautiful Garden, and then sadly tell how sin began on earth and why he and Eve had to leave the Garden. Perhaps he said to them, "It is because of my sin, my disobedience to God, that you are sinful and there is evil in the world. It is because of sin that Cain had to leave home."

He may also have said, "Because of sin we bring an animal sacrifice to God. God told me that the punishment for sin is death, but because God loves us, He will accept the death of an animal in our place and forgive our sin. He wants us to love and obey Him. He has promised to send a Savior someday who will defeat Satan and sin."

When Adam died, his sons and grandsons continued to pass on God's Word as they had heard it from Adam.

3. Enoch does not die. (Genesis 5:1-27; Hebrews 11:5,6)

(Remove stick figures or flash cards one at a time as Bible verses are given, leaving the one which represents Enoch.)

Do you remember that God told Adam if he disobeyed and ate the fruit of the tree in the Garden he would die? When Adam disobeyed, he was separated from God and put out of the Garden. Adam lived to be very old, but eventually his body died. Since all people born into the world are sinners because of Adam's disobedience, their bodies eventually die too.

Look in Genesis 5 where we can read about some of the men in Adam's family. What does verse five tell us about Adam? How old was he? *(930)* After he had lived for 930 years, what happened to him? Yes, Adam died. *(As time permits, read the following verses aloud: 5:8, 11, 14, 17, 20, 27—or have different children read them. Ask what each verse says about the man who is described. If you are using the flash cards, write each man's age on the appropriate card—or on a separate age card you attach temporarily to the flash card.)*

What does the Bible say about each one of these people? Yes, that each one died. Now read verse 23. *(Have someone read it aloud.)* What was different about Enoch? *(He did not live as long as the other men.)* Now let's read verse 24 together. What happened to Enoch? *(God took him away.)* Why did Enoch not die? *(He walked with God or had faith in and obeyed God.)* What happened to him? We read in the New Testament (Hebrews 11:5,6) that "by faith" Enoch was taken out of the world so he would not die like everyone else did.

Where does faith come from? Our Bible verse tells us it comes from hearing the Word of God. But where had Enoch heard the Word of God? He may have heard it from Adam, for Adam did not die until Enoch was more than 300 years old. Of course, Adam told others who could have told Enoch. The Bible says that Enoch walked with God and that he pleased God. Let's see what we can learn about Enoch and what did happen to him.

4. Enoch is taken to heaven. (Genesis 5:21-24; Hebrews 11:5,6; Jude 14-15)

(Enoch 51, groups 52, 92, 93.)

Enoch believed and obeyed all that he was taught about what God had said they should do *(place 51 on board)*. He must have brought an animal sacrifice as an offering to God as Abel had done. The New Testament book of Jude tells us that Enoch was a preacher. He warned the people around him that God was going to punish them for their sinful ways if they did not return to Him and obey His Word *(add 52, 92, 93)*.

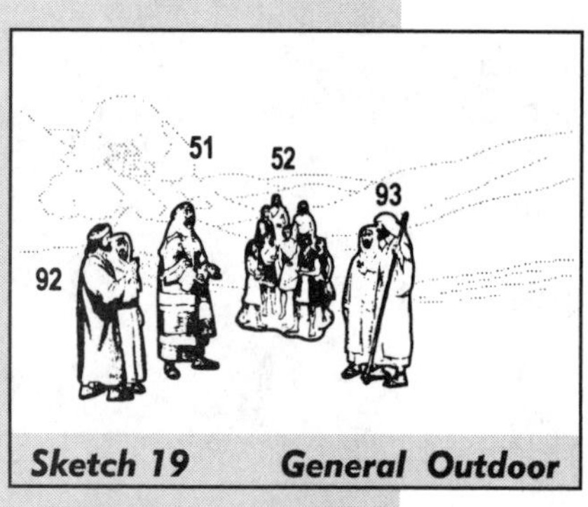

Sketch 19 General Outdoor

Because everyone was a sinner, even those who believed in God began to get farther away from Him. They forgot about the animal sacrifices and God's promise of the Savior to come. They began to be more like those in Cain's line of unbelief. They did not like to have Enoch tell them about their sin, but he preached God's Word anyway.

Perhaps the people laughed at Enoch when he would not join them in doing sinful things. Perhaps they got angry with him when he told them that the Lord would come some day to punish them. But Enoch listened to God's voice and obeyed, even when no one else did. He walked with God.

One day no one could find Enoch anywhere, for God had taken him away *(remove 51)*. What do you think his friends and neighbors thought then? We do not know, but they never saw him again. Because Enoch faithfully listened to God and obeyed His Word, God took him to heaven without dying (vs. 24)!

Conclusion

Summary

(Memory verse visual, boy 13, BELIEVE 53, OBEY 54; chalkboard and chalk or newsprint and markers.)

Do you think that God can speak to us today as He did to Adam and Enoch? How did God talk with them? They didn't have the Bible to read, so God spoke directly to them, probably in a voice they could hear with their ears. Why did God do that? So they would know what He wanted them to do. Enoch was willing to hear God's voice and obey it. He walked with God when hardly anyone else did.

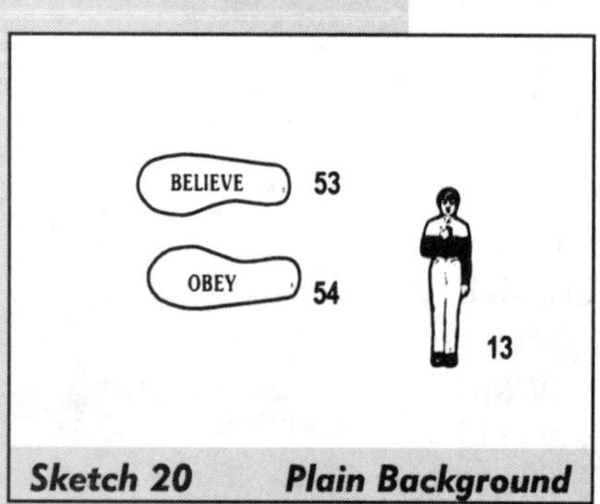

Sketch 20 Plain Background

How does God talk to us today? *(Through His Word, the Bible.)* As we hear and read what the Bible says, it is as if God "speaks" to us from the printed page to give us His instructions. Our memory verse says that by hearing God's Word, we receive faith to believe and obey what He tells us to do. *(Display the verse visual as you review its words and meaning with the children.)*

Application

When God speaks to you through the Bible, what are some things He might tell you? *(Print responses on chalkboard or newsprint for all to see. Have some idea starters in mind; e.g., to obey my parents, to love others, to pray, to tell the truth.)*

God will never say anything to us in our hearts that does not agree with what is written in His Word, the Bible. One day you might read that God wants you to always tell the truth. Then God might remind you that you to lied to your teacher by telling her you had lost your homework, when instead you had not finished it.

What should you do then to make things right? *(Allow for response.)* First, confess to God that you lied to your teacher and ask Him to forgive you. Then, tell your teacher the truth, even if it means failing that assignment. It's hard to do something like this, but God promises He will help us obey Him. He also promises that when we obey His Word in faith, He will give us joy. Are you reading the Bible every day so that you can know what God is saying to you? Are you then obeying what He tells you? Let's ask God now to help us want to hear and obey what He says to us in the Bible.

Response Activity

Give opportunity for children to accept God's forgiveness and receive Jesus as Savior as their first step in obeying what God tells them in His Word.

Give each one a ***Bible reading form*** *(see Materials to Gather) and encourage them to listen and obey God as He speaks to them when they read His Word in the coming week.* ▲#5

▲ Option#5:

Prepare a large Bible reading form on newsprint and do an example reading with them in class so they will understand how to do it at home.

Have the children think quietly about whether they have been disobedient to God's Word. Encourage them, if they have, to ask God to forgive them and then make things right this week. Next week give them opportunity to share what happened as a result.

This is an excellent time to present individual Bible studies designed for children and encourage your boys and girls to use them at home. Consider BCM's "Bible Study Helps" for Genesis or Mailbox Bible Club correspondence lessons (available from BCM International Distribution Center).

HELPS FOR YOUNGER CHILDREN

Bible Content 3: Omit the suggested oral reading of the verses and use only Genesis 5:5 and 5:23,24. Read these aloud to the children, using the questions in the text. Simplify the questions about Enoch. Ask them to tell his age and what happened to him.

God Destroys the World by a Floo

Theme: God Calls Us — To Safety In Jesus

Lesson

6

BEFORE YOU BEGIN...

All children long for physical safety and emotional security, but many don't find it in their families or their world. Your class may be the only refuge some of your children have—the only place where someone takes the time listen to them, to affirm them, to make them feel as though they belong. Trust God to help you provide a secure and loving atmosphere for them.

More importantly, have they found an eternal refuge in Jesus Christ? Have they trusted Him as their Savior? Use the story of how God provided safety for Noah in the ark to point the way to the safety God has provided for them in the Lord Jesus. Encourage them to trust Him as Savior today, for Jesus said, "I am the way, the truth, and the life. No one comes to the Father except through Me" (John 14:6, NKJV).

AIM:

That the children may

- Know that receiving Jesus Christ as Savior is the only way to be safe from the punishment for sin.
- Respond by receiving Christ as their Savior from sin and claiming assurance of forgiveness.

SCRIPTURE: Genesis 6:1-9:19

MEMORY VERSE: John 10:9a

I am the door; by me if any man enter in, he shall be saved.

MATERIALS TO GATHER

Visual for John 10:9a
Backgrounds: Review Chart, Plain, General Outdoor, Rough Sea, Hilltop
Figures: R1-R6, 3, 11, 14, 25, 36, 39, 44, 52, 55, 56, 57, 58, 59, 60, 61, 62, 63, 84, 92, 93, 107, 116 *(Carefully cut around the door of heaven 25 so you can open it; use a small amount of tape to secure cross 84 behind it.)*
Special:

- ***For Conclusion:*** "Door" take-home tokens.
- ***For Options:*** Additional materials for any options you choose to use.
- ***Note:*** To make "Door" take-home tokens, use copy machine to duplicate pattern R-10 found on page 162.

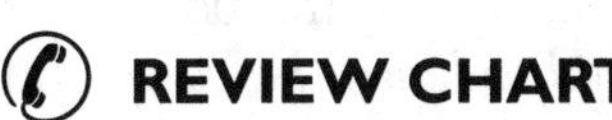

REVIEW CHART

Display the Review Chart with R1-R4 in place. Place R5 on the Chart as you review the verse and theme with the group. Have R6 (To Safety in Jesus) ready to use as indicated. Use the following questions to review Lesson 5.

1. What does it mean to have faith in God? *(To believe what He says and obey)*
2. Which child born to Adam and Eve would encourage his children and grandchildren to have faith in God? *(Seth)*
3. How was Enoch different from all those who had lived before him? *(He went to heaven without dying.)*
4. Why did Enoch not die? *(Because he walked with God and pleased God, God took him.)*
5. How does God speak to us today? *(God speaks to us as we read the Bible or listen to someone who teaches about the Bible.)*
6. What is one thing God says to us from His Word.

Today we are asking a second question about God: Why does God call us? Or, What does God tell us to do when He speaks to us? The first answer is that God calls us to safety in Jesus. *(Place R6 on chart.)*

We all need to feel safe and protected from danger on this earth. More importantly, God wants us to know how we can be sure we will be with Him forever, safe in heaven one day. Today we will learn how we can be safe from God's punishment for sin.

 **Review Token:**

♥ MEMORY VERSE

Use the visual from Bible Verses Visualized *to teach John 10:9a.*

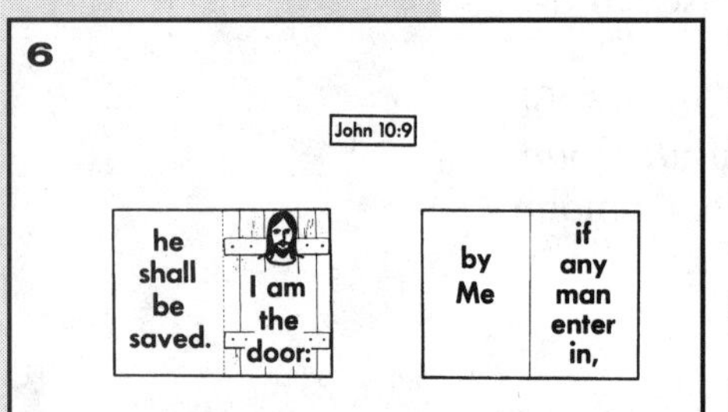

When Jesus was here on earth, He once told His disciples that He was the door. *(Display verse visual and read it together.)* What do you think He meant when He said He was the door? *(Allow students to respond. Use the door to your class room as a visual aid. Open and close it; have children walk in and out. Discuss the purpose for a door in a room or building.)* ▲#1

Of course, Jesus did not mean He was an actual door like this one in our classroom. He was using the door to explain the way to heaven. Just as the only right way to enter this room is to come in through the door, so the Lord Jesus is the only way we can come to God to be saved and go to heaven someday. We go through this "door" when we believe that Jesus died and rose again to take the punishment for our sin, and accept His forgiveness for our sin. Then we can know we will be forever safe from God's punishment for sin because we have come through God's "door," the Lord Jesus. *(Use the verse visual to learn the verse and review its meaning.)* ▲#2

▲ Option#1:

On construction paper or poster board trace around a pair of large shoes to make a series of footprints. Print several words of the verse on each one and cut out. Tape the footprints to the floor (keeping the verse in correct order) so that they lead from outside the classroom through the doorway and into the room. Take the students outside the room and have them follow the footprints back into the room and then go to their seats.

Discuss how they got into the room, where the footprints led them, and why it was important to follow them. Talk about the meaning of the verse in light of the activity; i.e., following Jesus who is the Door—or the only way—to heaven.

BIBLE LESSON OUTLINE

God Destroys the World by a Flood

Introduction

A place of safety.

Bible Content

1. The condition of the human race.
2. God speaks to Noah.
3. Noah obeys God:
   a. He builds and preaches.
   b. He enters the ark.
4. The flood comes upon the earth.
5. Noah and his family praise God.

Conclusion

Summary

Application

Choosing to receive Jesus as the only way to safety from God's punishment for sin.

Response Activity

Entering into assurance of salvation through John 10:9.

BIBLE LESSON

Introduction

A place of safety.

Have you ever been in danger and needed a safe place to go? Perhaps you got caught in a severe thunder storm and you needed to get inside quickly, away from the rain and lightning. Or maybe you were chased by a big fierce dog.

Something like that happened to Bill one evening when he was on his way home from ball practice. It was almost dark and he was late for supper, so he took a shortcut he usually avoided because of a mean dog that lived on that street.

"Oh, well," he thought, "it's on a chain. I'll just run fast!" But as he ran down the alley, Bill heard a familiar snarl and then, to his horror, the dog came right over the fence after him. It was loose from its chain! Could he get home before the dog caught up to him? He ran as fast as he could with the dog barking and chasing after him.

Just as he thought he couldn't run another step, Bill saw that the door of his house was wide open. His father had heard the dog barking and was looking for Bill. What did Bill do? He picked up speed and raced right through the open door as fast as he could go! His father quickly closed the door with a bang, and the fierce dog was left barking on the outside. Why did Bill run in through the doorway? Because he knew he would be safe inside. He needed a place of safety.

Today we will learn how God provided a place of safety for Noah and his family when a great flood came on the earth. We will also learn how each of us can be sure we have entered through God's door to be forever safe with Him.

Bible Content

1. The condition of the human race. (Genesis 1:31; 6:5; Matthew 24:37,38)

(GOD 14, world 3, verse visual for Romans 5:19, Noah 55; plain background.)

Listen to Genesis 1:31 to find out what God thought about the world that He had made. *(Place 14 above 3 on left side of board; read, or have a child read, the verse aloud.)* What did God see? *(That everything He made was good)* Let's say it together: Everything He made was good. ▲#3

Now listen to Genesis 6:5. *(Have the verse read aloud.)* What did God think about the world at this time? *(That the wickedness of the people was VERY great)* How can it be that everything God saw was wicked when He had originally made everything good? ▲#4

Do you remember Romans 5:19? *(Display the verse visual on the right side of the board as you say the verse together.)* Because of Adam's sin these people were sinners, and so the things they did

▲ Option#2:

Learning the verse: Use the footprints you taped to the floor as a learning visual. Have children repeat the verse as they walk on the footprints. Or, take up the footprints and pass them out in random order. Have class members put them in order on the floor.

- Take away 1 or 2 footprints at a time as the group repeats the verse.
- Mix footprints on the floor and have some children put them in order as the rest check to make sure they are correct.
- Say the verse together.

▲ Option#3:

Print Genesis 1:31 and 6:5 on newsprint or chalkboard so entire class can read and respond.

▲ Option#4:

When teaching younger children, simply say that the people forgot God and became very sinful. Omit the other details.

were sinful and wicked. By this time the earth was filled with sin: fighting, lying and quarreling. People no longer believed in God or brought animal sacrifices to Him to show that they were sorry for sin. Their minds were filled with wrong thoughts all the time. They hardly ever thought about God or His promise to someday send a Savior.

When God saw this, He was sorry that He had made people. His heart was very sad. He said, "I will destroy all human beings and all living creatures on the earth, for I am sorry I made them."

▲ Option#5:

Use generation cards from Lesson 5 and add a card for Noah. Have children hold them in order to show Noah's relation to Enoch.

2. God speaks to Noah. (Genesis 6:8-22)

As God looked at the earth and its wickedness he saw one man *(place 55 in the center of the board)* and his family who had stayed true to Him: Noah and his wife, with their three grown sons and their wives. The Bible says that Noah walked with God when everyone else lived in sin and unbelief.

We learned about another man who walked with God when those around him did not. Who was he? Yes, Enoch. He was Noah's great grandfather. ▲#5

Noah was born soon after God had taken Enoch to heaven. As Noah was growing up, he must have heard God's Word from his father and his grandfather. They probably told him about his great grandfather Enoch and how he had walked with God and been taken to heaven without dying. Noah began to walk with God, and he chose to obey God rather than join in the wickedness of those around him.

▲ Option#6:

Print this information on a poster or newsprint. Show pictures to help the children "visualize" the size.
The Ark...
- was taller than a four-story building;
- was longer than 12 school buses or an American football field (300 ft.); about the length of five great blue whales end to end;
- was wider than a four-lane divided highway;
- could hold as much as 522 railroad boxcars (13,960 tons) and could have housed more than 45,000 animals.

Because Noah walked with God, God could talk with him and Noah would listen. God told Noah He was going to destroy the whole world because it was so wicked. He said He would do this by sending a flood on the earth that would destroy every living thing.

Because Noah did what was right, he pleased God. So God also said that He would save Noah and his family from the flood. He would start the world over again. God told Noah to build an ark (a large boat) out of wood to be a place of safety for him and his family when the flood came. God told Noah exactly how to build it and what size to make it. It was to be large enough to be a home for Noah and his family plus many animals and all the supplies they would need.

Sketch 21 **General Outdoor**

3. Noah obeys God.
a. He builds and preaches (Genesis 2:5-6; 6:22; Hebrews 11:7; 2 Peter 2:5).

(Noah 55, FAITH 44, Noah's sons 56, 116, 62; groups 52, 92, 93.)

We learned last week that if a person is to walk with God, he must believe God's Word and obey it. The Bible tells us that Noah did just that *(place 55 on board)*. We do not know if Noah lived near the sea or any large body of water, but we do know that up to this time no one had ever seen a flood of waters such as God had promised. It is possible that no one had ever seen rain as we know it today.

What God said must have sounded very strange and terrible to Noah, but Noah believed God and started right away to obey Him. He got the exact kind of wood God told him to use and began to build the ark according to God's design. ▲#6

The ark was to be very large: 450 feet long (equal to one and a half football fields), 75 feet wide and 45 feet high, as large as some ocean ships today. It had one window that could be closed and opened (it appears to have been just under the roof and all the way around the ark) and only one door. To make it watertight, Noah put pitch or tar over the wood, both inside and out.

Noah and his family *(add 56, 116, 62)* worked very carefully, doing everything exactly as God had said. The New Testament tells us that Noah did all this by faith (Hebrews 11:7; *place 44 above Noah*). He had heard God's Word and even though he had never seen a flood he believed God would do what He said.

The Bible calls Noah "a preacher of righteousness" (2 Peter 2:5). Probably all the time he and his sons were working, Noah tried to tell the people around them what God had said to him *(add 52, 92, 93)*. He warned them about what was coming. Do you suppose they laughed and made fun of him for building an ark when there had never been a flood? Maybe they did. ▲#7

Even though he worked and preached day after day, not one person believed what Noah said or turned to God. Noah and his little family were the only people on the earth who believed and obeyed God! It must have been difficult to keep on trusting God! ▲#8

▲ Option#7:

Ask the class what reasons they think the people had for not believing Noah. Then ask why it took such faith for Noah to obey God. List their answers to both questions on newsprint.

▲ Option#8:

Have class members act out the scene of neighbors asking questions as Noah and his sons build the ark, one child saying what Noah might have told them was going to happen and several others questioning and scoffing as neighbors. Point out the parallel between this and what often happens when we try to tell others about Jesus.

b. He enters the ark (Genesis 7:1-16).

(Ark 57, animals 58.)

After they finished building, Noah and his family had to load lots of food into the ark for themselves and the animals. Then God told Noah, "Go into the ark with your whole family and take with you every kind of animal and bird and living creature that breathes on the earth. Seven days from now I will send rain on the earth for 40 days and nights." Again, Noah and his family did all that God commanded them. They took seven pairs of certain animals that would be needed later for food and for sacrifices to God, but only two—a male and female pair—of all the others.

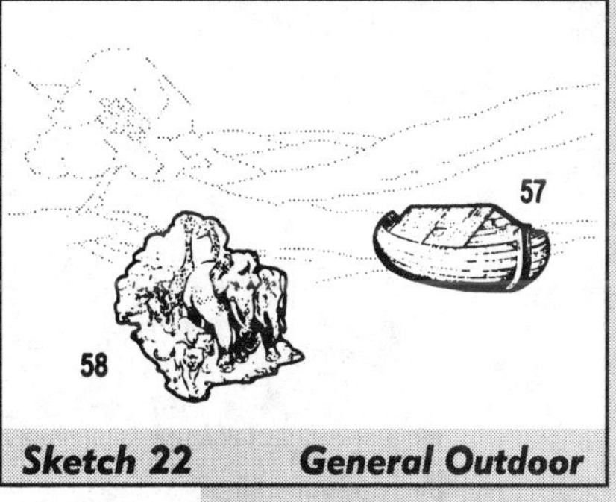

Sketch 22 **General Outdoor**

God must have made the animals come willingly without fighting. All the creeping things (like lizards and snails), all the birds and fowl, all the animals and every living thing that breathed on the earth went into the ark along with Noah and his family. Then God shut the door. They were safe inside the ark.

Probably a crowd of people watched all this, but they still did not believe. And since God had shut the door, no one else could get in now, even if they had wanted to.

4. The flood comes upon the earth. (Genesis 7:17 - 8:14)

(Ark 57, dove 59, olive branch 60, raven 11.)

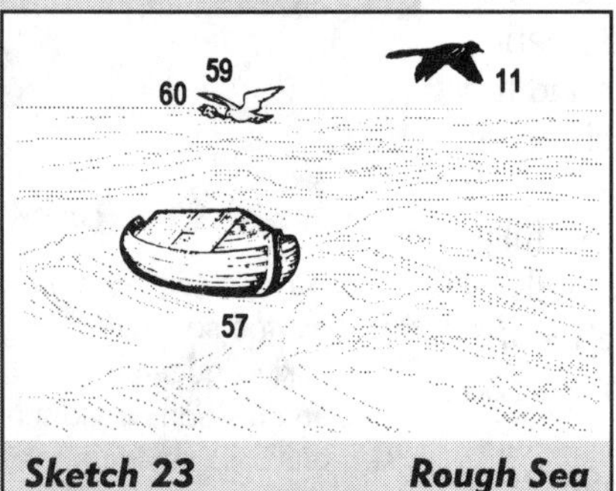

Sketch 23 **Rough Sea**

When they all were in the ark, God sent the rain. It rained for 40 days and 40 nights without stopping! The Bible says that it rained very, very hard, and great forces of water rushed up out of the oceans in tidal waves. The waters rose up over the land until all the hills and mountains were covered. Every living thing died, both animals and people, except those who were safe inside the ark. The water that destroyed the earth lifted up the ark, and it floated as a ship does at sea. There was nothing to see in any direction except water!

After 40 days and nights the rain finally stopped. The ark floated for 150 days (about five months) while the water was going down. About seven months after they had gone into the ark, it settled on the top of a high mountain named Ararat. Finally the tops of the mountains began to show above the water.

One day Noah opened the window of the ark and sent out a raven *(add 11)*. It did not come back. He must have thought the raven was a strong bird and could fly back and forth until the waters dried up. He sent out a dove *(add 59)*. It soon returned to the safety of the ark because the water was still covering the earth and it could not find a place to stop and rest.

One week later Noah sent the dove out again. In the evening it came flying back with an olive leaf in its beak *(add 60)*. Then Noah knew that the ground was drying out and that trees and bushes were beginning to grow leaves again. Seven days later Noah sent the dove out a third time. This time it did not return. It had found a place to nest.

5. Noah and his family praise God. (Genesis 8:15-9:16)

(Noah 55; Noah's sons 56, 116; altar 36; women 61, 107; Noah's son and wife 62; rainbow 63.)

Sketch 24 **Hilltop**

After they had been in the ark more than a year, God spoke again: "Noah, come out and bring the animals." What a sight that must have been! Out streamed the animals, free to run and make their own homes once more.

The very first thing Noah and his family did after leaving the ark was build an altar and offer animal sacrifices to God. Perhaps they knelt together to give thanks to God who had brought them safely through this great flood. Then, as they looked up into the sky, they saw the very first rainbow *(add*

63). God had put it there to remind them that He had promised He would never again destroy the world with a flood. Now, whenever we see a rainbow in the sky we can remember God's promise and that He has kept it.

Conclusion

Summary

(Noah's family 55, 56, 61, 62, ark 57, people 92, 93; Bible verse visual, John 10:9a; heaven 25, cross 84; "Door" take-home tokens.)

(Place figures 55, 56, 61, 62 on board.) What did God ask Noah and his family to do when He saw all the sin on earth? *(Build an ark.)* They had to believe what God said, obey by building an ark *(add 57)* and go into the ark through the one door–their only way to safety.

Why did all the other people die *(add 92 and 93)*? They chose not to believe what God said and never entered the ark.

Sketch 25 **Plain Background**

Application

Will you choose, as Noah and his family did, to believe God's Word and obey it? Or will you choose, as the rest of the people did, to go your own way? Let's say our verse together and think about this choice we all must make. *(Display visual; say verse together.)*

What do these words of Jesus mean? *(Response.)* The cross inside this door *(add 25 with 84 behind the door)* reminds us that Jesus died to take the punishment for our sins. It also reminds us that Jesus is the only way to come to God to be safe from the punishment for sin and know we will live with Him someday in heaven.

How can you enter through the "Door"? First, by trusting God, as Noah did, and believing that Jesus is the only way to safety from God's punishment for sin. Then, by admitting you are a sinner and can't save yourself. And finally, by walking through that "Door," by receiving Jesus as Savior from your sin. Have you entered God's "Door," the Lord Jesus? You must choose. No other person can do it for you.

Response Activity

Invite those who have never been saved to accept Jesus today.

Lead those who have previously accepted Christ to be assured of their salvation by trusting what God says in John 10:9.

Give each child a ***"Door" take-home token*** *(see Materials to Gather). Have them write their names on the line if they have "gone through" the Door by accepting Christ as their Savior.*

Review the memory verse again.

God Confuses the Language

Theme: God Calls Us — To Obey Him

Lesson

7

BEFORE YOU BEGIN...

Unfortunately, the word consequences is seldom heard today. It seems as though few children are taught that every choice, every action, whether right or wrong, has a consequence, either good or bad. And they grow into adults who live by the "rule" that anything goes unless you get caught, giving no thought to the consequences of their choices or their behavior.

The people of Babel had a similar problem. Their willful disobedience to God's command resulted in consequences that affected not only them, but also all future generations of the world. Through this lesson help your children understand that there are always consequences when we disobey God and that these consequences affect others as well as ourselves. "Do not be deceived, God is not mocked; for whatever a man sows, that he will also reap" (Galatians 6:7, NKJV).

AIM:

That the children may

- Know that disobeying God's Word is sin.
- Respond by choosing to obey God when others try to influence them to disobey Him.

SCRIPTURE: Genesis 9:1-19; 11:1-9; (chapter 10 as reference)

MEMORY VERSE: Acts 5:29b

We ought to obey God rather than men.

MATERIALS TO GATHER

Visual for Acts 5:29b
Backgrounds: Review Chart, Plain, Hilltop, Plain with Tree, General Outdoor
Figures: R1-R7, 1, 13, 14, 21, 28, 32, 36, 39, 45, 55, 56, 62, 63, 64, 65, 92, 93, 106, 107, 116
Special:
- ***Memory Verse:*** Newsprint & marker or chalkboard & chalk.
- ***Bible Content 1:*** New word strips: Fill the earth with people, Rule over animals, Eat meat for food, Not kill people, Promised to never again destroy earth by flood, Gave rainbow as a sign.
- ***Bible Content 6:*** Old Testament map showing Mt. Ararat.
- ***For Conclusion:*** 4- x 6-inch cards; pencils.
- ***For Options:*** Materials for any options you choose to use.

REVIEW CHART

Display the Review Chart. Place R1-R6 as you briefly review the lesson themes. Use the following questions to review Lesson 6. ▲#1

True or False?
1. Noah thought of the idea of building the ark all by himself. *(False)*
2. Noah's family refused to go with him into the ark. *(False)*
3. God decided to destroy the world because it was very wicked. *(True)*
4. When Noah and his family were safe in the ark, God shut the door. *(True)*
5. Noah was kept safe because he obeyed God. *(True)*
6. Noah and his family forgot about God when they left the ark. *(False)*
7. The sign God gave as a reminder of His promise to never again destroy the world by a flood was a rainbow. *(True)*

Review Token:

▲ Option#1:

Use the "Who Am I" questions on page 60 to review Lessons 1-6.

♥ MEMORY VERSE

Have at hand R7 to add to the Review Chart and the visual from Bible Verses Visualized *to teach Acts 5:29b.*

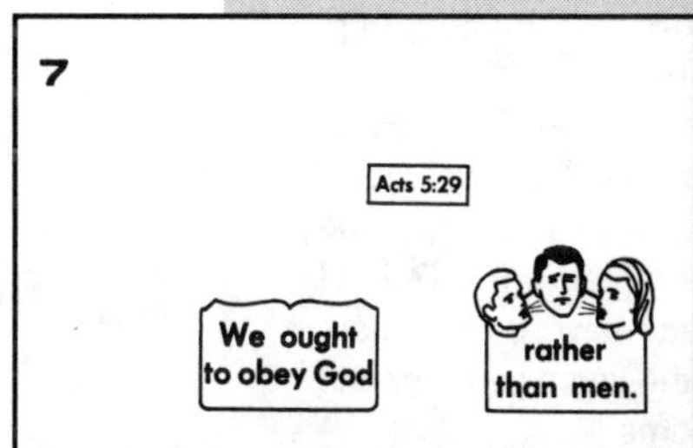

Today's memory verse gives us the next answer to our question, Why does God call us? Let's read the verse together to discover what God wants us to do. *(Display the verse visual and read it aloud together with the children.)* What does God want us to do? Obey Him. *(Place R7 on chart.)*

What new thing does this verse tell us about obeying God? *(That we should obey Him rather than men.)*

Who would like to tell us what this verse means? *(Encourage responses.)* Does it mean that we should not obey our parents or teachers or the police? No. When should we refuse to obey or go along with someone? Right! When they want us to do something God's Word says is wrong. If we do that, we sin against God.

Can you think of a situation in which you should obey God rather than people? *(Write responses on newsprint or chalkboard for all to see.)* ▲#2 Have friends ever wanted you to do something you knew God's Word said was wrong to do? Did you go along with them or say no? Did they make fun of you so much that you finally did it, even though you knew it was wrong? That's obeying people instead of God.

We need to know what God says in His Word so we know what He wants us to do. Then we need to obey what He says. *(Take time to learn the verse together, encouraging the children to tell its meaning in their own words.)* ▲#3 ▲#4

▲ Option#2:

Have the children act out or pantomime one of these situations or one of their own.

▲ Option#3:

Learning the verse: Divide the class into two sections and assign half the verse to each. Have each group say their part aloud, and all say the reference together. Then have groups switch parts and repeat the process.

▲ Option#4:

Collect several small cardboard boxes. Print one word of the verse on each box and the reference on the last one. "Build" the verse from the bottom up, having the children say each word as it is added. Knock the "building" down and choose a section of the class to rebuild it. Repeat until all have participated. Say the verse together one final time.

BIBLE LESSON OUTLINE

God Confuses the Language

■ Introduction

Tom has to choose.

■ Bible Content

1. God makes a covenant with Noah and his sons.
   a. God's new instructions.
   b. God's covenant promise.
2. The human race grows after the flood.
3. The people choose their own way.
4. God comes down to see the city and the tower.
5. God confuses their language.
6. The nations begin.

■ Conclusion

Summary

Application

Understanding choices and consequences.

Response Activity

Taking the first step of obedience by receiving Christ as Savior.

Using verse reminder card to remember to obey God.

BIBLE LESSON

■ Introduction

Tom has to choose.

One morning Tom's dad said, "Tom, I want you to stay home from school today. An important package will be delivered while I'm at work and someone has to be here to take it." Tom did what his dad told him to do, but he was upset because he knew he wasn't supposed to be absent from school unless he was sick.

The next day Tom's dad wrote a note saying that Tom had been been absent because he was sick. Tom said, "Dad, that's not true!" But his dad said, "Your teacher will never know the difference; just give her the note."

Tom was a Christian. As he walked to school he was troubled. He knew the note was a lie, and yet he knew he should obey his dad.

What were Tom's choices? *(Discuss Tom's situation and the possible choices. You will deal with the results later in the application.)* ▲#5

In our Bible lesson today we will learn about a group of people who had to make difficult choices like Tom's. Let's see what choices they faced and what they decided to do.

▲ Option#5:

Help two children role play Tom's experience with his dad.

■ Bible Content

1. God makes a covenant with Noah and his sons. (Genesis 9:1-17)

(Noah 55, Noah's sons 56, 116, GOD 14, rainbow 63, new word strips: Fill earth with people, Rule over animals, Eat meat for food, Not kill people, Promised to never again destroy earth by flood, Gave rainbow as sign.)

Sketch 26 **Hilltop**

After the flood there were only eight people alive in the world. Who were they? *(Noah and his wife; their three sons—Shem, Ham and Japheth—and their wives)* In Genesis 9 *(encourage children to open their Bibles and follow along)* we read that God blessed Noah and his sons and gave them some new instructions. Then he made a covenant with them. Let's look first at the instructions He gave them.

a. God's new instructions. ▲#6

Place word strips on board as you teach.

1) They were to multiply (have children) and fill the earth with people (9:1,7).
2) They were to rule over the animals (9:2). Before this time, people were not afraid of animals and animals were not afraid of people, but now God placed a fear of man within animals and all other living creatures.
3) They were to eat meat for food (9:3,4). Before the flood people had eaten only plants, like vegetables and fruits. After the flood God allowed them to kill animals for food, but commanded them never to eat the blood with the meat.
4) They were not to kill people (9:5,6). God said that anyone who killed (murdered) another person should be put to death. God made man in his own image and human life is precious to Him. This law was given by God and is to be obeyed even today.

▲ Option#6:

Before class, print the instructions on a chart and temporarily cover lines with strips of paper; remove each strip as you discuss the instruction.
Or, write each instruction on chalkboard or newsprint as you teach.

▲ Option#7:

Definition Word Card:
Print "Covenant = Sacred promise" on newsprint or flash card. (On a flash card, print "Covenant" on the front and "Sacred promise" on the back.)

▲ Option#8:

Cut two 10- inch circles from light-weight cardboard. On one print "Destroy all by a flood." Draw a slash across it (like a traffic sign). On the second, color a rainbow and print "God's sign."

b. God's covenant promise.

A covenant is a sacred promise—a promise made by God that will never be broken. There were two parts to the covenant God made with Noah and his sons after the flood. ▲#7

1) God promised He would never again destroy every living creature with a flood (9:8-11). And He told Noah and his family that as long as the earth remained, there would be different seasons of the year— spring, summer, autumn and winter—as well as day and night (8:22). ▲#8
2) God gave them the rainbow as a sign that He would never again destroy the earth with a flood. God said to them, "Whenever I see a rainbow in the clouds, I will remember My covenant with you and all living creatures. Never again will I destroy the earth with a flood." And so every rainbow we see today also reminds us that God keeps His Word.

2. The human race grows after the flood.

Noah's three sons, Shem, Ham and Japheth, all had sons and daughters of their own. More and more babies were born until there were many people filling the land. As their families grew, Noah and his sons passed on to them the Word of God and the records of the past generations.

God's plan was that the people, as they increased in numbers, should spread out all over the world and fill it up again, but they did not obey Him right away. For a long time after the flood they tried to stay together and live in one place. Let's see what happened when the people didn't scatter as God told them to do. Turn in your Bibles to Genesis 11.

3. The people choose their own way. (Genesis 11:1-4)

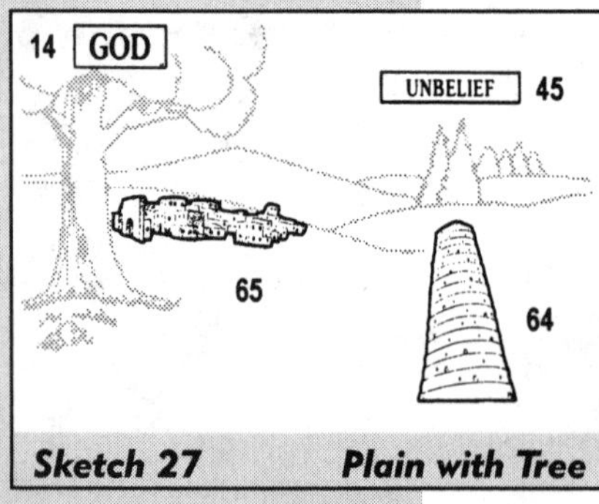

Sketch 27 **Plain with Tree**

(City 65, tower 64.)

Sometime after the flood the people traveled toward the east. They were one large family, all speaking the same language, so that each one could understand all the others. They came to a large plain they liked very much. It was located between two rivers, the Tigris and the Euphrates. They built their homes and settled there to live together, disobeying God's command to fill up the whole earth.

The people became very proud. One day they decided to build a city and a tower whose top would reach to the heavens. The Bible says they decided to do this in order to make a name for themselves and so that they would not be scattered all over the earth.

These people knew what God wanted them to do, but they went ahead with their own plans anyway. They were rebelling against God. Let's read verses 3 and 4 and count the number of times they said "we" or "us" or "ourselves." *(Have a child or helper read these verses aloud while the rest of the class counts the words as they are read.)* They never mentioned God in their plans. ▲#9

Many workmen labored together to build the city and the tower. They made bricks of mud and dried them in the sun. Then they cemented them together with mud or tar to form the walls.

▲ Option#9:

Print verses 3 and 4 on newsprint for all to see. Have the class read them aloud together, looking for "we," "us" or "ourselves." Use a colored marker to circle or color each word they find.

4. God comes down to see the city and the tower. (Genesis 11:5)

(Add God 14 and unbelief 45 to Sketch 27.)

One day the Lord came down to see the city and the tower *(place 14 over city)*. The people had not invited Him, but He came anyway. How do you think it all looked to Him? Could He say it was good? Did He see obedience to His commands and faith in Him? No, because faith is believing and obeying what God says, and these people did not believe or obey God. Instead of faith, we must put the word unbelief over this tower *(place 45 over tower)*. They left God out of their plans completely.

These people had heard how God sent the flood to punish the people of Noah's day for their wickedness. Did knowing that make them obedient? No, they too were sinful. They wanted their own way and refused to obey God. God had to punish them for their sin of disobedience, for He knew they would not change.

▲ Option#10:

If you have a bi-lingual friend or bi-lingual children in your class, ask them to speak to the class in their other language at this point to give the children a feel for what it was like not to understand each other.
Or, borrow a foreign language tape from the library and play a few minutes of it to give the same idea.

5. God confuses their language. (Genesis 11:6-9)

(People groups 62, 92, 93, man 106, woman 107.)

So that they would scatter out and fill up the earth, God did something quite amazing! He changed their language without any warning. Suddenly they were speaking different languages, even though they had never learned them. ▲#10

Sketch 28 **General Outdoor**

What do you suppose happened when the workers came to work on the tower? *(Encourage discussion.)* Would they understand each other? Would they understand the boss's orders? What would be the result? Probably a lot of noise, confusion and frustration—perhaps even fighting. The Bible tells us this city was called Babel, which means confusion.

Just think what it must have been like. The laborers couldn't work together on the city or the tower, friends couldn't talk to each other, children couldn't understand their teachers, neighbors couldn't communicate. It must have been sad and frightening as well as frustrating. Does it remind you of any problems we have in our school or our town or the world today? *(Discuss)* It would have been much better for the people to obey God in the first place.

God punished them for their rebellion and disobedience by confusing their language. In this way He also caused them to do what He had told them to do. We read, "So the Lord scattered them from there over all the earth."

6. The nations begin.

Note:

The events of Genesis 11:1–9 occurred before the development of the nations recorded in chapter 10. We know this is true because Genesis 11:1 says that all the world had one language while Genesis 10:5, 20, 31 speak of the nations having different languages. No doubt the events surrounding the tower of Babel took place early in the period of time covered by chapter 10.

(Old Testament map showing Mt. Ararat area in Turkey.)

Soon the people separated from each other and traveled to different places where they made homes for themselves and their families. Probably groups who spoke the same language moved together to a place of their own. They went in different directions, settling in many places, and so the different nations began.

We read the Bible record of how this happened in Genesis chapter 10. ⍓ Noah's sons (Shem, Ham and Japheth) and grandsons had many children. Probably several generations had passed by this time. Now Japheth's descendants moved to the north and west; from his family came the nations of Europe. Ham's descendants moved south; the many dark-skinned races descended from his family and spread through Palestine and into Africa. Shem's descendants moved to the east; from them came the Jewish and Arabian people.

■ Conclusion

Summary

(Memory verse visual, cross 1, boy 13, DISOBEDIENCE 28, OBEDIENCE 32, altar 36, lamb 39, tower 64, people 92)

What choice faced the people we've been talking about today? *(Allow for answers.)* Yes, whether to obey God and spread out to populate the earth or to stay together in one place.

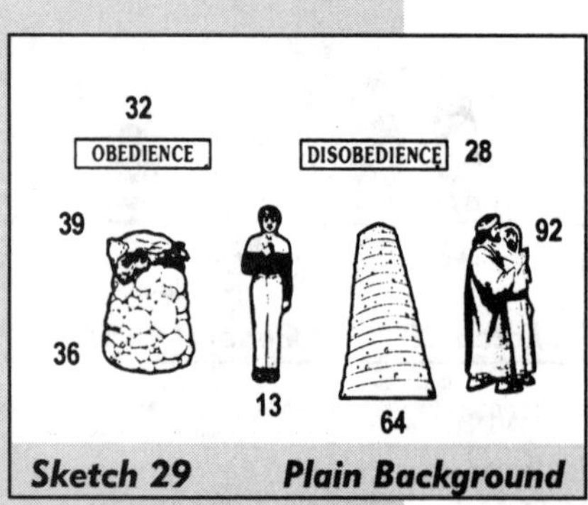

Sketch 29 **Plain Background**

What is God calling us to do today? To obey Him. *(Review memory verse, displaying visual or "building" the blocks again as a reminder. Review the meaning.)*

What did the people in our lesson choose to do? *(Allow response.)* They chose to listen to each other and stay together in one place. They chose to disobey God. What were the consequences of their choice? Their language was changed, they couldn't understand each other or work together and God scattered them across the earth. Going the way of DISOBEDIENCE to God always brings problems for us. We'll let this tower remind us of the people's choice to disobey. *(Place 64, 28 and 92 on one side of the board.)*

What other choice could the people have made? *(Response)* They could have chosen God's way of OBEDIENCE *(place 32 on other side of board).* They could have built an altar and made a sacrfice for their sins to show that they chose to obey God *(place 36 under 32).* Then they could have divided into groups and agreed in which direction each group would move so they would begin to fill up the earth.

Application

If we want to please God rather than men, which of these two ways should we choose? Yes, the way of obedience. *(Place 13 on side of obedience.)* Let's talk about Tom again. *(Briefly review Tom's situation and the choice he had to make.)* ▲#11

As a Christian what could Tom have done to obey God's Word? *(Responses)* Yes, he could have taken the note to the teacher but told her that he had also been helping his dad. Or he could have kept the note and told his teacher the truth. He would then have had to tell his dad what he had done. But he would have been obeying God. Why would it be wrong for him to do what his dad told him to do? *(Discuss)* Yes, what the note said was not true. Giving it to the teacher would have been disobeying God's Word which says that we should always tell the truth. In this kind of situation, "we ought to obey God rather than man."

What might be the consequences of Tom's choice? *(Responses)* Yes, Tom's dad might get angry and even punish Tom, but Tom would know he had chosen God's way.

How could Tom or you be strong enough to choose the right way—God's way? By asking God for help. God promises He will help us obey His Word and go His way when we ask Him.

Do you need God to help you choose to obey Him even when others want you to disobey? Do you need to ask God for His help right now? Or have you made a wrong choice and now you need God's help to make it right? Let's ask God right now to help us obey Him, even when our friends or family try to influence us to disobey.

▲ Option#11:

Allow several children to act out Tom's choices. Then have class decide the consequences of each and which would honor God.

Response Activity

Give the children time to pray—first silently and then aloud, if they desire—asking God to help them make right choices this week.

Either in class or one-on-one afterward, invite children who have never trusted Jesus as Savior to make this important choice today. Invite any who want to talk with someone about their choices to come to you after class.

Give each child 4- x 6-inch card or paper with the memory verse printed on it to take home and place where they will see it each day and be reminded to obey God. Ask them to write on the back one or more times during the week when they had to choose to obey God or people and what choice they made. Give them opportunity next week to share what happened.

HELPS FOR YOUNGER CHILDREN

Introduction: *Use the following story as an alternative to the one given in text.*

One day Peter was playing a game on the computer when his mother asked him to help her in the back yard. "Yeah, sure Mom," Peter answered, but he kept right on playing. Soon Mom called again, "Peter, please come here." "In a minute, Mom," he answered as he turned up the music on the stereo. After all, the game was too exciting to leave! When his mother called the third time, Peter answered back, "I can't hear you, Mom."

Peter found it hard to be obedient. Is it always easy for you to obey? No. Because we are sinners it is very easy to want our own way. Today we will learn from our Bible lesson that God calls us to obey Him. We will also learn that disobedience is a very serious sin before God.

Bible Content 1: When presenting the covenant, use part 1, "God's command to spread over the earth," and Part 5, "God's promise sealed with a rainbow." Omit the details of Parts 2-4.

Review Chart: To review Lesson 6, make the true-false statements into questions, requiring simple answers, such as,

1. Whom did God choose to build an ark?
   (Noah)
2. Why was God going to destroy the earth?
   (Because it was wicked and sinful.)

NOTES FOR TEACHERS

Review: *Use these "Who am I?" questions to review Lessons 1-6.*

Who Am I?

1. I was cast out of heaven because of my pride. *(Satan)*
2. I was used to deceive Adam and Eve in the garden. *(Serpent)*
3. I was the first mother. *(Eve)*
4. I told the Word of God to my children and grandchildren. *(Adam or any godly man through Noah and sons)*
5. My sacrifice was accepted by God. *(Abel)*
6. I was the first murderer. *(Cain)*
7. I was born after my brother Abel was killed and I encouraged others to have faith in God. *(Seth)*
8. I went to heaven without dying. *(Enoch)*
9. I was the oldest man who ever lived. *(Methusaleh)*
10. I obeyed God by building an ark. *(Noah)*

God Calls Abraham

Theme: God Calls Us — To Serve Him

Lesson

8

Probably some of the children in your class have learned by hard experience to distrust people, so they may find it difficult to trust you as their teacher and friend. Your Christlike example can pave the way for them to know the loving and faithful God who can always be trusted, no matter what!

In this lesson we see Abraham learning to trust God. We learn what it meant for him to look beyond his situation and problems and believe in a God he could not see. We discover that trusting God meant doing what God asked him to do. Help your children see that when Abraham stepped out in faith and obedience, God blessed him beyond what he could imagine. Then "build a bridge" from Abraham's experience to where they are right now and show them how they can put their trust in God today. "He who calls you is faithful, who also will do it!" (1 Thessalonians 5:24, NKJV).

AIM:

That the children may

- Know that God blesses those who are willing to serve Him obediently;
- Respond by deciding to obey God's call to serve Him in daily life.

SCRIPTURE: Genesis 11:10-12:9; Acts 7:2-5

MEMORY VERSE: Genesis 12:2

And I will make of thee a great nation, and I will bless thee, and make thy name great; and thou shalt be a blessing.

MATERIALS TO GATHER

Visual for Genesis 12:2

Backgrounds: Review Chart, Plain, Old Testament Map with locations added, Plain with Tree

Figures: R1-R8, 1, 2, 3, 13, 14, 31, 36, 39, 66, 67, 68, 69, 70,71, 73, 74, 75, 77, 78, 79, 80, 81

Special:

- ***For Introduction:*** New word strip SERVANT; large question mark drawn on newsprint or poster board with question underneath: What can I do right now to serve God?
- ***For Bible Content 1:*** A 24-inch piece of string or yarn for Time Chart.
- ***For Bible Content 2:*** New word strip ABRAHAM.
- ***For Bible Content 3:*** New word strips CANAAN, ISRAEL.
- ***For Conclusion:*** chalkboard & chalk or newsprint & markers; New word strip YES; individual question marks drawn on construction paper or cardboard for each child; pencils.
- ***For Options:*** Additional materials for any options you choose to use.

Review Token:

▲ Option#1:

Have Bible drill when presenting new review symbol, using 2 Chronicles 34:33, I Samuel 17:9, Joshua 22:5, Genesis 25:23, Exodus 3:12. When children have found and read all verses, see if they can identify the "key" word (the word repeated in each verse: serve).

Or, have several good readers find the verses ahead of time and read them aloud in class. Ask the group to identify the key word.

REVIEW CHART

Display the Review Chart with R1-R6 in place. Review Lesson 7, placing R7 on the chart as the children state the theme and verse. Encourage the children to tell how they obeyed God rather than people during the past week. Use the following questions to review Lesson 7.

1. What did Noah's family do to worship God after the flood? *(Built an altar)*
2. Why did the people build the tower? *(To keep from being scattered and to be remembered)*
3. What two things did God do because the people disobeyed His command? *(Confused their language and scattered them across the world)*
4. How can we come to God today? *(By receiving the Lord Jesus as Savior)*

Today we are learning that God calls us to serve Him *(add symbol R8).* ▲#1 *Explanation of the theme is given in the Bible Lesson Introduction.*

♥ MEMORY VERSE

Use the visual from Bible Verses Visualized *to teach Genesis 12:2 during the Bible lesson (see Bible Lesson Outline).*

BIBLE LESSON OUTLINE

God Calls Abraham

Introduction

What does it mean to serve?

Bible Content

1. God has a plan.
2. God calls Abraham.
3. God gives Abraham promises.
   Memory verse presentation
4. Abraham journeys to Canaan.
5. Abraham worships and obeys.

Conclusion

Summary

Application

Serving God as Abraham did

Response activity

Answering God's call to receive Christ.

Writing on a question mark what they promise to do this week to serve God.

BIBLE LESSON

Introduction

What does it mean to serve?

(Review Chart with R1-R7 in place; R8; new word strip SERVANT; large question mark with question.)

What do you think of when you see the word servant? *(Place word strip on board and encourage students to answer.)* ▲#2

A servant is a person who serves or works for another person. Waiters or waitresses in a restaurant serve by bringing meals to the table. Some people serve—or help—at the checkout in grocery stores. Nurses take care of—or serve— patients in the hospital.

Some servants work for money; others do jobs because they love and respect the person they serve. Our new message tells us that God calls us to serve Him. *(Display Review Chart; place R8 on it.)*

A servant seeks to please the one he serves by doing what he is told. Sometimes he may have to do something he doesn't enjoy or feel like doing. God wants us to serve Him by doing what He asks because we love Him. He promises us that He will reward us with joy as we serve Him, and others will see that we belong to Him.

The big question for us is, What can I do right now to serve God? *(Display question mark with question.)* Today we will learn about a

▲ Option#2:

Brainstorm. Ask the children what it means to serve others. List their ideas on chalkboard or newsprint. Or role play some situations which show examples of serving.

man who was willing to serve God right where he was. Let's see if we can discover how he served God and how we can serve Him, too.

Bible Content

1. God has a plan. (Genesis 3:15)

Use Time Chart from Lesson 1 (see Sketch 1): cross 1, eternity 2, world 3, piece of yarn or string. Place emphasis on the cross.

Do you remember the promise God made to Adam and Eve before He sent them out of the Garden *(display Time Chart; indicate world)*? What was it? *(Allow response.)* Yes, that He would someday send a Savior. Let's read that promise in Genesis 3:15. *(Have the group find the verse and read it aloud together or have it printed on large paper for all to see and read.)*

God was saying that sometime in the future a child would be born who would destroy Satan (who worked through the serpent in the Garden) and his power. The one who was to come—the Lord Jesus Christ—would take away the sin of the world and bring everlasting life with God *(indicate cross)*. God was working according to a plan to prepare the whole world for the time when Jesus would come as Savior.

2. God calls Abraham. (Genesis 11:31,32; 12:1-3; Joshua 24:2,3; Acts 7:2-5; Romans 4:3)

Sketch 30 Old Testament Map

(Abraham 66, new word strip ABRAHAM, GOD 14.)

Many years after making this promise to Adam and Eve, God did the next big thing in His plan. He called a man named Abram to be the father, or the leader, of a new nation of people *(place 66)*. The Savior would come into the world as part of this nation. God later changed Abram's name to Abraham *(add word strip ABRAHAM)* and that's the name we will call him.

Abraham was from the family of Noah's son, Shem. He lived in a city called Ur of the Chaldees *(locate UR on the map background)*. The people of Ur worshiped many gods or idols, but their main god was the moon. In fact, Ur was the center of moon worship at that time. When people don't know the true God in heaven, they make up gods to pray to and worship. Sometimes they make a statue out of wood or stone or something else and call it their god. Anything that people worship other than the true God in heaven is called an idol.

One day God appeared to Abraham (Acts 7:2; *place 14 on top of board opposite Abraham*). The Bible does not tell us how God came to him. In those days before the Bible was written down, God sometimes came to people in a human body they could see. At other times He spoke to them in dreams. He spoke to some others in a voice they could hear with their ears, even though they couldn't see Him.

We don't know all that God said to Abraham. Perhaps He said, "I am greater than the moon or the so-called moon god, for I made the moon. I made you and I love you. I have a plan for your life. Follow Me; trust Me." Whatever God said to Abraham about himself, it was enough to cause Abraham to listen when God said, "Leave your country and your family and friends and go to a land I will show you." Abraham believed and obeyed God, even though he had no idea where God was leading him (Acts 7:2-5).

3. God gives Abraham some promises. (Genesis 12:1-3,7)

(NATION 67, LAND 68, NAME 69, BLESSING 70, new word strips CANAAN, ISRAEL, Bible 71, JESUS 31; verse visual for Genesis 12:2; see Sketch 30.)

When God called Abraham to go to this new land, He also gave Abraham some wonderful promises. These promises are very important, for they tell what God would do for Abraham and his family forever. They are called a covenant—or sacred promise. *(Review the meaning of "covenant.")*

Abraham was to be the leader of a new group or nation of people. God called these people His chosen people. We know them today as the Jewish people or the nation of Israel.

The human race continued to fill the world with more and more people, but the rest of the Old Testament tells us mainly about God's chosen people, this new nation of which Abraham was the beginning and the head. Let's see what the promises were.

A. "I will make of you a great nation" (vss. 2,4; *place 67 on board. Have class say each of the promises aloud as they are presented*). Even though Abraham was 75 years old and had no children when God called him, God promised that Abraham would have children and become a great nation. Has that promise come true? Yes, the nation of Israel is descended from Abraham and today there are many, many Jewish people living all over the world, as well as in the country of Israel.

B. "I will give you a land" (vs. 7; *place 68 on board; have children repeat promise together*). God had the right to give the land to Abraham. In Genesis it is called the land of Canaan; today, we call it Israel *(place word strips CANAAN and ISRAEL).* God gave it to Abraham and his descendants, God's chosen people, forever. Many Jews, no matter where they live in the world, desire to someday live in this promised land of Israel.

C. "I will make your name great" (vs. 2; *place 69; have children repeat together*). Today the name of Abraham is known by millions of people, even by many who do not believe in the name of Jesus. The Jewish people honor Abraham as their father; Arabs and other muslim people honor Abraham's name, even though they do not believe that Jesus is the Savior. Christians respect and honor Abraham, too.

▲ Option#3:

Learning the verse: Have the class read the verse aloud. Then allow one child to remove a piece of the visual and hand it to another child. Ask for a volunteer to say the verse without the missing piece. Have the one who succeeds remove another piece of the visual and hand it to a different child. When all the pieces are off the board, have the ones holding the pieces put them back in correct order. Read the verse together. Remove it all from the board and say it one more time. Be sure to review its meaning as you go.

D. "I will bless you...and you shall be a blessing" (vs. 2; *place 70; repeat promise together*). When God blesses someone, He does special things to show His approval of that person. He works for him and helps him and gives him special work to do. God told Abraham two things: 1) He would bless Abraham, and 2) through Abraham He would bless all people of the world. What did God mean? The rest of the Bible tells how God kept His Word and describes the blessing that was to come to all the world through Abraham and his family.

Abraham was a blessing to the whole world in two ways:

1) The Bible came to us through the nation of Israel *(place 71)*. God's Word was not written down when God called Abraham, but it had been passed down through the families that believed and obeyed God. God wanted it written down so that it would not be lost. He chose good men from the nation of Israel to do this so that we would have God's Word in written form. Every place the Bible goes throughout the whole world it brings blessing to those who read it.

2) The Lord Jesus Christ was born into the world through Abraham's descendants, the nation of Israel. Jesus' mother Mary was Jewish *(place 31)*. Jesus brought blessing to all the people of the world by taking the punishment for their sin so they could someday live with God forever. Every person who trusts in Jesus as his Savior from sin is blessed by God.

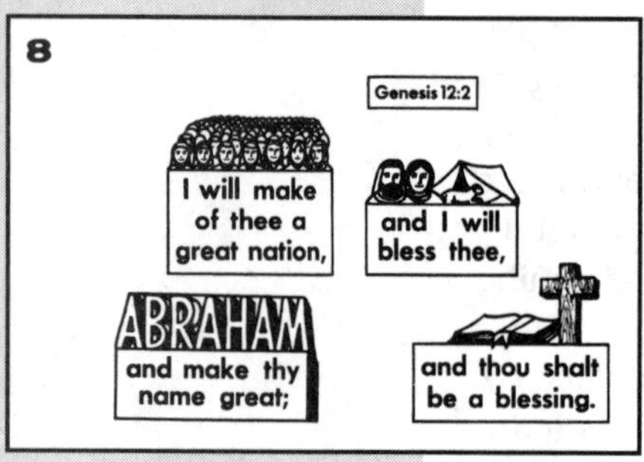

Now let's read Genesis 12:2 together. *(Remove figures; display verse visual and have class read.)* This verse tells us three of the promises God gave to Abraham. What are they? *(Encourage response.)* God made these promises to Abraham and his family (the nation of Israel) forever. They did not depend on Abraham or what he did. They depend on God who is faithful. God always keeps His promises. This important verse is our memory verse for today. ▲#3

4. Abraham journeys to Canaan. (Genesis 11:31,32; 12:4-6)

(Abraham 66; servants 77, 78; flocks and herds 74, 75.)

Abraham has always been known as a man of great faith because he believed and obeyed God. He left Ur with his wife Sarah, his father and his nephew Lot. They probably traveled along the Euphrates River until they came to a place called Haran. They stopped there and stayed until Abraham's father died. Then, in obedience to God, Abraham, Sarah and Lot started out once more toward the land of Canaan. They probably walked or rode their donkeys or camels. *(As you teach, trace Abraham's route and note the places he visited on the map you're using as a background. Temporarily attach—with a small roll of masking tape—a small flag or other marker at each place.)*

Sketch 31 Old Testament Map

Abraham was a wealthy man. He had many sheep, oxen, camels, donkeys and cows and needed many servants to take care of them.

He also had servants to care for his family by cooking the meals, making and washing clothes and doing many other jobs. It must have been a long procession that left Haran. Since they were not able to travel very far in a day, it must have taken a long time to get to Canaan.

5. Abraham worships and obeys. (Genesis 12:7-9)

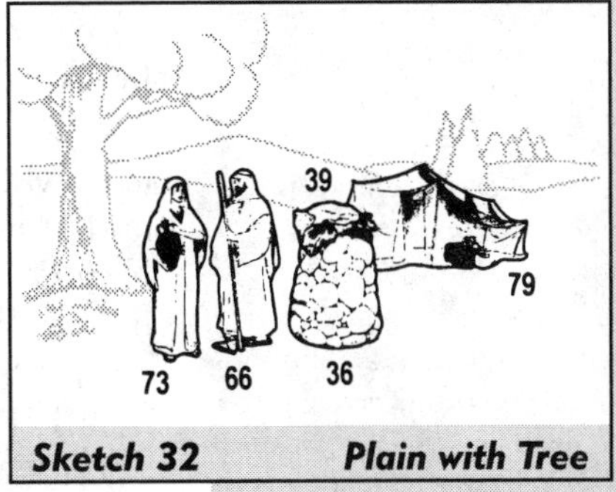

Sketch 32 **Plain with Tree**

(Abraham 66, Sarah 73, tent 79, altar 36, offering 39.)

During their long journey, and even when they got into the land God had promised them, Abraham and Sarah and their servants lived in tents. Why was Abraham willing to give up his lovely home to live in a tent, to make such a long journey to a land he had never seen? Because he was following and serving God (Hebrews 11:9,10,13). By living in a tent, rather than a house of stone or brick, Abraham showed that he trusted God and was ready to move whenever God told him to.

When Abraham reached Canaan, God appeared to him again and said, "I will give this land to your descendants"—the people we now know as the Jewish nation. Abraham still had no children. But he believed that God was able to do what He had promised. He showed that he believed God by building an altar and offering a sacrifice. No doubt Abraham was grateful to God for bringing him into the land safely and for promising to give it to him and his descendants. He worshiped God with a thankful and trusting heart.

Conclusion

Summary

(Chalkboard & chalk or newsprint & markers; cross 1, Abraham 66, GOD 14, tent 79, altar 36, lamb 39, word strips 67-70, boy 13, FAMILY OF GOD 80, CHRISTIAN 81, large question mark from Introduction, new word strip YES; question marks and pencils.)

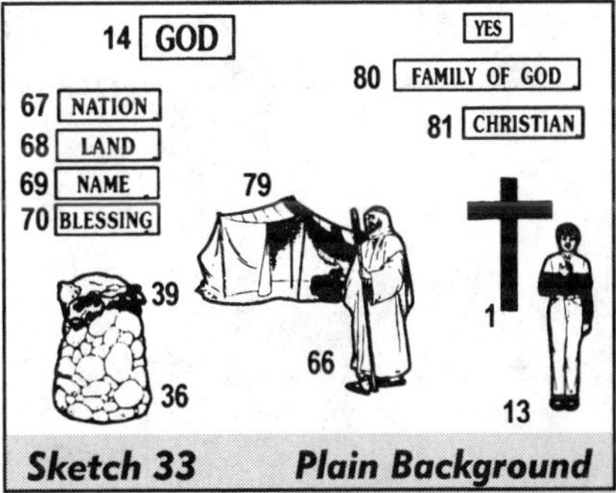

Sketch 33 **Plain Background**

Abraham lived long before the Lord Jesus came to this earth. *(Place 1 and 66 on board.)* How did he show God love and obedience? *(Allow for responses.)* By saying yes to God's call to serve him *(add 14)*, by following God to an unknown place *(add 79)*, and by worshiping God at the altar *(add 36 and 39)*.

God also gave Abraham some special promises. Who can tell us what they were? *(Allow students to place word strips 67-70 as they give the promises. Then have four different students explain what the promises mean.)*

Let's think about these promises as we say our verse together. God would begin the nation of Israel through Abraham. And God's Son, the Lord Jesus Christ, would come to earth through that nation.

Application

How are we like Abraham? *(Add 13; encourage response.)* We are on a journey through life and God wants us to follow Him. God has made a way for us to come to Him through believing in the Lord Jesus. When we receive Him as our Savior, we are born into God's family and are given the special name of Christian *(add 80 and 81).*

God promised blessings to Abraham. He also promises good things to us who belong to His family. Let's name some of them. *(Brainstorm with the class, writing responses on chalkboard or newsprint. Include, if they don't, forgiveness of sin, a home in heaven, God's help to live each day for Him, peace and joy even in hard situations.)*

How can we serve God right now? *(Show large question mark here.)* First, we must say yes to God's call *(add YES word strip).* Then how shall we serve him? *(Write responses on chalkboard or newsprint for all to see. Have some ideas in mind: reading and studying the Bible, doing the best job we can in school, helping others, obeying those who are in charge of us, pleasing God with our words and actions, telling someone about Jesus.)*

Response Activity

Encourage any who have not done so to answer God's call by coming to the Lord Jesus Christ as Savior.

Hand out the prepared question marks; make pencils available. Have those who are willing to serve God now write yes on the front of their question marks and sign their names; then write a specific thing they will do (from the list on the board or from an idea they may have) on the back of their question marks. Encourage them to ask God to help them keep their promise. Give them opportunity next week to tell how God helped them. Let them take the question marks home as a reminder of their decision.

If some of your children are not yet ready to say yes to God's call, encourage them to pray that God will help them be willing to serve Him. Have them take their question marks home so they can write yes and sign their names whenever they are ready.

HELPS FOR YOUNGER CHILDREN

Memory Verse: Shorten the verse to " I will make of thee a great nation and I will bless thee." Teach the promises in Bible Content.

Conclusion: Use Summary, paragraphs 1-3 and Application, paragraphs 3, 4. Give yes cards to children and have them sign them if they want to serve God this week. Discuss ways they can do that.

Abraham and Lot Choose

Theme: God Calls Us — To Make Right Choices

Lesson 9

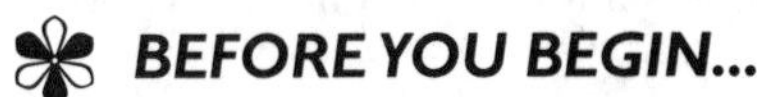

BEFORE YOU BEGIN...

Choices....consequences! This theme runs through Genesis. God gave us the right to choose. He gave us His Word as a standard to help us make good choices that honor Him. Now He holds us responsible for the choices we make. Abraham and Lot are examples of this truth. They made very different choices and experienced very different consequences. Their choices affected their families and generations after them. They also affected what other people thought about their God.

Use this lesson to teach your boys and girls that God holds them responsible for their choices, too. And that their choices affect other people besides themselves. Help them learn how to pray and think through a life situation with God's help and then make good choices that will honor God. "Choose for yourselves this day whom you will serve,... But as for me and my house, we will serve the Lord" (Joshua 24:15, NKJV).

AIM:

That the children may

- Know the importance of making right choices that honor God;
- Respond by asking God to help them make right choices every day.

SCRIPTURE: Genesis 13; 17:1-8; 18; 19; 2 Peter 2:7,8

MEMORY VERSE: Joshua 24:15

Choose you this day whom ye will serve.

MATERIALS TO GATHER

Visual for Joshua 24:15
Backgrounds: Review Chart, Plain, Old Testament Map, General Outdoor, Plain with Tree, City Street
Figures: R1-R9, 28, 32, 36, 39, 45, 65, 66, 72, 73, 74, 75, 79, 82, 83, 85, 86, 92
Special:

- ***For Bible Content 3:*** New word strip: BELIEF.
- ***For Conclusion:*** New word strips: CHOICE, RIGHT, WRONG; "Choice" response forms and pencils.
- ***Note:*** To make "Choice" response forms, use a copy machine to duplicate pattern R-5 found on page 158.

REVIEW CHART

Review Token:

Display Review Chart and have R1-R9 ready to use as indicated. Ask the following questions to review Lessons 1-8.

1. How did God make the world? *(By speaking; "And God said...")*
2. Who were the first man and woman? *(Adam and Eve)*
3. Where did the first man and woman come from? *(God made Adam from soil and Eve from Adam's rib bone.)*
4. What was the result of Adam and Eve's disobedience then and now? *(Sin entered the world then; all people today are sinners.)*
5. What promise did God give to Adam and Eve? *(He would send a Savior.)*
6. Which sacrifice pleased God—Cain's or Abel's? *(Abel's)*
7. What must we do to come to God today? *(Receive Jesus as our Savior from sin)*
8. What two special things does the Bible teach us about Enoch? *(He walked with God and God took him to heaven without dying.)*
9. What promise did God give to Noah after the flood? *(That He would never again destroy the earth by a flood)*
10. What sign did God give to remind Noah (and us) that He would keep His promise? *(A rainbow)*
11. What did God do when people stayed in one place and built the tower of Babel instead of spreading out and covering the earth as He had told them to? *(He confused their one language into many languages and forced them to move apart.)*
12. What four promises did God give to Abraham? *(Land, nation, name, blessing)*
13. What are some ways we can serve God today?

Review themes and verses from Lessons 6-8 by mixing up R6-R8 on a table. Ask for volunteers to choose a symbol and place it on the review chart as they recite the verse. If you have time, review Lessons 1-5 in similar manner. Present the new theme (To Make Right Choices) when teaching the memory verse.

♥ MEMORY VERSE

Display Review Chart and have R9 ready to use as indicated. Use the visual from Bible Verses Visualized *to teach Joshua 24:15.*

Our memory verse gives us a clue to the next answer to our question, Why does God call us? Let's find it in our Bibles: Joshua 24:15. *(Or display verse visual.)* What does it tell us we must do? Yes, we must choose. *(Place R9 on review chart and encourage students to answer your questions.)*

To choose means to decide between two or more things. Joshua lived many years after Abraham. Like Abraham, he chose to love and serve God. He became one of the great leaders of God's people, the nation of Israel. In our verse he is urging them to choose or make a choice. As we read the verse together, find the choice they had to make. *(Display verse visual and read aloud together.)*

What was the choice? Yes, they had to choose whom they were going to serve: the one true and living God or the false gods of the nations around them. No one could choose for them. They had to decide for themselves.

God had faithfully shown His people that He was the only living and powerful God and that He was worth serving. God was willing to help them choose to love and serve Him, but He could not make the choice for them.

It is the same for us. We must choose to serve God by obeying Him and living the way He teaches us in His Word, or to go our own way, living the way we want. *(Work on learning the verse and reviewing its meaning.)* ▲#1

▲ Option#1:

Learning the verse: Read verse and reference aloud together. Have children choose partners and give pairs a few minutes to practice saying the verse to each other without looking. Ask for a volunteer pair to stand and say the verse together. Have that pair choose another pair to do the same and so on until all have said the verse. You could also give each pair paper and marker to see if they can write the verse from memory.

BIBLE LESSON OUTLINE

Abraham and Lot Choose

Introduction

How do we make choices?

Bible Content

1. Abraham and Lot travel together.
2. Abraham and Lot choose.
3. Abraham and Lot live as they chose.
4. Abraham prays for Lot.
5. God judges Sodom and Gomorrah.
6. Lot loses and Abraham gains.

Conclusion

Summary

Application

Learning how to make right choices

Response Activity

Choosing to obey God today

BIBLE LESSON

Introduction

How do we make choices?

We make many choices every day. Can you think of some? *(Allow response.)* Some are simple: what clothes we will wear or what food we will eat. Some are more important: to do homework or go out to play; to obey our parents or do whatever we want; who will be our friends; how we will behave in school.

Some of our choices are right or wise; others are wrong or foolish. Choices have consequences, or results. Some are good and some are bad, depending on how we have chosen.

Tell the following story. Then use the following questions to discuss Andy's options and the choice he had to make. Don't give an answer. You will come back to this discussion at the end of the lesson.

Andy had to make a choice one day. He and some friends were walking home from school when one of them said, "Hey, let's go get some candy bars." ▲#2

▲ Option#2:

Have children take the parts of Andy, his friends and a store clerk and act out this story. Stop at the point of choice.

Andy said, "You go on. I don't have any money with me."

"That doesn't matter," his friends said. "You keep the clerk busy and we'll get the candy."

What do you think the boys were planning to do? What choices did Andy have? As a Christian, what should he do?

We don't have to depend on ourselves for wisdom to make right choices. God tells us in His Word what pleases Him. He also promises to guide us to make choices that honor Him when we ask for His help.

Today we will look at some people in the Bible who made choices and what the consequences of those choices were. We will also discover how God can help us make right choices in our own lives.

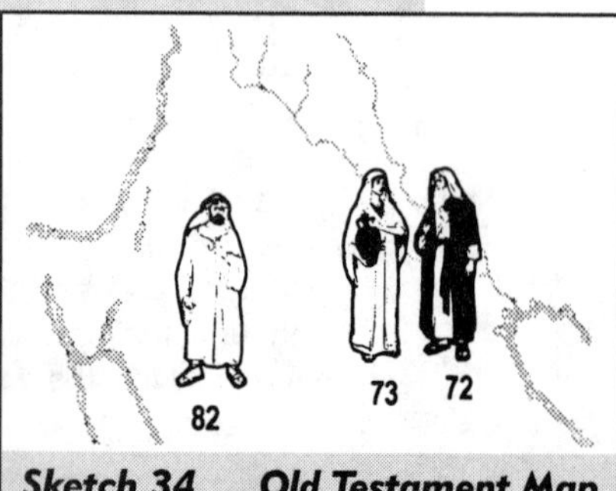

Sketch 34   Old Testament Map

Bible Content

1. Abraham and Lot travel together. (Genesis 11:31)

(Abraham 72, Sarah 73, Lot 82)

When Abraham left Ur to make the long journey to the land of Canaan, his wife Sarah and his nephew Lot went with him. *(Place 72, 73 and 82 on map; review the route of their trip.)* Lot's father had died. Perhaps he now looked to his uncle Abraham as a father.

Lot knew why Abraham was taking this journey, and he chose to go with him. Lot had seen his Uncle Abraham build altars and offer sacrifices. It's possible he too had offered sacrifices. He knew what God had said, and he believed it was the living God who had spoken to Abraham and given him those wonderful promises.

2. Abraham and Lot choose. (Genesis 13:5- 18)

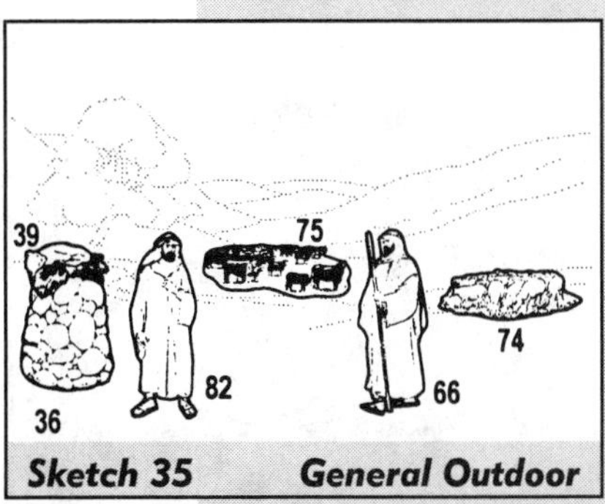

Sketch 35 **General Outdoor**

(Abraham 66, flocks and herds 74,75, Lot 82, city 65, altar 36, offering 39.)

Abraham and Lot were both rich men with many flocks of sheep and herds of cattle. Both sheep and cows eat a lot of grass. Even though the new land was large, there was not enough grazing land for all the animals. Lot's shepherds and Abraham's shepherds began to argue with each other. Each group wanted the best pastures for their flocks and herds.

Abraham soon heard about the problem. He knew that quarreling was not pleasing to God so he said to Lot, "Let's not have any quarreling between us or our servants, for we are relatives." Then he suggested that they move away from each other, each choosing a part of the land where he wanted to live and then settling there with his family and flocks.

Since Abraham was older he had the right to choose land first. Instead, he kindly and unselfishly said to Lot, "You choose first." Lot wasn't concerned about Abraham or what was right. He looked over the land to find the very best part for himself and his family. He finally decided to go toward the east where the Jordan river flowed through a valley—or plain—where the grass was very green and good for grazing. There were also cities there. ▲#3

Lot left his Uncle Abraham, took his family and flocks and herds and settled in this new area among the cities of the plain. He pitched his tents near a city called Sodom. We read in the Bible that the men of Sodom were very wicked and sinned greatly against the Lord. Even today the name Sodom is sometimes used for a place that is very wicked.

Apparently Lot did not stop to think about how growing up near such a wicked place would affect his children or how difficult it would be for them to follow God there. He did not choose by faith. Instead, he chose by what his eyes could see and what his heart wanted. He made a selfish choice.

Abraham loved Lot. He and Sarah must have missed him and his family after they moved away. Perhaps Abraham felt bad that Lot had chosen so selfishly. But after Lot moved, God spoke to Abraham again:

▲ Option#3:

Use a detailed map of the area to show these places. Allow individual children to trace Abraham's journey from Ur to Canann, locate the Jordan River, Sodom and Gomorrah. Show a present-day map of that area (or that area on a world map) and point out current names of these Bible locations to help children realize the reality of the Bible history you are teaching.

"Look all around you—east and west, north and south. I will give all the land you can see to you and your family forever. There will be more people in your family than there are specks of dust on the earth."

When Abraham heard this amazing statement—that all the land, even the part Lot had chosen, would someday belong to his family—he built an altar and worshiped God. God rewarded Abraham for choosing well—for choosing to trust Him and obey Him.

3. Abraham and Lot live as they chose. (Genesis 13:13; 17:1-8; 2 Peter 2:7,8)

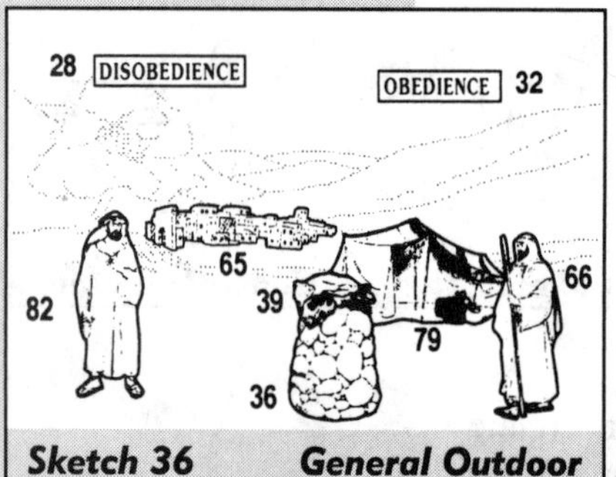

Sketch 36 ***General Outdoor***

(Lot 82, tent 79, city 65, Abraham 66, altar 36, offering 39, OBEDIENCE 32, DISOBEDIENCE 28)

In their new home Lot *(place 82 and 79 on board)* and his family began to meet the people who lived nearby, including some who lived in Sodom *(add 65)*. Perhaps they were at first shocked by all the sinful activities they saw there, but gradually they must have gotten used to them. ▲#4

Eventually they chose to leave their tents *(remove 79)* and move right into that wicked city! *(Move 65 closer to 82.)* Soon they made friends and two of Lot's daughters married men who lived there.

Sometimes Christian boys and girls have experiences something like Lot's. Perhaps you met some new friends you liked a lot, but then were shocked to hear them use swear words or to see them stealing. At first what they are doing seems so wrong, but after awhile, if you keep going around with them, it can seem normal. Then it's very easy to start saying the same words they say or do the same things they do without it feeling wrong at all. The friends we choose can make a big difference in our lives. They can help us or get us into trouble.

▲ Option#4:

Have the children look up Genesis 13:13 and 2 Peter 2:7,8 to discover what Sodom was like.

Lot became an important man in Sodom, something like a member of the city council, and people looked up to him. In the New Testament we read that Lot was righteous; that is, he believed in the living God. He probably became angry at the evil all around him. Perhaps he even tried to tell the people about God, but they would not listen. Lot believed in God, but he didn't obey Him *(add 28)*, so he suffered the consequences of his wrong choices.

During the years that Lot lived in Sodom, Abraham *(place 66 on board)* continued to trust and obey God. He lived in a tent *(add 79)* and moved from place to place as God told him. Wherever he went,he built an altar and offered animal sacrifices *(add 36 and 39)* to show that he believed in God. Abraham obeyed God *(add 32)*. When Abraham was 99 years old God appeared to him again. God reminded Abraham of the promises He had given him: that He would make Abraham and his family a great nation and give them this land.

4. Abraham prays for Lot. (Genesis 18)

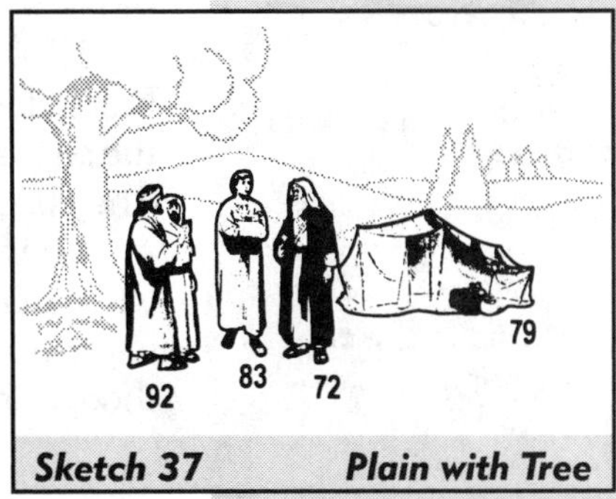

Sketch 37 **Plain with Tree**

(Group 92, Abraham 72, tent 79, angel 83.)

One day Abraham was sitting by the door of his tent when three men he had never seen before came to visit him. He welcomed them and got water for them to wash their feet, as was the custom in those days, while his servants prepared food for them. They ate under the shade of a tree and talked with Abraham for awhile. The Bible tells us that these men were visitors from heaven—two angels (19:1) and the Lord Himself (18:25). When they got up to leave, Abraham walked along with them. As they went, the Lord told Abraham that He had come to destroy the cities of Sodom and Gomorrah because of their great sinfulness. Then the two angels left and started toward Sodom. ▲#5

Immediately Abraham thought of Lot in that wicked city. He turned to the Lord and asked, "Will You destroy the righteous people—people who trust You—along with the wicked? Would that be right? If You found 50 righteous people in the city, would you spare it for their sakes?" The Lord said that He would.

Then Abraham asked if God would save the city for 45 righteous people, and God said yes. Abraham kept asking: Would God save the city for 40 people who believed in Him? Yes, He would. Would He save it for 30 people? For 20? Even for 10? Each time God said He would save the city if He found that many people there who believed in Him. Abraham stopped asking at 10. Maybe he was embarrassed to ask anymore. Or maybe he thought there would be at least that many righteous people among Lot's family and friends and that the city would be spared.

▲ Option#5:

Print numbers 50, 45, 40, 30, 20, 10 on separate sheets of construction paper or 4- x 6-inch cards. Distribute these to children before class. Have the children come to stand before the class, holding their cards, as you mention their number.

5. God judges Sodom and Gomorrah. (Genesis 19:1-26)

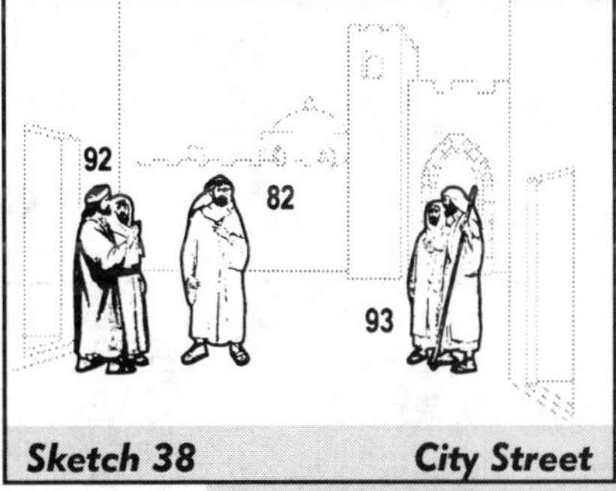

Sketch 38 **City Street**

(Angels 92, Lot 82, men 93)

Lot was sitting in the gateway of the city in the evening when the two angels who had visited Abraham arrived at Sodom. *(Place 82 and 92 near the city gate.)* Though they were angels sent by God, they looked like ordinary men. Lot welcomed them and, because there were no motels in those days, invited them to come to his house to stay overnight *(remove figures)*.

At home Lot prepared a meal for his visitors. Before they could go to bed, a large group of homosexual men from the city surrounded the house *(place 93 at door)* and began shouting, demanding that Lot send his visitors out so they could have sex with them.

God's Word says that it is a sin for any two people who are not married to each other to have sex together. Were these men married to the angels? *(Of course not)* Homosexual sex is always wrong because God never intended for two men or two women to be married to each other.

When Lot refused to send his visitors out, the angry men tried to break down the door to get inside. Suddenly, the two angels caused the wicked men to be struck blind so that they could not find the door. They became so confused that they left.

Then the angels told Lot that God had sent them to destroy this wicked city, and that he must escape with his family. Lot hurried off to warn his married daughters and their husbands. But the husbands thought he was joking and none of them came with him.

▲ Option#6:

Print LOT on one side and ABRAHAM on the other side of newsprint or chalkboard. Underneath list the consequences of their choices as they are given. LOT: a home in a wicked city, leadership, lost home & wife, lived in cave; ABRAHAM: received God's promises, God's answers, God's blessing.

6. Lot loses and Abraham gains. (Genesis 19:29, 30)

86 85

Sketch 39 ***General Outdoor***

(City 65, Lot & family fleeing 86, Lot's wife & flaming city 85)

Early the next morning, the angels took Lot, his wife and their two unmarried daughters by the hand and led them out of the city. "Run for your lives," they said, "and don't look back! Go to the mountains or you will be destroyed!" Lot and his family ran, but Lot's wife disobeyed the angels. She must have been thinking about all the things she was leaving behind. She turned to look back at the burning city and immediately became a pillar of salt. Lot and his daughters escaped to a cave in the mountains.

The day after the heavenly visitors came to his tent, Abraham got up early in the morning *(perhaps to pray)* and went to a place where he could see the entire valley. Great clouds of black smoke like the smoke from a huge furnace rose from where the cities of Sodom and Gomorrah had been. Then he knew there had not been even ten righteous people in Sodom. God had destroyed it completely.

But we read in the Bible that when God destroyed the wicked cities, He remembered His promises to Abraham and saved Lot out of the destruction. God answered Abraham's prayer for Lot.

▲ Option#7:

Review Andy's story by having several children act it out.

■ Conclusion

Summary

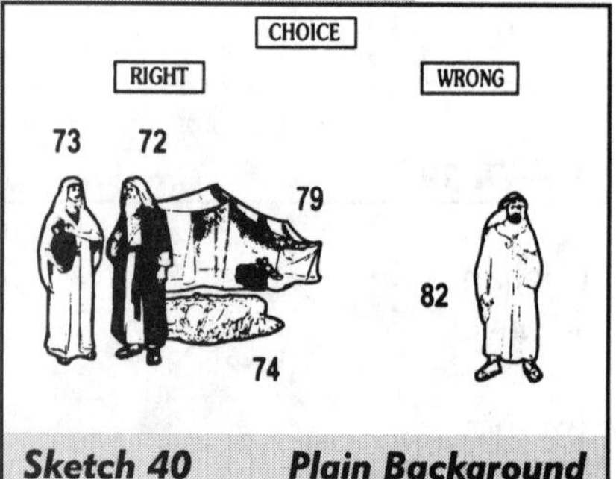

CHOICE
RIGHT WRONG
73 72 79 82 74

Sketch 40 ***Plain Background***

(Lot 82, Abraham 72, Lot and daughters 86, Sarah 73, tent 79, flock 74, new word strips: CHOICE, RIGHT, WRONG; "Choice" response forms and pencils.)

Today we've been learning about Abraham and Lot, two men who knew the living God. Both followed God at first. God blessed both of them and made them wealthy. When their flocks and herds got too large, they both had to choose where they would settle.

Let's think about the choices they made. *(Place word strips CHOICE, RIGHT and WRONG on board. Have the students place figures under appropriate headings as they answer questions.)*

Who chose first? *(Lot)* Where did he choose to settle? *(Near best pasture and wicked cities)* What kind of choice was it? *(A selfish and wrong choice)* He chose what looked best, without asking God's help.

What kind of choice did Abraham make? *(A right and wise choice)* He believed God even though it looked as like he was getting less.

What were the results of Lot's choice? ▲#6 He and his family lived in the city and Lot became an important leader there. But in the end Lot lost all his possessions and even his wife. He and his daughters had to flee to a cave in the mountains. *(Replace 82 with 86.)*

What were the consequences of Abraham's choice? God came to talk with him. God renewed the promises He had made to him. God answered his prayers for Lot. In the end Abraham had more than he ever had before. *(Add 73, 74, 79.)*

Application

Remember the story of Andy? *(Review briefly.)* ▲#7 What did his friends want him to do? Was it right or wrong? Would anyone have known? What do you think he did? What would you do? Why?

Let's look at what God says Andy should do. Find Exodus 20:15 and Romans 13:9,10. *(Or, before class write these verses on newsprint so all can see them. Discuss what Andy should do.)*

God calls us to make right choices, too, just as He did Lot and Abraham long ago. Maybe you have learned, as Lot did, that making wrong or selfish choices creates problems. God wants to help us make right choices every day. As we study His Word in class and read it at home, we learn how God wants us to live. When we ask God to help us obey what His Word says, He guides us in making right choices. Then God will be pleased with our lives as He was with Abraham's.

Response Activity

Encourage any who have never trusted Christ as Savior to receive Him today as the first step in choosing to obey God.

Ask, What are some choices you might have to make this week? List responses. Pray that God will help them make right choices.

*Hand out **"Choice" response forms** (see Materials to Gather). Ask children to write on form during the week one choice they had to make, how they chose, and the result of their choice—and then bring the form back next week to share what happened.*

HELPS FOR YOUNGER CHILDREN

Bible Content 4: Omit the details and introduce the angels and their visit in part 5 (p. 75).

Note:

The Bible clearly teaches that God established marriage in the beginning for one man and one woman for both fellowship and procreation (Genesis 2:21-24; 1:26-28). Paul instructed, "Let each man have his own wife, and let each woman have her own husband" (1 Corinthians 7:2-7).

Repeatedly, Scripture condemns homosexual behavior along with fornication, adultery and other sexual sin (Leviticus 18:19-25; 20:12-16, 22, 23; Romans 1:22-27; 1 Corinthians 6:9, 10; 1 Timothy 1:8-11).

Paul emphasizes that God loves and extends His mercy to anyone, including the homosexual, who will turn to Him in repentance. Notice what he writes concerning the Corinthian believers: "And such were some of you. But you were washed, but you were sanctified, but you were justified in the name of the Lord Jesus and by the Spirit of our God" (1 Corinthians 6:11, NKJV).

Abraham Learns to Trust God

Theme: God Calls Us — To Trust Him

Lesson **10**

Part One: Ishmael and Isaac Are Born

BEFORE YOU BEGIN...

Promises kept, promises broken—both impact our lives and influence our ability to trust. Children who live with broken promises find it difficult to trust people or God. But God calls to His children, I love you; trust me with all your heart; don't lean on your own ability to figure it out! Abraham struggled with this. Years had gone by and still the promised son had not been born. Had he misunderstood God? Or trusted in vain? Finally he "leaned on his own understanding," agreed with Sarah's plan and Ismael was born—bringing joy, but leading to strife when God gave Isaac, the promised son, to Sarah. Abraham learned the hard way that he could trust God with all his heart!

Continually remind your children that God is faithful. Teach them that His ways are higher than our ways, that they will not always understand what He is doing, but that He is always working for their good. Encourage them to trust Him, to walk daily in the footsteps of faith and obedience. "He who calls you is faithful, who also will do it" (1 Thessalonians 5:24, NKJV).

AIM:

That the children may

- Know that God always can be trusted to do what He promises.
- Respond by trusting God instead of relying on what seems right to them.

SCRIPTURE: Genesis 15-18;21

MEMORY VERSE: Proverbs 3:5

Trust in the Lord with all thine heart; and lean not unto thine own understanding.

 **MATERIALS TO GATHER**

Visual for Proverbs 3:5
Backgrounds: Review Chart, Plain, Plain with Tree
Figures: R1-R10, 14, 67, 68, 69, 70, 72, 73, 78, 79, 87, 88
Special:

- ***For Memory Verse:*** Chalkboard & chalk or newsprint & marker.
- ***For Bible Content 1:*** Pictures of the night sky.
- ***For Bible Content 2:*** New word strips ISHMAEL and GOD HEARS.
- ***For Bible Content 3:*** New word strips ABRAHAM, FATHER OF MANY NATIONS, ISAAC, LAUGHTER.
- ***For Options:*** Additional materials for any options you choose to use.

 **REVIEW CHART**

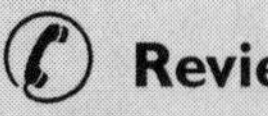 **Review Token:**

Display the Review Chart with R1-R8 in place. Briefly review the theme and verse from Lesson 9, having the child who says the verse place the token on the Chart. Have R10 ready for use as indicated.

To review the last few lessons, ask for volunteers who will pretend to be one of the Bible characters you have already studied. Use the questions below (and/or questions you or the children write) to interview the volunteer characters.

NOAH:

1. Why did you build an ark? *(Because God told me to build it and gave me the plans.)*
2. Why did you feel safe in the ark? *(God promised to keep me and my family safe through the flood He would send.)*

LOT:

1. Why did you and your family choose to live near Sodom? *(Sodom was in the best part of the land.)*
2. What happened to your wife when she looked back at Sodom? *(She became a piller of salt.)*

ABRAHAM:

1. What were the four promises God gave to you? *(I will make of you a great nation; I will give you a land; I will make your name great; I will bless you...and you shall be a blessing.)*
2. Tell us one thing God asked you to do that required you to have great faith. *(Leave my home and go to a land He would show me.)*

Briefly introduce the new theme and place symbol R10 on the review chart. You will give a fuller explanation of its meaning as you teach the memory verse.

♥ MEMORY VERSE

Use the verse visual from Bible Verses Visualized *to teach Proverbs 3:5.*

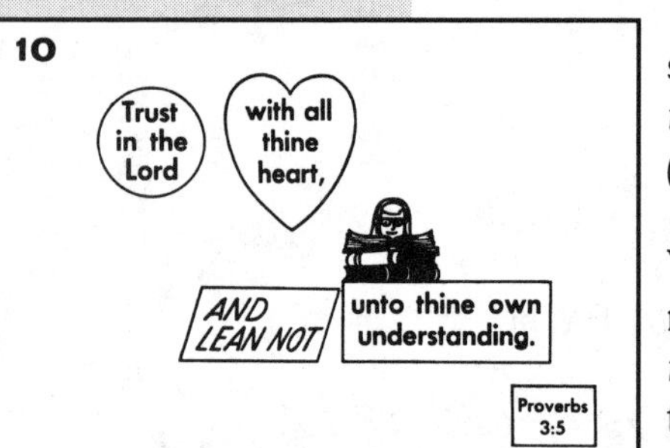

Can you think of a time when you had to trust someone? *(Suggest some examples to start their thinking.)* What did it mean for you to trust that person? *(Encourage response.)*

To trust someone means you depend on that person. You know he will do what he says. The first part of our memory verse speaks about trusting someone. *(Display the first part of the verse visual.)* Who does it say we are to trust? *(The Lord)* How does it say we are to trust Him? *(With all our heart)* To trust someone with all your heart means to trust that person completely, with no doubts.

Let's read the first part of this verse twice. The first time we will use the word *trust*. The second time we will use the words *depend on* in its place to help us better understand its meaning. *(Read this part of the verse together aloud.)* God wants us to depend on Him all the time, for we can trust Him to do only what is best for us.

(Display the second part of the visual.) What does our verse tell us God does not want us to do? Yes, it's lean on our own understanding.

To lean on also means to depend on, like leaning against a table, trusting it to hold us up. The Bible tells us not to depend on our own understanding—our own knowledge or abilities—because when we do, we often make wrong decisions. Instead, our verse commands us to trust in God for everything and to depend on His wisdom and help. *(Work on drilling the verse and reviewing its meaning.)* ▲#1

▲ Option#1:

Learning the verse: Have the group say the verse several times emphasizing a different word—trust, Lord, all, heart, lean not, own—each time.

For variety, specify groups to say it each time: e.g., all wearing the same color, those wearing tennis shoes, those who are oldest children, or youngest, etc.).

BIBLE LESSON OUTLINE

Ishmael and Isaac Are Born

■ Introduction

Having a "best friend."

■ Bible Content

1. God renews His promise of a son for Abraham.
2. Sarah suggests a plan; Ishmael is born.
3. God keeps His promise; Isaac is born.
4. Ishmael and Hagar leave.

■ Conclusion

Summary

Application

Trusting in God.

Response Activity

Asking God to help us trust Him instead of ourselves.

BIBLE LESSON

Introduction

Having a "best friend."

What makes a person your "best" friend? *(Encourage response.)* Our best friends are those we play with and can trust enough to tell important things we wouldn't want everyone to know.

The Bible tells us that Abraham had a "best friend." Who do you think it was? Yes, his Friend was God. The Bible says that Abraham was called the "friend of God" (James 2:23). He loved to walk and talk with God. Because Abraham trusted God with all his heart, God told him things He didn't tell anyone else.

Our memory verse tells us to "trust in the Lord." Can we trust God like we trust our best friend? Let's discover just how God called Abraham to trust Him and how we, too, can learn to trust God today.

Bible Content

1. God renews His promise of a son for Abraham. (Genesis 15)

(Abraham 72, GOD 14, nation 67, land 68, name 69, blessing 70; pictures of the night sky.)

God gave Abraham four promises. Let's see if we can remember all four. *(Have children give promises as they place word strips on the board. Encourage them to explain the meaning of each promise.)* God promised to make of Abraham a great nation, give him a land, make his name great, and make him a blessing to the whole world.

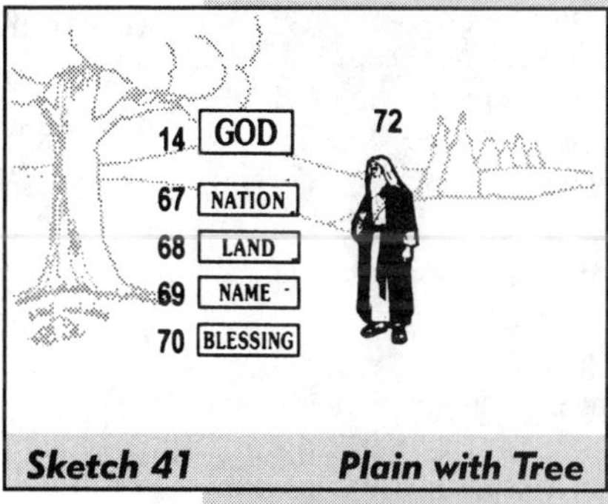

Sketch 41 ***Plain with Tree***

Abraham probably wondered many times how God was going to keep His promise to make him a great nation. He and his wife Sarah had no children and they were now getting too old to have a baby. Still, Abraham believed God and trusted Him to keep His promise.

Because Abraham was God's friend, he could tell God anything. One night when God came to talk with him, Abraham told God how concerned he was because he had no children to fulfill the promise. He said, "You have not given me even one child."

Then God said to Abraham, "But I will give you a son of your very own." Then He took him outside and said, "Look up at the heavens and see if you can count the stars. That's how many descendants you will have." *(Show pictures of the night sky to emphasize God's promise.)* What did God mean by that? *(Encourage children to respond.)* Not only would Abraham have a son, he would have so many descendants he would not be able to count them. What a wonderful promise! Abraham believed this even when it was hard to see how God would do it. God also repeated His promise to give a great land to Abraham and his family.

2. Sarah suggests a plan; Ishmael is born. (Genesis 16)

(Sarah 73, Abraham 72, Hagar 78, tent 79; new word strips ISHMAEL, GOD HEARS.)

Sarah knew about God's promises and she knew how much Abraham wanted a child. She also thought she would never have a child because she was now too old. Perhaps she thought God had forgotten His promise to Abraham. So she made a plan of her own.

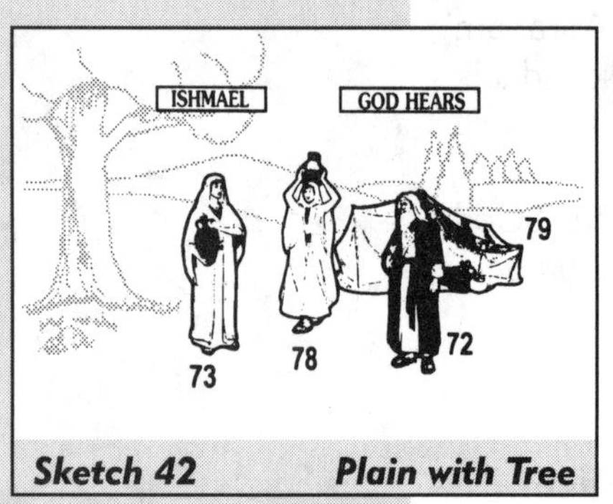

Sketch 42 **Plain with Tree**

One day Sarah said to Abraham: "God has not given me any children. I have an idea. Perhaps you should take my servant Hagar to be your wife. Then you could have a child with her."

Abraham thought Sarah's plan sounded like a good idea. He didn't stop to ask his best friend, God, what he should do. Instead, he took Hagar to be his wife. Maybe he was afraid that God wouldn't keep His promises and decided to trust what seemed right to him instead.

Although men in those days sometimes had more than one wife, that was never God's plan. In the beginning God gave Adam one wife and said that a man should leave his father and mother and be united to his wife. Doing something other than what God says is right and good always leads to trouble.

Hagar became pregnant and soon began to look down on Sarah because she had no children and couldn't get pregnant. When Sarah mistreated her for acting that way, Hagar ran away into the desert. It was a lonely place, full of dangers, but God watched over Hagar for the sake of His friend Abraham, even though Abraham had been impatient.

The angel of the Lord found Hagar sitting beside a well of water. He told her to go back to Sarah and be obedient to her. Then he said, "You will have a little son; name him Ishmael." *(Place word strip ISHMAEL on board.)* The name Ishmael means God hears. *(Add second word strip, GOD HEARS.)* Hagar knew then that God had heard her and was taking care of her.

Hagar obeyed God. She returned to Abraham's home and was obedient to Sarah. Before long her baby boy was born. Abraham named him Ishmael. Abraham was 86 years old when his son Ishmael was born and he was glad to finally have a son. As Ishmael grew, Abraham probably taught him all kinds of practical things, like how to hunt with a bow and arrow and how to obey cheerfully. He also taught him about the true and living God whom he had come to know and love.

3. God keeps His promise; Isaac is born. (Genesis 17:1-19; 21:1-13)

(GOD 14, Abraham 72, Sarah 73, Isaac 87; Hagar and Ishmael 88, new word strips ABRAHAM, FATHER OF MANY NATIONS, ISAAC, LAUGHTER.)

Note:

From a survey of Old Testament references to "the angel of the Lord," many believe the angel is Jehovah Himself. In fact, the terms "the LORD" and "the angel of the LORD" are used interchangeably in many passages.

Others maintain that the Lord speaks through the angel. Still others hold that the angel of the Lord was a special angel divinely delegated to speak God's messages as though he were God.

We are using the term "the angel of the LORD" wherever it occurs in the biblical account. To avoid confusing children, you may wish to use "the Lord" when "the angel of the LORD" is mentioned.

When Ishmael was 13 and his father was 99, the Lord appeared to Abraham again *(place 14 and 72 on board)*. Abraham bowed in worship as God said: "I am God Almighty. I will keep My promises to you and you will become the father of many nations. You are not to be called Abram any more, but Abraham." Abraham means *father of many nations. (Add word strips ABRAHAM and FATHER OF MANY NATIONS.)* Then God repeated His promises to make a great nation from Abraham and his descendants and to give him a land.

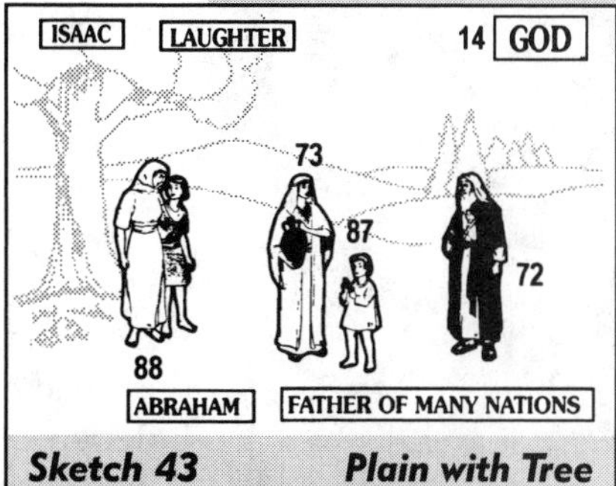

Sketch 43 ***Plain with Tree***

God also said, "I will bless Sarah and give her a baby son." Abraham could hardly believe this because they were too old to have children. He thought that God would keep His promises through Ishmael.

God said, "I will bless Ishmael because he is your son, and make a great nation come from him, too. But the promises will come true through the son I will give to you and Sarah. Name him Isaac." *(Remove 14 and word strips; add 73.)*

Everything happened just as God said. Sarah had a baby boy , and Abraham named him Isaac which means laughter. *(Add word strips ISAAC and LAUGHTER.)* They were so happy! Isaac's birth was a miracle of God, for Abraham was 100 years old and Sarah was 90– much older than your grandparents and even some of your great-grandparents!

When Isaac was still a little boy *(add 87)*, his father held a feast for him. A feast was something like a party with many good things to eat. Everyone paid attention to little Isaac, and big brother Ishmael became angry and jealous. He began to tease Isaac and make fun of him.

Sarah became very angry and said to Abraham, "Send Hagar and Ishmael away from here!" *(Add 88.)* Abraham was upset. He loved Ishmael, too. He asked God what to do. God said, "Do what Sarah wants and do not feel sad. It will be better this way. Because he is your son, I will take care of Ishmael and he will become a great nation also." *(Remove all figures but 72 and 88.)*

4. Ishmael and Hagar leave. (Genesis 21:14-21)

Early next morning Abraham gave Hagar some food and a container of water and sent her away with Ishmael. They wandered in the desert until their water was all gone. Then they both became weak and sick from lack of water.

Hagar helped Ishmael to the shade of a desert shrub. Then she sat down and cried. She was afraid they would die in the desert. Suddenly the angel of the Lord who had met Hagar before Ishmael was born called to her from heaven: "Don't be afraid, Hagar. God has heard Ishmael's crying. He will live and become a great nation."

Then God opened her eyes to see a well of water there in the desert. She quickly filled the water bottle and gave Ishmael a drink. Both of them lived because God took care of them.

Ishmael grew up in the wilderness and learned to use a bow and arrow to hunt animals for food. He became a strong, rugged man and married a girl from Egypt. They had twelve sons.

God kept His Word to Abraham. Ishmael's family grew into a nation of people living in the deserts of Arabia. Today we know them as the Arab nation. They too are descendants of Abraham, but God's special promises to Abraham were given to Isaac and his descendants.

■ Conclusion

Summary

Abraham followed Sarah's suggestion to take Hagar as his wife instead of trusting God completely to give him the promised son. He depended on his "own understanding." What were the results? Ishmael was born, and Hagar, Sarah and Abraham all suffered much sadness and trouble. But God promised to bless and take care of Ishmael in spite of Abraham's lack of trust. How loving and merciful God is!

Application

Can you think of a time when you, like Abraham, knew what God wanted you to do, but you did what someone else wanted instead? *(If necessary, suggest, Maybe your mother asked you to do a job, but your friend convinced you to come and play. Or, while at a friend's house you watched a TV program you knew your parents' didn't approve of.)* How did you feel afterward? What were the results? ▲#2

In such situations, how can you show that you are trusting God? And what would show that you are "leaning on your own understanding"? *(Through discussion help the children realize the vital link between trusting God and everyday living.*

God has put wise rules for living in His Word. To trust God is to do, or obey, what He has told us there.

▲ Option#2:

Before class, prepare several children to help you act out one or more of these situations, or situations the class suggests. Then encourage boys and girls to suggest how they would show trust in God rather than "leaning on their own understanding." Act out these responses as well.

Response Activity

Let's ask God right now to help each of us trust Him and obey Him this week when it would be easier to do what we want to do.

Invite class members to pray, asking God to help them trust and obey Him instead of doing what they think is best. Recite the memory verse together and then pray that God will specially help each child in the coming week. Next week encourage them to talk about what happened.

Abraham Learns to Trust God

Theme: God Calls Us — To Trust Him

Lesson

10

Part Two: God Gives Abraham a Test

BEFORE YOU BEGIN...

Children have tests in school. They understand the pressure of having to "pass" or what it's like to worry about what will happen if they fail. Some of them live with the "tests" of an abusive or broken home or abandonment by an absent parent. Others face rejection by friends or their peer group because they're somehow different. Or simply because they want to live for Jesus. It's hard to understand why God allows such hard things...and easy to wonder why God allows them if He really loves us.

Abraham must have wondered, too, on that three-day trip to the mountain where God had told him to sacrifice his only son Isaac. But God had a purpose. Help your boys and girls see that this test was Abraham's opportunity to demonstrate how much he really loved and trusted God. And that God sometimes allows us to go through hard things—whether big or small—to see if we will trust Him and obey Him and let Him help us through them. "For He Himself has said, 'I will never leave you nor forsake you.' So we may boldly say: 'The Lord is my helper; I will not fear. What can man do to me?'" (Hebrews 13:5,6. NKJV).

AIM:

That the children may

- Know that they can trust God when tests come in their daily lives.
- Respond by learning to recognize tests when they come and to trust God for victory.

SCRIPTURE: Genesis 22:1-14

MEMORY VERSE: Proverbs 3:5

Trust in the Lord with all thine heart; and lean not unto thine own understanding.

MATERIALS TO GATHER

Visual for Proverbs 3:5
Backgrounds: Review Chart, Plain, General Outdoor, Hilltop
Figures: R1-R10, 1, 14, 31, 36, 72, 87, 89, 90, 93, 96
Special:

- ***For Introduction:*** New word strip or flash card TEST.
- ***For Conclusion:*** New word strips TRUST, OBEY; picture of an empty tomb; newsprint & marker or chalkboard & chalk; 4- x 6-inch cards; pencils.
- ***For Options:*** Additional materials for any options you choose to use.

REVIEW CHART

Review Token:

Display the Review Chart. Quickly review R1-R10 with the children, placing the symbols as you go. Use the following questions to review last week's lesson.

1. What did God promise to give to Abraham? *(A name, a land, a son, a nation and blessings)*
2. Why did Sarah advise Abraham to marry Hagar? *(She thought she was too old to have a baby herself.)*
3. What mistake did Abraham make? *(He listened to Sarah's advice and had a child with Hagar instead of asking God what he should do.)*
4. What was the result of Abraham's leaning on his own understanding? *(Ishmael was born; this created problems between Sarah and Hagar and forced Abraham to send Hagar and Ishmael away.)*
5. How did God keep His promise to give Abraham a son? *(He gave Sarah a baby boy when she was 90 years old and Abraham was 100.)*
6. What did Abraham and Sarah name their son? *(Isaac)*

♥ MEMORY VERSE

Use the verse visual to review Proverbs 3:5 and its meaning. ▲#1

BIBLE LESSON OUTLINE

God Gives Abraham a Test

■ Introduction

Do you like to take tests?

Bible Content

1. God tells Abraham to do something difficult.
2. Abraham obeys God.
3. God provides a sacrifice.

Conclusion

Summary

Application

Trusting God as Abraham did.

Response activity

Making sure they have passed the first test of receiving Christ. Writing down a test they need to trust God for this week and asking for His help.

BIBLE LESSON

Introduction

Do you like to take tests?

Have you ever had to take a really hard test? *(Place new word strip TEST on flannelboard.)* What kind of test was it? *(School subject, sports try-out, etc.)* What made it so difficult? *(Encourage response throughout.)* You may not have known the answers or maybe it was worded so you could not understand the questions. Or maybe you didn't study. How did you feel when you finished?

We've been learning that God sometimes gives "tests" in life to His people. Can you think of a test Abraham had to take in the lesson we had last week? Yes, he had to choose whether he would listen to his wife or God. Did he pass the test? No, he failed. Why? Right, because he listened to Sarah's advice instead of asking his best friend, God, what he should do about Sarah's suggestion. He "leaned on his own understanding" about how to get a son instead of waiting on God to keep His promise.

Have you ever failed a test? How did it make you feel? How do you think Abraham felt when he realized he had failed to trust God? When we fail a test, we have to go back to our books and study some more before we take the test again. We might even have someone help us until we understand. Sometimes we have to retake the test more than once until we get it right. God is a good teacher. When He tests us and we fail to trust Him, He faithfully continues to teach us and prepare us to take the test again.

Sometimes when we have difficulty with a test it's because we think it's unfair, that it contains questions we didn't know about. Do you think Abraham's test from God was unfair? Do you think God ever gives unfair tests? In our Bible lesson today we will learn about another test God gave Abraham.

▲ Option#1:

Learning the verse: Play a review game.

Read the verse together as a group, then remove one piece of the visual.

Ask who can say the verse with that piece missing.

Allow the child who can do it to remove the next piece.

Continue until all the visual has been removed.

Have the children say the verse once more as a group. Then distribute visual pieces to the group to put back on the board in order.

■ Bible Content

1. God tells Abraham to do something difficult. (Genesis 22:1, 2)

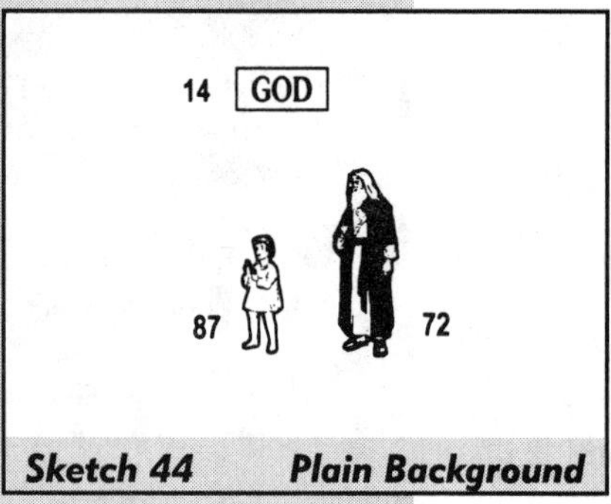

Sketch 44 **Plain Background**

(Abraham 72, Isaac 87, God 14.)

When Isaac was still a young boy, Abraham probably began teaching him about the true and living God *(place figures on board)*. As he grew up Isaac learned why they offered animal sacrifices. He learned about the promises God had given to his father and that they were going to be fulfilled through him. Isaac came to love and trust the living God just as his father did *(remove 87)*.

God knew that Abraham trusted Him. But God gave Abraham a very difficult test to see if he loved God more than he loved Isaac and if he would trust God completely.

One day when Abraham was alone with God, God said to him, "Take your son Isaac, whom you love, to the land of Moriah. There offer him as a burnt offering on a mountain I will show you."

To offer Isaac as a burnt offering, Abraham would have to kill him and burn his body on an altar as a sacrifice to God.

2. Abraham obeys God. (Genesis 22:3-10; Hebrews 11:17-19)

(Abraham 72, Isaac 96, servants 93)

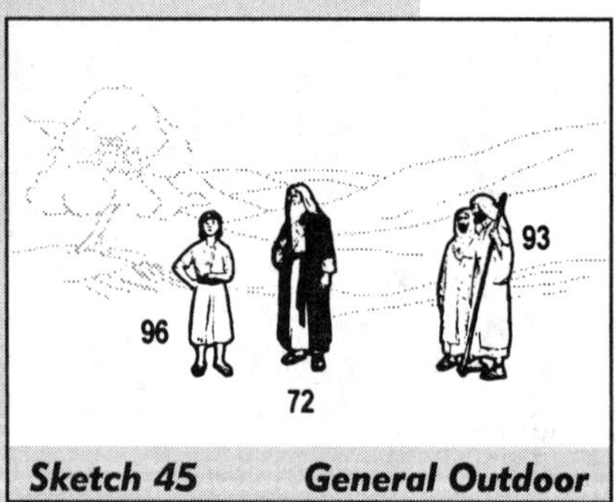

Sketch 45 **General Outdoor**

Can you imagine how Abraham must have felt when God asked him to do this? He knew that the people of other nations sometimes sacrificed their children to their idols, but surely the Lord wouldn't want him to kill the son for whom he had waited so many years. God had told Noah that people were not to murder other people because human life is precious to Him. Today human life is still precious to God. He is never pleased when one person murders another or parents abuse their children.

But Abraham had finally learned his lesson. He had learned to trust God so well that he was willing to obey even when he did not understand why God was telling him to do this. Early in the morning, he got up, split wood for the sacrifice, saddled his donkey and set off on the trip with Isaac and two men servants. They traveled for three days.

Abraham must have wondered how God's promise that he would make Isaac the father of a great nation would come true if Isaac were to die now as a sacrifice on an altar. But the Bible tells us that he believed God was able to keep His promise, even if it meant raising Isaac from the dead.

On the third day, Abraham saw the mountain where God had told him to go. He told the servants to stay and wait with the donkey *(remove 93)* while he and Isaac went on a little farther to worship.

"Then," he said, "we will come back." ▲#2

Abraham put the wood for the offering on Isaac's back. He took fire (perhaps hot coals in a pan) and a knife and they started up the mountainside together.

Isaac had often seen his father offer sacrifices; he knew what was needed. He said to his father, "We have the wood and the fire, but where is the lamb for the sacrifice?"

How hard it must have been for Abraham to answer his son, knowing what God had told him to do. But his answer showed his complete trust in God. He said, "My son, God himself will provide a lamb for a burnt offering." Isaac did not know that he was to be the offering.

▲ Option#2:

Before class, prepare children to take the parts of Abraham and Isaac and act out this story as you read aloud Genesis 22:7-13.

3. God provides a sacrifice. (Genesis 22:11-14)

(Abraham and Isaac 89, altar 36, ram 90)

When they reached the place where God had told him to go, Abraham built an altar and laid the wood in place. Then he tied Isaac's arms and legs and laid him upon the wood on the altar. He must have told Isaac what God had told him to do. Isaac was probably a young man by this time and could have escaped from his father who was old, but he loved his father very much and was used to obeying him. He knew that his father trusted God completely and would not ask anything of him that was not right or good. He, too, trusted God and believed God would care for him.

Sketch 46 **Hilltop**

Abraham put out his hand and took the knife. Just as he was about to kill Isaac, the angel of the Lord called to him from heaven: "Abraham! Abraham!"

Abraham answered, "Here I am." He was exactly where God had told him to be, doing what God had told him to do.

The angel of the Lord said, "Don't harm the boy. Now I know that you love God, because you have been willing to give your only son to Me."

Quickly Abraham untied Isaac. Perhaps he even held him tightly in his arms, for it was as though Isaac had been given back to him from the dead. As he looked around, Abraham saw a ram *(add 90)* caught in the bushes by its horns. He caught the ram and offered it, instead of Isaac, as a burnt offering to God. He and Isaac worshiped God together with thankful and happy hearts.

The angel of the Lord spoke to Abraham again: "Because you did not keep your only son from Me, I promise you that someday there will be more people in your family than there are stars in the sky and grains of sand on the beach!" Through Abraham all nations of the earth would be blessed. After this, Abraham and Isaac went back to the servants and they all went home together.

■ Conclusion

Summary

(Abraham and Isaac 89, altar 36, ram 90, cross l, JESUS 31; new word strips TEST, TRUST, OBEY; memory verse visual; picture of an empty tomb; newsprint and marker or chalkboard and chalk; 4- x 6- inch cards, pencils.)

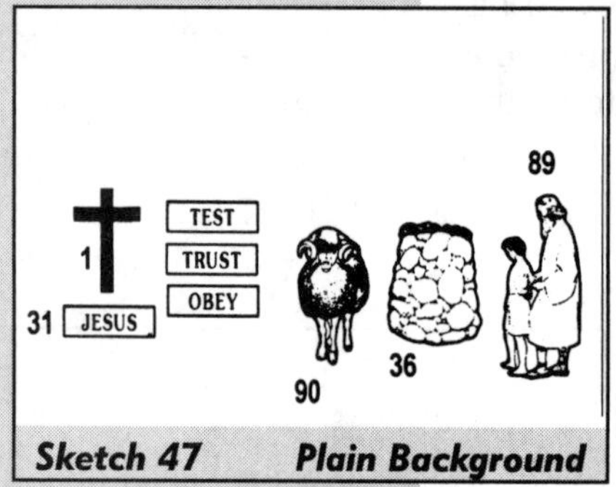

Sketch 47 **Plain Background**

What kind of test did God give Abraham? *(Place word strip TEST on board; add 89 and 36 as children respond.)* Was it a fair test? *(Encourage response.)* Why did God ask Abraham to sacrifice his son Isaac? *(God wanted to see if Abraham would trust Him completely.)* Did Abraham pass the test? *(Yes)* How did Abraham pass God's test? *(He was ready to sacrifice his son, not knowing that God would send a ram and save Isaac.)*

Abraham showed that he trusted God completely rather than his own understanding or his own way of doing things. He is a good example of what our memory verse means. *(Display verse visual.)* Let's say it together.

Application

If Abraham had "leaned on his own understanding," as our verse tells us not to do, what might he have done? *(Allow response.)* He might have begged God not to ask him to give up his son, or he might have given excuses why he could not obey God. He might have tried to think of other things he could sacrifice instead of his son. Or he might have said to God, "Explain this to me. I'll be glad to obey you if I only understand why You are asking this."

Have you ever acted like that when you knew God wanted you to do a difficult thing? Sometimes we offer to do something else to make God happy instead of doing what God shows us in His Word. It shows that we don't really depend on God to help us do things that are difficult for us. Abraham showed his trust in God by doing what God told him to do, even when he could not understand why. *(Place word strips TRUST and OBEY under TEST.)* God then provided a ram *(add 90)* to take Isaac's place.

God is calling us to trust Him today. How can we do this? First, we must see how much He loves us and how He showed that love by sending His only Son, the Lord Jesus, into the world. Jesus died on the cross to take the punishment for our sin *(add cross 1 and JESUS 31)*. He rose again from the dead *(I Corinthians 15:3,4; show picture of empty tomb)* and now He lives in heaven. The first "test" God gives each of us is, Will you trust in My Son Jesus as your Savior? Have you passed this test?

After we have been born into the family of God by trusting Jesus as our Savior, we need to trust Him with our lives here on earth.

Sometimes he sends "tests" to see if we will trust Him. Then He continues to show His love to us by helping us in these difficult times. Like Abraham, we have to trust God when something happens that just doesn't make sense to us. Can you think of some problem or situation like that?

Write the children's responses in brief form on newsprint or chalkboard to be used later in the Response Activity. If they don't suggest anything, mention experiences like parents getting a divorce, mother getting sick with cancer, best friend moving away, house burning down, having their bike stolen, someone mistreating them, family needing money to pay bills while parent is out of work, needing help in a school subject that is hard for them, being tempted to use bad words like the kids around them do.

When you or I have hard tests, it is very important to do what our verse tells us. Let's say it together aloud. *(If time permits, repeat the verse several times, each time emphasizing a different word: "TRUST in the Lord...."; "Trust in the LORD...."; "Trust in the Lord with ALL your heart...."; "Trust in the Lord with all your HEART...."; "....LEAN NOT....")*

God wants us to trust Him with all our heart. That means to believe that He knows what is happening and is right there with us; that He will never go away and leave us, but will take care of us and help us live the way He wants us to through the test. It also means to obey Him each day and thank Him that He is helping us.

Response Activity

Encourage your children to make sure they have "passed" the first test of personally accepting Christ as Savior. Invite them to pray sentence prayers, thanking God for sending Jesus. Give opportunity for any who have not yet trusted Christ as Savior to do so today.

Pass out pencils and 4- x 6-inch cards. Have each child write a test he or she is facing or will face during the coming week on one side of the card and copy the memory verse on the other side. Let them look at the list of situations you have written on the newsprint or chalkboard if they need to. Then allow time for each one to silently ask God for help with their specific test. Encourage them to pray and trust God to help them each day and then to share in class next week what God did for them.

HELPS FOR YOUNGER CHILDREN

Bible Content: Emphasize that God did not want Abraham to take his son's life, but rather wanted Abraham to show that he loved and trusted God enough to give up the son he loved.

Isaac and Jacob Learn God's Ways

Theme: God Calls Us — To Learn His Ways

Lesson

11

Part One: Jacob and Esau Are Born

BEFORE YOU BEGIN...

What child doesn't want to be like Dad or Mom or a favorite teacher or sports figure? Children unconsciously (or consciously) pattern themselves after the models they're exposed to. Parents are the original role models, but today children are exposed to many others through media and experience. Some choose to follow poor examples who lead them to wrong actions and lifestyles.

Through this lesson aim to communicate clearly this basic truth: We reap what we sow! Talk with your group about some of their role models and whether they are planting "good" seeds or "bad" by the way they live. Emphasize the importance of planting good seeds in their own lives and following the example of people who walk in God's ways. Show them how God honored Abraham and Isaac because they chose to follow Him. "But now the Lord says:... Those who honor Me I will honor, and those who despise Me shall be lightly esteemed" (1 Samuel 2:30, NKJV).

AIM:

That the children may

- Know that the law of sowing and reaping is one of God's ways and it is wise to sow good seeds early in life.
- Respond by choosing to sow a specific "good" seed in their lives in the coming week.

SCRIPTURE: Genesis 23:1–25:28

MEMORY VERSE: Galatians 6:7

Be not deceived: God is not mocked; for whatsoever a man soweth, that shall he also reap.

MATERIALS TO GATHER

Visual for Galatians 6:7
Backgrounds: Review Chart, Plain, Old Testament Map, Plain with Tree
Figures: R1-R11, 14, 67, 68, 69, 70, 72, 79, 91, 94, 95, 96
Special:

- ***For Memory Verse:*** Several fruits and/or vegetables (real, artificial or pictures) and corresponding seeds or seed packets.
- ***For Conclusion:*** Newsprint & marker or chalkboard & chalk; "We Reap What We Sow" response forms.
- ***For Options:*** Additional materials for any options you choose to use.
- ***Note:*** To make "We Reap What We Sow" response forms, use a copy machine to duplicate pattern R-6 found on page 159.

REVIEW CHART

Display the Review Chart on the flannelboard. Place R1-R5 on the Chart as you briefly review the themes of the first five lessons. Using R6-R10, review the themes and verses of the next five lessons by having the class recite the verse for each symbol as a child places it on the board. Have R11 ready to use as indicated.

Use the following questions to review Lesson 10.

1. Who was called the friend of God? *(Abraham)*
2. Why was Abraham called God's friend? *(He believed and trusted God.)*
3. What does it mean to trust God with all our hearts? *(To trust in Him completely, without doubting)*
4. What test did God give to Abraham? *(He told him to sacrifice Isaac.)*
5. Why did God test Abraham? *(To see if Abraham would trust Him completely)*
6. Name some tests God might give to us today and tell how we can pass them. *(Example: Copying homework from a friend when we don't feel like doing it or doing it on our own, asking God to help us do our best.)*

Today's answer to our question Why does God call us? tells us that God wants us to learn His ways *(place R11 on Chart)*. Have you ever had to learn someone else's way of doing something? Maybe the way your mother wanted you to wash the dishes or how your father wanted you to clean up the yard? You might have preferred to do it your own way, but later you discovered that their way was better.

The Bible says that God wants us to learn about Himself and His ways. We don't always understand His ways or agree with them. But we will see that He has a purpose in them for our good.

♥ MEMORY VERSE

Use the verse visual from Bible Verses Visualized, *fruits and vegetables (real,artificial or pictures) and corresponding packages of seeds to teach Galatians 6:7.*

Can you think of a new thing you learned to do recently? How did you learn it? *(Encourage response.)* ▲#1 Usually someone has to tell you how to do a new thing and you have to follow instructions. If you try to do it your own way, you don't learn it very well.

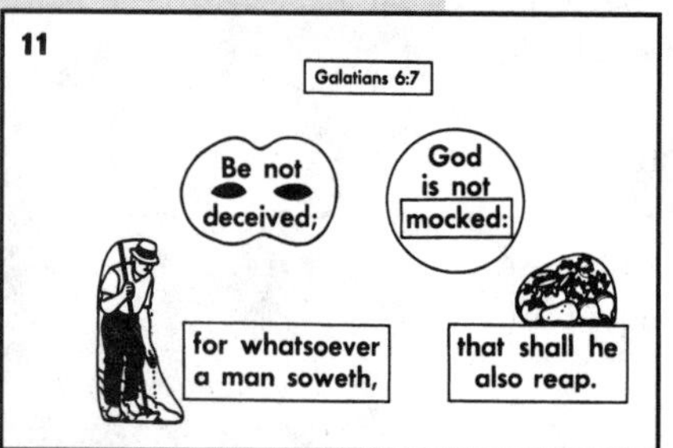

God wants us to learn His ways,but they are not like our ways. We learn about God's ways in the Bible. Our memory verse tells us one of them. What is it? *(Display verse and have it read aloud.)*

The word *deceived* means *tricked* or *fooled*. We are not to be fooled or tricked into thinking we can say or do anything we want without God seeing or knowing about it. He is not mocked or fooled by us, for He sees our hearts and knows us better than even our parents or teachers do. We can never get away with ignoring or disobeying God's laws. Sooner or later the consequences (results) are always unpleasant.

God uses gardening to help us understand this truth. In the springtime we plant (or sow) our gardens. When the plant is grown, we reap (or harvest) the vegetable or fruit. If you sow lettuce seed in a row, what will grow there? *(Show seed packets and corresponding fruits and/or vegetables.)* If you sow cucumber seeds, what will grow? Can I sow onion seeds and get tomatoes? No, the things that grow are the same as the seeds that were planted. ▲#2

The things we think and say and do are like seeds. Whatever we "sow" into our lives now will increase and become part of us as we grow older. For example, what will I reap (or what will be the result) if I sow kindness or helpfulness to others? *(Usually kindness or helpfulness or appreciation)* Or if I sow obedience to parents and teachers and respect for those who are over me? *(I'll be respected and able to work well with others.)* But what if I treat others with disrespect and refuse to do anything I don't want to do? *(People will not respect me and I'll be in trouble with those over me.)*

What will I reap if I sow good and thankful thoughts in my mind? *(A happy attitude and good relationships with others)* What if I think bad or selfish thoughts, or say angry mean words? *(I won't be a nice person and probably won't have any friends.)* We reap what we sow. This is one of God's laws or "ways." *(Work on drilling the verse and reviewing its meaning.)* ▲#3

▲ Option#1:

Ask for volunteers (one or more) to demonstrate how to do something they recently learned and tell how they learned it.

▲ Option#2:

Allow children to pick out and match seeds or seed packets with actual fruits, vegetables or plants.
Or, plant some seeds in flower pots and put the pots in a window where the children can watch the plants come up and grow. Be sure to keep the soil moist. Place the seed packets by the pots so the boys and girls can see that they are "reaping" what they planted.

BIBLE LESSON OUTLINE

Jacob and Esau Are Born

Introduction

Ashley goes to a new school.

Bible Content

1. Isaac marries Rebekah.
2. Isaac and Rebekah have twins.
3. Isaac receives God's promises.

Conclusion

Summary

Application

Are you sowing the good seeds of trust and obedience?

Response Activity

Using an activity sheet to sow a specific "good seed" this week.

BIBLE LESSON

Introduction

Ashley goes to a new school.

Ashley had to go to a new school when her dad got a job transfer. She tried to make friends, but the girls in her new class ignored her. Then they teased and made fun of her. Sometimes Ashley cried all the way home from school.

But Ashley was a Christian, so she asked the Lord to help her. Then she remembered that the Bible says we should be kind to those who treat us unfairly. That seemed hard, but she asked God to help her be kind to the girls who were teasing her and not get angry.

God did help Ashley. She kept on saying hi to the girls. She invited them to her house, even though they always refused. She often felt very lonely, but God helped be kind to them day after day.

Two months later, Ashley met Sally on the way home from school. Ashley said hi and expected to be ignored as usual. Instead, Sally asked Ashley how she could be nice to them when they had been so mean to her. Ashley was amazed, but gladly told Sally about Jesus and how He had been helping her. She and Sally soon became friends. When the other girls saw this, they also became more friendly.

What was Ashley "sowing" in her life? Why was it so difficult? What did she finally "reap" from what she sowed? Why?

Listen to our Bible story to see what the people we talk about were sowing in their lives and what they reaped as a result.

▲ Option#3:

Learning the verse: Divide the class into four sections and assign one part of the verse to each section. Give them time to "design" an action for their part: e.g., cover eyes for "Be not deceived."

Have the class say the reference together; then each section stand to say their part while doing the motion they planned. When all have done their part, remove the verse visual from the board and go through the process again. Finally, have class say the whole verse and do all the motions.

Extra: Say the reference together; then have groups do their motions in turn without saying the words.

Bible Content

1. Isaac marries Rebekah. (Genesis 23, 24)

(Abraham 72, Isaac 91, Eliezer 106.)

Some years after God tested Abraham, Sarah died. She was 127 years old. Abraham and his family had lived in this land of Canaan for many years *(place 72 near Canaan on map)*. God had promised to give it to him and his descendants, but he did not own any of it yet. So he bought a cave from some of the people in the land and buried Sarah there. He and Isaac *(add 91)* grieved for her and were very lonely.

Though Isaac was almost 40 years old, he was not married. Abraham was concerned. He knew Isaac needed a wife, but God would not be pleased if Isaac married someone nearby. These people all worshiped idols of wood and stone. Isaac needed a wife who worshiped the true God.

It is just as important that God's people today marry only those who have trusted in Jesus as their Savior and belong to the living God. Believers who marry unbelievers—or become close friends or partners with them—often turn away from following God.

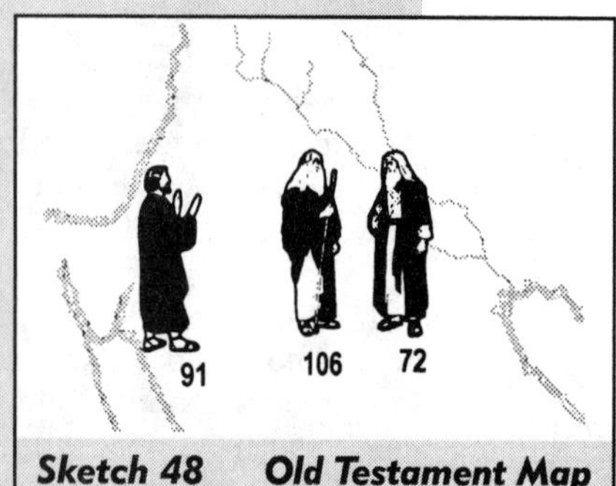

Sketch 48 Old Testament Map

Abraham called Eliezer *(remove 91, replace with 106)*, his most trusted servant (Genesis 15:2), and asked him to do an important task. "Go to my relatives in the land we came from (indicate Haran area on map) and find the right kind of girl to be Isaac's wife."

The "right kind of girl" would worship the true God, be willing to go where Isaac was and be a faithful wife to him. Together they would worship and follow God and teach their children to believe in Him. These are good things to look for in a husband or wife today.

Eliezer had some questions. "What if the girl doesn't want to come?" he asked. "Should I take Isaac to her?"

Abraham answered, "The Lord will send His angel before you so that you can get a proper wife for Isaac. Don't take Isaac there. God promised *this* land to him." So Eliezer promised.

It was a long trip to the town of Nahor *(about 450 miles which may have taken eight to ten weeks; indicate the route on the map)*. Eliezer, his servants and camels finally arrived at the home of Abraham's relatives. At home, Abraham and Isaac waited, praying and wondering what was happening. Eliezer also prayed, asking God to lead him to the right girl for Isaac.

God answered prayer. He showed Eliezer that He wanted Isaac to marry a young woman named Rebekah from the family of Abraham's brother. The whole family listened eagerly as the servant told them about Abraham and his family in Canaan.

God worked in Rebekah's heart so that she was willing to leave her family and travel to the land of Canaan. She married Isaac, and the Bible says that Isaac loved her very much. Eliezer was happy that God helped him keep his promise to Abraham.

What "seeds" did Abraham, Isaac and Eliezer "sow"? *(Obedience to God and trust in God)* And what did they reap? *(Answered prayer and Isaac's wife who believed in God)*

▲ Option#4:

Choose three children to read aloud the three "I will" statements God made to Isaac (Genesis 26:3-4). Place 67-70 on the board as they read.

2. Isaac and Rebekah have twins. (Genesis 25:19-28)

(Tent 79, Rebekah 94, Jacob 95, Esau 96, Isaac 91.)

When Isaac and Rebekah had been married for almost twenty years, they still had no children, even though they must have prayed many times that God would give them a baby. Isaac didn't give up. Perhaps he thought about how long his father and mother had to wait before he was born. He knew it was God's plan for the promises to be passed on to his son, so he kept praying. At last God answered his prayer by giving Rebekah twin boys!

Sketch 49 **Plain with Tree**

When the babies were born, the first one was red and covered all over with fine hair. They named him Esau (hairy) and his brother, Jacob. Isaac had sowed trust in God and reaped answered prayer. How happy he and Rebehah–and grandfather Abraham—must have been with these two little boys!

3. Isaac receives God's promises. (Genesis 25; 26:1-5)

(Abraham 72, Isaac 91, word strips: GOD 14, NATION 67, LAND 68, NAME 69, BLESSING 70.)

Abraham lived 175 years—until Esau and Jacob were 15 years old. He had trusted and obeyed God throughout his long life, even when it was not easy to do. Today, 4,000 years later, Abraham is known as the "friend of God."

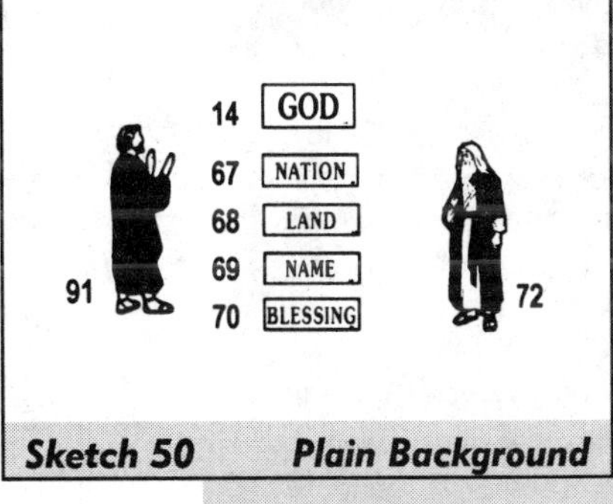

Sketch 50 **Plain Background**

When Abraham died, Ishmael came from his desert home in the east. He and Isaac buried their father in the cave where Sarah had been buried years before.

After Abraham's death, the Lord appeared to Isaac and said, "I will be with you and bless you. I will give this land to you and your descendants. I will make your descendants as many as the stars in the sky, and through them all nations on earth will be blessed." ▲#4

All the promises God had given to Abraham he now gave to Abraham's son Isaac. Through Isaac's descendants Jesus Christ, the Savior, would come into the world (Galatians 3:16), and the Word of God would be given to all people. Isaac was now the leader of God's chosen people. He was responsible to offer sacrifices and to teach his family the Word of God.

▲ **Option#5:**

Secure three 8 1/2" x 11" cards. Print one name on each: Abraham, Eliezer, Isaac. Place on table, floor or wall.

Prepare several blank cards or papers, half the size. Print SOW at the top of some; REAP at the top of others.

As children respond, write their answers on a SOW or REAP card. Have the children match the SOW and REAP cards with the Abraham, Eliezer or Isaac cards.

▲ **Option#6:**

Prepare response sheets by drawing a line down the center and labeling one column SOW and the other, REAP.

In class, write each child's name on a sheet along with whatever he says he sowed and reaped during the week.

Keep these sheets and add to them over several weeks, allowing other students to take part as they respond.

■ Conclusion

Summary

(Chalkboard and chalk or newsprint and marker; "We Reap What We Sow" response forms, pencils.)

Let's think back over our story and tell what kind of "seeds" Abraham, Eliezer and Isaac were "sowing" in their lives. ▲#5 *(Brainstorm, writing responses on the chart you have drawn on newsprint or chalkboard. Mention, if the children do not: Abraham sent Eliezer to find a wife for Isaac; sowing obedience to God and trust in God. Eliezer made the long journey to find a wife for Isaac, praying that God would lead him; sowing respect and obedience toward his master and trust in God. Isaac waited and prayed at home, sowing patience, obedience and trust in God.)*

What were some of the things these men "reaped" from what they sowed? *(Continue to brainstorm, writing responses on newsprint or chalkboard in the REAP column, especially "answers to prayer" and "Rebekah, a wife for Isaac.")* God blessed them because they "sowed" the good seeds of trust and obedience in their lives.

Application

What are you "sowing" in your life? Did you plant good thoughts and helpful deeds at home or school today? Did you obey God by telling the truth or being kind instead of fighting? Or did you plant some "bad" seeds? *(Allow children to share.)*

God blessed the men in our story and answered their prayers when they sowed the good seeds of trust and obedience. When we sow the good seeds of trusting Him and obeying what we learn in His Word, God will bless us and help us, too. Let's say our memory verse together to remind us how we know this is true.

Response Activity

Let's pray right now about these things. If you planted some bad seeds today, like lying or fighting or disobeying or thinking bad thoughts or saying bad words, confess that to God and ask Him to forgive you. *(Allow time for the children to pray silently.)*

*Give each child a **"We Reap What We Sow" response form** (see Materials to Gather). Encourage them to write something specific in the blank (like "telling the truth," "coming when my mother calls," or "being kind to my little sister") and agree to ask God each day to help them do it. Be sure to give them opportunity at your next meeting to tell what they "reaped"—how God helped them.* ▲#6

Isaac and Jacob Learn God's Ways

Theme: God Calls Us — To Learn His Ways

Part Two: Jacob and Esau Reap What They Sow

BEFORE YOU BEGIN...

"We reap what we sow" is a life principle established by God, but many have never seen how it relates to their everyday lives. Last week we saw this truth positively illustrated in the lives of Abraham and Isaac. They "sowed" trust in God and obedience to His commands and "reaped" God's blessing. This week, teach by contrast the negative aspect of the principle as illustrated by Jacob and Esau. Each chose to do things his own way and later reaped heartache and sorrow.

What an important concept for our children to understand! They need it when relating to other people or when relating to God. Through the example of Jacob and Esau help your boys and girls see clearly the relationship between what they "sow," whether good or bad, and what they "reap" as a result. Use the true-to-life illustrations to help them transition the truth from the Bible story to their own situations. Encourage them to make right choices and "sow" good, God-honoring actions and thoughts in their lives. "And let us not grow weary while doing good, for in due season we shall reap if we do not lose heart" (Galatians 6:9, NKJV).

AIM:

That the children may

- Know that when they sow bad seeds in their lives, they will reap the bad results sooner or later.
- Respond by identifying the bad seeds they have already sown, confessing them and choosing not to sow them any longer.

SCRIPTURE: Genesis 25-27

MEMORY VERSE: Galatians 6:7

Be not deceived: God is not mocked; for whatsoever a man soweth, that shall he also reap.

MATERIALS TO GATHER

Visual for Galatians 6:7
Backgrounds: Review Chart, Plain
Figures: R1-R11, 30, 32, 44, 45, 97, 98, 99, 100, 101
Special:

- ***For Review:*** Seeds and fruits/vegetables or pictures used last week.
- ***For Conclusion:*** Three 7-inch-wide hearts cut from red or white felt or flannel; new word strips JACOB, ESAU, KIND ACTIONS, GOOD THOUGHTS; newsprint & marker or chalkboard & chalk; "Heart and Seed" handouts; pencils; glue sticks.
- ***For Options:*** Additional materials for any options you choose to use.
- ***Note:*** To make "Heart and Seed" handouts, use copy machine to duplicate pattern R-8 found on page 160.

Review Token:

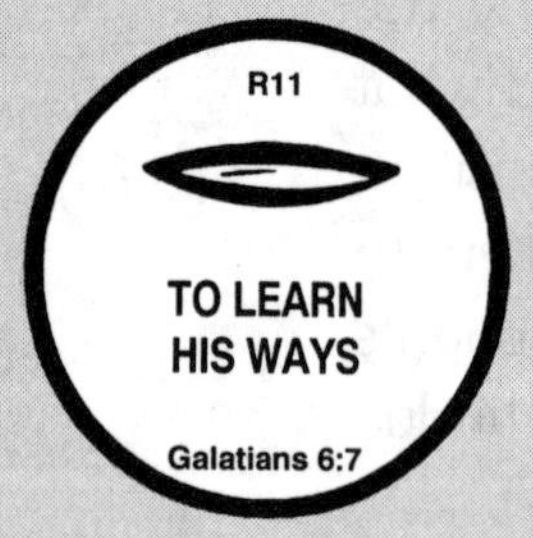

REVIEW CHART

Display the Review Chart with symbols R1-R5 in place. Have the children place R6-R11 on the Chart as you briefly review the verses from Lessons 6-11. Use the following questions to review last week's lesson.

1. What was the name of the wife God gave to Isaac. *(Rebekah)*
2. What special thing did Isaac ask God for after he had been married a long time? *(For Rebekah to have a baby)*
3. How did God answer Isaac's prayer? *(He gave Rebekah twin boys.)*
4. What "way" of God did Abraham and Isaac learn as they walked with Him over many years? *(He rewards those who trust Him and obey Him. We reap what we sow.)*

♥ MEMORY VERSE

Review Galatians 6:7, using the visual from Bible Verses Visualized. *Use the seeds and fruits or vegetables (or pictures) from last week's lesson as you discuss how this verse applies to what happened in that Bible story.* ▲#1

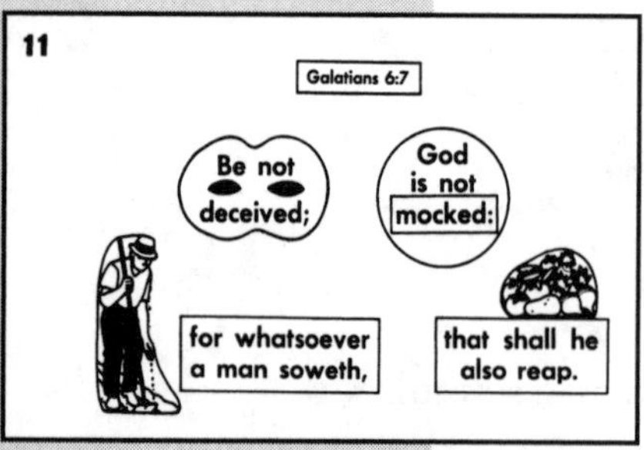

BIBLE LESSON OUTLINE

Jacob and Esau Reap What They Sow

Introduction

Jason and the hockey team.

Bible Content

1. Esau and Jacob grow up.
2. Esau sells his birthright.
3. Jacob deceives Isaac.

Conclusion

Summary

Application

Choosing what to "sow" in life.

Response Activity

Asking God to help us "sow" a specific action or attitude.

BIBLE LESSON

Introduction

As you listen to this story about Jason, look for what he was sowing in his life and how it grew, or became a problem for him. ▲#2

Jason and the hockey team.

Jason loved to play hockey! He was one of the best players on the team and was in line for the position of goalie. So was Kevin, one of his best friends. When the coach made his choice, it was Kevin. Jason couldn't believe it! He felt so hurt! Then he was jealous. He allowed these feelings to grow until every time he looked at Kevin he became more upset and angry. Finally he didn't want to play with him or even be around him.

Others on the team could see how Jason felt. Before long people were staying away from him. It was no fun playing with someone who was always angry. Jason's parents tried to talk with him, but he didn't want to listen. Because he claimed to be a Christian they reminded him that God promises to help us if we will trust Him and obey Him. But Jason still wouldn't listen. His attitude got worse and worse, until during practice one day he tripped on another player's stick and his anger boiled over! He swung his own stick and hit the player in the legs! Immediately the coach removed Jason from the game. Still, he wouldn't calm down. Instead, he began to talk and act disrespectfully toward the coach and other team members. Eventually he was thrown off the team.

▲ Option#1:

Reviewing the verse: Print verse and reference on several different-colored sheets of construction paper. Cut each sheet into puzzle pieces and hide them around the room ahead of time.

Divide the class into groups; give each group the color of one of the hidden puzzles. At a signal, have them look for their pieces (being careful not to touch other colors), put them together into a completed puzzle and then compete to see which group can say the verse correctly.

▲ Option#2:

Help several children prepare ahead of time to pantomime Jason's story as you read it from the text.

What was Jason sowing in his life? What result did he reap? How did it grow and become a problem for him? *(Discuss with the children.)* What could he have done to prevent it from happening?

This week we're going to learn about the twins, Esau and Jacob. Let's listen carefully to identify some of the seeds they sowed in their lives and what thy reaped as a result.

■ Bible Content

1. Esau and Jacob grow up. (Genesis 25:19- 28). ▲#3

▲ Option#3:

Draw a line down the center of chalkboard or newsprint. Write Jacob on one side; Esau, on the other. Draw stick figures to represent them. Add descriptive phrases under each as the Scripture passage is read or as you tell the story.

Before Esau and Jacob were born, God told Rebekah that she would have twin boys and that nations would come from both of them. He said that one nation would be stronger than the other, and that the nation from the older twin would serve the nation from the younger one.

The boys had the same parents and grew up in the same home, but they were very different. Esau loved to be outdoors and became a skilled hunter. Jacob was quieter and enjoyed working around home. He eventually became a shepherd.

Isaac especially loved Esau because he brought home such good meat when he went hunting. Jacob was Rebekah's favorite. It's very sad when parents love or pay more attention to one child than another, and it always causes problems, just as it did in this family.

Esau and Jacob were different in another way, too. They must have heard their grandfather Abraham (who lived until they were 15 years old) tell many times how God called him to leave Ur about 100 years before, about the promises God had made to him and how those promises would be passed on to them through their father Isaac. They had seen their grandfather and their father worship the Lord God by offering animal sacrifices. But only one of them believed.

The Bible tells us that Jacob believed God's promises and wanted them for his own. But Esau was not interested in the wonderful things his grandfather told him about God. He never believed what God said or obeyed His commands.

2. Esau sells his birthright. (Genesis 5:27-34; 26:34, 35)

One day when Esau came back from hunting he was very hungry. Jacob was cooking a stew and its delicious aroma made Esau hungrier than ever. He said to Jacob, "Quick, give me some of that stew. I'm so hungry I'm afraid I'll faint!"

Jacob said to Esau, "I'll give you some stew if you will sell me your birthright."

Both Jacob and Esau knew what the birthright was. It belonged to the oldest son in the family. It meant that he would receive twice as much of the inheritance when their father died and that he would then be the head of the family with the right to offer sacrifices. It also meant he would receive the wonderful promises God had given Abraham and Isaac regarding the nation, the land, and the blessing. Esau said to Jacob, "I'm so hungry I'll die if I don't get some food, and what good will the birthright be to me then? Take the birthright; just give me the stew." So Jacob gave Esau the food he wanted in exchange for the birthright.

The Bible says that Esau despised his birthright. That means he thought it wasn't very important or worth much. Esau's heart was not right toward God. He did not value the birthright; he was just thinking about his stomach.

But was it right for Jacob to cheat his brother? Why didn't he just give Esau the stew? Before the boys were born God had told their mother Rebekah that Jacob would be the head of the family someday. In His time God would have given the birthright to Jacob if he had waited. Jacob was wrong to trick his brother, and he suffered for it later. But he did believe in God and valued the birthright. When Esau was 40 years old, he went to the people living nearby who did not believe in God and married two of their women. When he brought them home, his parents were very sad. They knew God was not pleased, for He wanted His people to be separate from the godless nations around them. He did not want them to marry women from these nations.

3. Jacob deceives Isaac. (Genesis 27:1-41)

Sketch 51 **Plain Background**

(Isaac 97, Jacob 98, Esau 99.)

One day when Isaac was an old man and nearly blind, he called for Esau and said, "I may not live much longer and I want you to do something for me. Take your bow and arrows and go hunting. Cook the fresh meat the way I like it and bring it to me. Then I will give you my blessing before I die." Esau left at once to obey his father.

Remember that Esau was Isaac's favorite, even though he had despised the birthright and married heathen women. Who was Rebekah's favorite? *(Jacob)* Rebekah overheard what Isaac said. She called Jacob and told him what was happening. "Go to the flock and get two of our best young goats so I can prepare some food the way your father likes it. Then you can take it to him to eat so that he can give you the blessing he plans to give Esau."

Jacob said, "But if my father feels my hands and face, he will know that I am not Esau, because my skin is smooth and Esau's is hairy. Then I will be in serious trouble."

His mother said, "I'll take the blame; just do what I tell you." So Jacob went to get the goats.

Rebekah cooked the meat just the way Isaac liked it. Then she told Jacob to put on Esau's clothing. When he was dressed, she used some of the goats' skins to cover Jacob's hands and neck so that they would feel hairy like Esau's.

Jacob took the cooked meat into the room where his father was resting. Isaac heard him coming. Because he could not see he asked, "Who is it?"

Jacob answered, "It is Esau. I have done what you told me to do. Please sit up and eat some of my meat so that you may bless me."

Isaac asked, "How did you find it so quickly, my son?"

Jacob answered, "Because the Lord helped me"– a terrible lie!

Isaac said, "Come close to me so I can touch you and really know if you are Esau." After he had touched Jacob, Isaac said, "It sounds like Jacob, but it feels like Esau. Are you *really* Esau?"

Again Jacob lied: "Yes, I am."

So Isaac ate the food that Jacob served him and afterward he gave Jacob his blessing, thinking he was giving it to Esau. He told Jacob that he would be the head of the family and rule over his brother. This blessing was not meant just for him, but for his sons and grandsons and all his descendants. It was part of the birthright.

Esau came in from hunting just as Jacob left his father. He prepared the meat he had caught and brought it to Isaac saying, "Father, please sit up and eat some of my meat and then give me your blessing."

Isaac was very surprised and asked, "Who are you?"

Esau answered, "I am Esau, your firstborn son."

Isaac began to tremble as he said, "But I already ate before you came. Your brother deceived me; I have given him my blessing and I cannot take it back." Esau cried bitterly and began to hate his brother Jacob after that.

Both Rebekah and Jacob had done wrong and they would suffer for it. If they had been willing to trust God and wait for Him to keep His promise, He would have given the birthright to Jacob without lies, deceit and hurt. Jacob believed in God and he valued God's promises, but he had a lot to learn about walking in God's ways. He sowed lies, deceit and hurt instead of trust in God.

Later we will learn how God made Jacob a man of faith, even though he had been deceitful. But Esau never became a man of faith. In the New Testament he is called a godless person who did not value his birthright or the promises of God (Hebrews 12:16, 17).

Conclusion

Summary

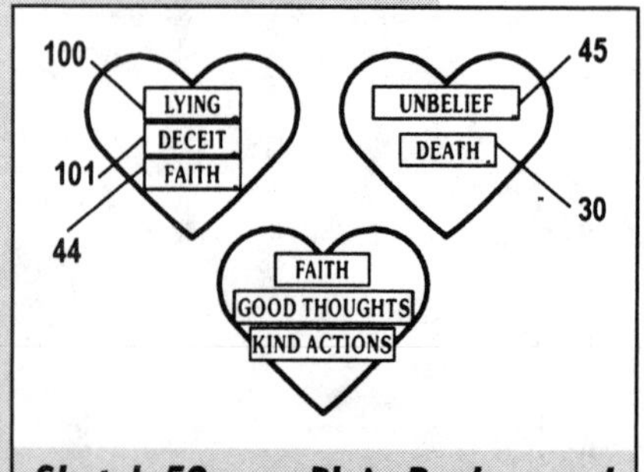

100
LYING
DECEIT
FAITH
101
44
UNBELIEF
DEATH
45
30
FAITH
GOOD THOUGHTS
KIND ACTIONS

Sketch 52 **Plain Background**

(Three 7-inch red or white felt or flannel hearts; word strips FAITH 44, LYING 100, DECEIT 101, UNBELIEF 45, DEATH 30, OBEDIENCE 32; new word strips KIND ACTIONS, GOOD THOUGHTS.)

What does our memory verse tell us about God? *(Display verse and say it aloud together. Encourage response.)* He is not fooled by anything we say or do. He sees what is in our hearts and knows all about us.

We will let one of these hearts stand for Esau; the other, for Jacob. *(Place two hearts on flannelboard; add word strips JACOB, ESAU.)* When we talk about our heart, we do not mean the organ that pumps blood, but the part of us that thinks and feels and makes choices. Let's discover what God saw "growing" in their hearts because of the choices they had "planted." ▲#4

When God looked at Esau's heart, what did He see? Did He see faith? Did Esau think about God, or believe in Him or want to follow Him? *(No, he didn't.)* Esau sowed UNBELIEF in his heart and it continued to grow there. *(Have children put this and other word strips on board.)* He had no desire to learn about God and His ways. Unbelief filled his life. When such a person refuses to come to God, his end is death, which is separation from God forever. *(Add DEATH to heart.)*

What did God see in Jacob's heart? Had he "sowed" anything there that did not please God? What was it? *(Tricked Esau into selling his birthright for stew; lied to his father and deceived him to get the blessing)* We must put LYING and DECEIT on Jacob's heart. *(Put word strips on the Jacob heart.)* Jacob wanted God's promises and was willing to do whatever he had to do to get them. But lying and deceiving people are sins. God was not pleased, and Jacob "reaped" the consequences of unhappiness and trouble for himself and others. We'll learn more about this next week.

Did God see anything in Jacob's heart that did please Him? What was it? Yes, God saw that Jacob believed in Him and valued His promises. He had faith in God. *(Place FAITH on heart.)* Because of this, God could see Jacob as he would be someday, a man of faith, learning God's ways and obeying them.

Jacob would suffer for his sin of deceit, but because he continued to believe in God and grow closer to Him, He became one of those people who passed faith in God "down the line," preparing for the time when God's Son, the Lord Jesus, would come.

▲ Option#4:

Make two large posterboard hearts. Print JACOB on one; ESAU, on the other. Have two children hold them in front of the class. Put tape or plasti-tak on the back of the word strips so children can put them in place.

Or cut out three "seeds"; print UNBELIEF, LYING, DECEIT on them. Make two plants; print DEATH on one; UNHAPPINESS and TROUBLE, on the other. Have children place them—and word strip FAITH—on hearts as they're mentioned.

Application

This third heart stands for your life and mine. *(Place third heart on board.)* We cannot fool God either. He knows what is in our hearts. ▲#5

What does God see when He looks in your heart today? Does He see faith in His Son because you've trusted Jesus as your Savior? *(Add FAITH strip to third heart.)* Does He see that you are "sowing" good attitudes and actions that please Him? Or things that displease Him and hurt others?

Sometimes, even when we belong to the Lord Jesus, we think wrong and disobedient thoughts and we do wrong things. But if we love God and want to obey Him, God sees our faith as he saw Jacob's

▲ Option#5:

Prepare a third posterboard heart, similar to the Jacob and Esau ones. Use here in the same way.

▲ Option#6:

Use the following Bible verses to help the children discover some of God's ways for us: Exodus 20:7; Deuteronomy 6:5; Psalm 31:1; Proverbs 15:1; Ephesians 4:15; 4:32; 6:1; Colossians 3:20.

Discuss the possible good results of these actions. Remind them that they may not see the results right away. Encourage them to be patient and trust God to bring results.

Have each one think of one good thing they need to "sow" in their lives right now and spend a few minutes asking God to help them do this during the coming week. Next week invite the children to share what happened.

and He is willing to forgive us when we confess our sins to Him.

Let's think about some of the wrong kinds of "seeds" boys and girls are sowing in their lives today. What can you think of? *(Encourage children's responses. If they do not mention them, bring up current problems facing children in society; e.g., taking drugs, drinking alcohol, smoking cigarettes, sexual impurity—immorality, preoccupation with sex or sexual perversion—watching TV trash, violent behavior, abuse, spiritism.)* Have you sown any of these "seeds" in your life? If you have, you will reap bad and hurtful results sooner or later. "Whatsoever a man soweth, that shall he also reap" is one of God's ways.

But you can choose to confess these sins to God now and ask Him to forgive you and change your life. Will you do that? *(Allow time for questions and silent prayer. Invite the children to come talk to you or a helper later if they need help.)*

And you can begin choosing to "sow" good things in your life that please God. Then you will "reap" good results and God's blessing. What are some things we should be "growing" in our hearts and lives? *(Allow children to place GOOD THOUGHTS and KIND ACTIONS on the heart. Write their responses on blank strips you have brought so they can put those on the heart as well.)* God will see these things in our hearts and others will see them in our lives by what we do.

Will you choose to learn God's ways from the Bible and then sow "seeds" of obedience in your life by doing what you learn? This is the way to please God.

Response Activity

Invite those who have not received Christ as Savior to do so now, "planting" that first seed of faith in their life.

With the children's help, make a list on newsprint or chalkboard of "God's ways" for them—things they should be putting into their lives. Use specific examples drawn from class or from the following list: thinking kind thoughts, telling the truth, forgiving others, having right attitudes, being obedient to parents and teachers, being honest. ▲#6

Give each child a **"Heart and Seed" hand-out** *(see Materials to Gather) and a pencil. Have them write their names on the hearts, choose one thing (from the list you've made or from their own thoughts) they want to "sow" in their lives this week and write it on their seeds, then use glue sticks to paste the seeds to the hearts.*

Jacob Learns God's Ways

Theme: God Calls Us — To Make Us Like Jesus

Lesson

12

Part One: Jacob Begins to Know God

BEFORE YOU BEGIN...

Every child knows what it means to fail. Some have failed often enough that they've given up trying at all. And many have had someone give up on them when they failed. They are left, then, with no confidence and—more seriously—no hope. How wonderful for them to discover a loving God who forgives and NEVER gives up on them no matter how they fail!

Jacob failed God terribly by outright disobedience. Yet God forgave him and continued to work in his life, carrying out His great plan for Jacob and his descendants. Seeing how God worked in Jacob's life will encourage your children to believe that God will never give up on them, but will continue to carry out His plan to make them like Jesus. "For whom He foreknew, He also predestined to be conformed to the image of His Son" (Romans 8:29, NKJV).

AIM:

That the children may

- Know that God does not give up on His children, even when they fail Him.
- Respond by accepting God's loving forgiveness when they confess sin and by trusting God to make them more like Jesus as they obey Him.

SCRIPTURE: Genesis 28-30.

MEMORY VERSE: Philippians 1:6

He which hath begun a good work in you will perform it until the day of Jesus Christ.

MATERIALS TO GATHER

Visual for Philippians 1:6
Backgrounds: Review Chart, Plain, Old Testament Map, Plain with Tree
Figures: R6-R12, 74, 75, 79, 94, 97, 102, 103, 104, 105, 106, 107
Special:
- ***For Bible Content 2:*** New word strips BETHEL, HOUSE OF GOD.
- ***For Conclusion:*** "Statement of Purpose" response forms and pencils.
- ***For Options:*** Additional materials for any options you choose to use.
- ***Note:*** To make "Statement of Purpose" response forms, use a copy machine to duplicate pattern R-7 found on page 159.

Display the Review Chart with symbols R1-R5 in place and symbols R6-R11 mixed up on one side of the board. Have the children work in pairs, one child choosing a symbol, the other saying the corresponding verse, and the first then placing the symbol in its position on the Review Chart.

Use the quiz below to review the highlights from Lessons 6-11. Encourage the children to make up their own descriptions for the questions. Have R12 ready to use where indicated.

"I'm Thinking of ... "

1. ... someone who is God's enemy. *(Satan)*
2. ... the book of the Bible called the book of beginnings. *(Genesis)*
3. ... the verse that tells us where faith comes from. *(Romans 10:17)*
4. ... the wife of Abraham. *(Sarah)*
5. ... the woman who helped her son deceive his father. *(Rebekah)*
6. ... the animal God provided to take Isaac's place. *(Ram)*
7. ... the thing Esau gave to his brother for a bowl of stew. *(Birthright)*
8. ... the man whose wife turned into a pillar of salt. *(Lot)*

We have been learning answers to the question Why does God call us? Our next answer to this question is God calls us to make us like Jesus *(place R12 on chart)*. Today we will see how God worked to make Jacob into a godly man, and how we, too, can become more like God's Son, the Lord Jesus.

♥ MEMORY VERSE

Use the verse visual from Bible Verses Visualized *to teach the memory verse as part of the Lesson Introduction.*

BIBLE LESSON OUTLINE

Jacob Begins to Know God

Introduction

Greg's experience in art class

(Memory Verse Presentation)

Bible Content

1. Jacob leaves home.
2. God talks with Jacob.
3. Jacob meets his mother's family.
4. Jacob marries Leah and Rachel.
5. Laban treats Jacob unfairly.

Conclusion

Summary

Application

Learning to cooperate with God.

Response Activity

Completing a statement of purpose to do a particular thing that pleases God.

BIBLE LESSON

Introduction

Greg's experience in art class.

(Verse visual for Philippians 1:6.)

Greg was working hard on his picture in art class, sketching, erasing and trying again. He seemed frustrated, but he kept working. When his teacher asked what he was drawing, Greg said it was a space station. She said, "That's nice," but wondered if it ever would look like one. But the finished picture was beautiful–in full color and complete with identifying markings. Greg was proud of his picture, and his teacher was proud of Greg, especially because he didn't give up, but completed what he had begun.

The new symbol on our review chart tells us that *God calls us to make us like Jesus.* Greg's story can help us understand how God works with us. Greg knew what he wanted to make and didn't stop till he was finished. Just so, God has a plan for us; He wants to make us like His Son Jesus. *(Add R-12 to Review Chart.)*

We don't look like Jesus and can't perform miracles. God wants us to be more like Jesus on the inside. For example, to always tell the truth as Jesus did, to be kind to others, to trust God and do what He wants, as Jesus did here on earth. It takes time to learn this and we can be thankful that God does not give up on us as our memory verse tells us this. *(Display verse visual and read verse together; encourage children to answer your questions.)*

12

Philippians 1:6

He which hath begun

a good work in you

will perform it

until the day of Jesus Christ.

What does the verse tell us God is doing in us? *(A good work)* What does it promise God will do? *(Perform it until the day of Jesus Christ; He will keep on doing it; He will complete it.)* God began that "good work" the same day we accepted Jesus Christ as our Savior.

We can never be completely like the Lord Jesus here on earth, for He is sinless and we are sinful. But when we were born into the family of God, He put His own life in us to help us live as we should, to please Him. His life in us makes us want to turn away from all that is sinful and do what is right.

The word *perform* means to do it or finish it. When the Lord Jesus comes back someday and takes us to heaven, God's work in us will be finished. Then we will really be like Jesus. Greg continued to work until he had finished his picture. In the same way God continues to work in us to help us become more like Jesus. Listen to our lesson to see how God began to do this for Jacob and how He can do it for us. *(Work on learning the verse and reviewing its meaning.)* ▲#1

▲ Option#1:

Learning the verse: Choose five children to hold the verse visual pieces in front of the class as everyone reads it aloud. Have one child take his visual and sit down. Ask for a volunteer to say the verse. Continue until all the children with visuals have sat down. Then have them go to the front again, but with the visuals scrambled. Allow class members to put them in correct order, saying the verse together each time. Finally, remove all the visuals and say the verse once more.

■ Bible Content

1. Jacob leaves home. (Genesis 28:1-10)

(Isaac 97, Jacob 103, Rebekah 94.)

God was working in Jacob even though Jacob had deceived his father and stolen his brother's blessing. God knew that one day would Jacob would learn to trust Him and obey, so He patiently worked with him. *(Place figures on foreground of map as you tell the story and show Jacob's route.)*

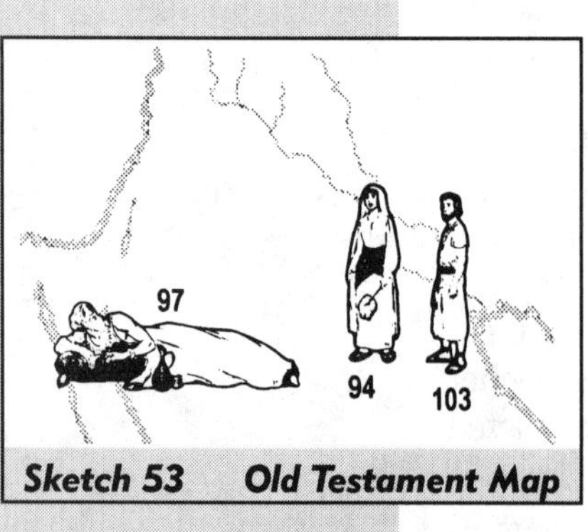

Sketch 53 Old Testament Map

After Jacob deceived his father, Esau threatened to kill him. Their mother was afraid, so she told him to go to his uncle's home in Haran saying, "I will send for you when Esau gets over his anger."

Then she said to Isaac, "We don't want Jacob to marry one of the women around here like Esau did." So Isaac sent for Jacob and said, "Don't marry a girl from the people around us who don't believe in God. Instead, marry a girl from your Uncle Laban's family." Then Isaac asked God to bless Jacob and watch over him, and he reminded Jacob of God's promises that were to come true through him.

Jacob left his father and mother, expecting to see them again very soon. He did not know that he was saying good-bye to his mother for the last time. He never saw her again because he was gone for a long time and she died before he returned.

2. God talks with Jacob. (Genesis 28:11-22)

(Jacob & ladder 102, Jacob 103; new word strips BETHEL, HOUSE OF GOD.)

Jacob started off alone, probably walking more than 400 miles to Haran. There were many dangers—wild beasts, robbers, very little food or water. He had a lot of time to think as he traveled under the hot sun and slept under the stars at night. I wonder if he thought that God had deserted him because of his sin.

One night, as he slept on the ground using a stone for a pillow, Jacob dreamed a wonderful dream. He saw a ladder that reached all the way from earth to heaven. Angels were coming down from heaven and going up from earth. The Lord stood at the top of the ladder.

God spoke to Jacob: "I am the LORD, the God of Abraham and of Isaac, your grandfather and your father." He repeated the promises that He had given to Abraham and Isaac: "I will give you and your descendants the land you are lying on; your descendants will be as the dust of the earth, spreading out in all directions. ▲#2 Through you and your descendants blessing will come to all the nations on the earth." These promises were not just for Jacob, but for the whole nation of Israel of which Jacob was now to be the head.

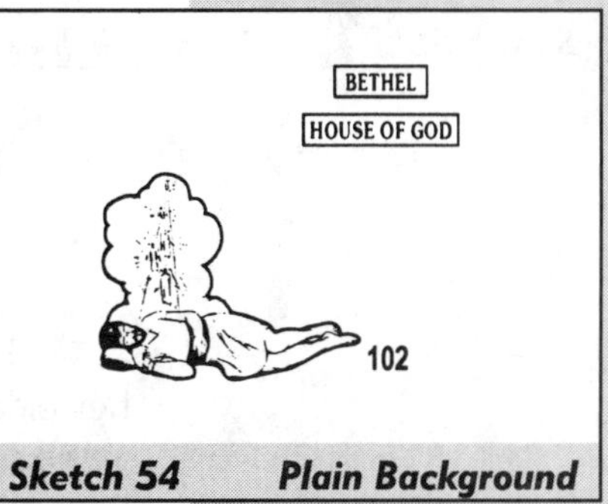

Sketch 54 **Plain Background**

Then God told Jacob some promises that were especially for him. Find Genesis 28:15 so we can look at them. *(Have the children read the verse and then give the promises.)* ▲#3 1) that He was with Jacob and would watch over him wherever he went; 2) that He would bring Jacob back to his own land; 3) that He would never leave Jacob until He had done all He promised.

Suddenly the ladder and the angels disappeared. When Jacob woke up he remembered the dream and knew that God had spoken to him. He said, "Surely God is in this place and I did not realize it."

Very early the next morning Jacob got up *(replace 102 with 103)*, took the stone he had used for a pillow and set it up as a marker to show the place where he had met God. He poured some oil over the top of the stone and named this special place Bethel, which means *house of God. (Place word strips on board.)* There Jacob solemnly promised God that if God would take care of him and bring him back home safely, he would worship God and give Him one tenth of everything he had.

As Jacob continued on his way towards Haran he must have thought many times of his dream and all that God had said to him. He knew now that God was taking care of him and had a plan for his life.

▲ Option#2:

Bring a jar of sand to class. Ask who would like to count the grains. Use this to help the children understand the number of Jacob's descendants.

▲ Option#3:

Before class, print Genesis 28:15 on newsprint so the group can read it together before discussing the promises.

Print the promises on newsprint or word strips to use as they are listed:
- God was with Jacob.
- God would bring him back.
- God would never leave him.

If you have time, allow an older child to print the promises on chalkboard or newsprint as you talk about them.

3. Jacob meets his mother's family. (Genesis 29:1-14)

(Jacob 103, well 104, Rachel 105, flock 74, Laban 106.)

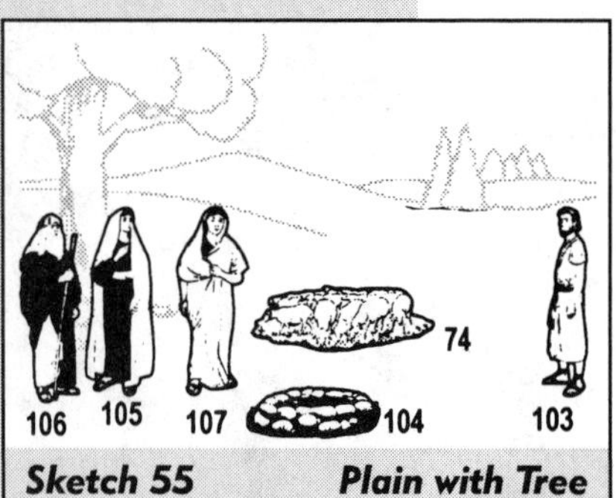

Sketch 55 **Plain with Tree**

After much traveling, Jacob came to a field where there was a well covered by a large stone. Three flocks of sheep were nearby, for shepherds would bring their animals here to be watered. Jacob talked with the men and learned that his uncle Laban lived nearby. "Look," they said, "here comes his daughter Rachel bringing her sheep to be watered."

Jacob went quickly to help Rachel. He rolled the heavy stone away from the well and watered her flock of sheep. Then he told her that he was her cousin and had come to visit her family. Rachel ran to get her father. They welcomed Jacob warmly and took him to their home.

4. Jacob marries Leah and Rachel. (Genesis 29:14-30:24)

(Remove well and flock; add tent 79; Leah 107.)

Laban had a large family of sons and two daughters, Rachel and her older sister, Leah. Jacob lived in his uncle's home as a guest. He was a good worker, and every day he helped care for the flocks. After a month had passed, Laban said to Jacob, "You shouldn't work for me for nothing just because you're my nephew. What shall I pay you?"

By this time Jacob was in love with Rachel, so he answered, "What I really want is to marry Rachel. I will work seven years for you if you will give her to me to be my wife." Laban thought that was a good idea so he agreed. The seven years didn't seem long at all to Jacob because he loved Rachel so much.

When the seven years were up, Laban invited many people to the wedding feast. Jacob thought he was marrying Rachel, but Laban tricked him by giving him Leah instead. Jacob was very upset! He went to his uncle Laban and said, "Why have you deceived me like this? I served you seven years for Rachel, not Leah!"

Laban just said, "It is not our custom for a younger sister to marry before an older one. If you will work for me another seven years, I'll give you Rachel, too." Jacob didn't have any choice. He agreed to his uncle's terms. After the week-long wedding celebration was over, he married Rachel also. He loved her more than Leah. Then he worked another seven years for Laban.

Remember how Jacob had deceived or tricked his own father? Now he had been deceived by his uncle. What does our memory verse say? Let's say it: "Whatsoever a man soweth, that shall he also reap."

In those days men sometimes had more than one wife, even though God never meant it to be that way. Sometimes people think that they know better than God, but doing what they want instead of what God says always leads to trouble. It did this time, too.

Jacob and Leah had four sons. Later Jacob married two more women, Leah's maid and Rachel's maid. They also had children. But Rachel had no children and became very sad. She prayed for a son. Eventually God answered her prayers by giving her a son whom she named Joseph. Jacob had a large family of eleven boys and one girl.

5. Laban treats Jacob unfairly. (Genesis 30:25-43)

(Remove tent 79, Rachel 105, Leah 107; add flocks and herds 74, 75.)

Jacob worked 14 years for his uncle Laban in exchange for his two daughters. After that he worked six more years and Laban paid him wages in animals—sheep, goats, cattle and perhaps camels—instead of money. Even then God watched over Jacob. If Laban said Jacob could have the speckled and spotted cattle for his pay, it seemed that all the baby calves were born speckled and spotted. So Laban's flocks and herds got smaller and Jacob's got larger.

Laban knew God had blessed him because of Jacob, for Laban had more flocks and herds than he ever had before. But Laban became jealous of Jacob and treated him unkindly. He changed his wages ten times in six years (Genesis 31:41). He made Jacob pay for any sheep or goats carried off by wild animals. Still, God watched over Jacob and continued to bless him. God did not give up on Jacob!

■ Conclusion

Summary

(Jacob 98, Jacob 103, promises 67-70; "Statement of Purpose" response forms and pencils.)

It looked as though Jacob got away with deceiving his father and stealing the family blessing *(place 98 on board)*, but what consequence did he suffer because of his wrong actions? *(He had to leave his family and home because Esau threatened him; remove 98.)*

How do we know that God did not give up on Jacob after this? *(Encourage response; add 103.)* That's right, God spoke to him in a dream and gave Him some promises. What were they? *(Add 67-70 as children respond.)* He promised to give the land where Jacob was lying to him and his descendants, to make them into a great nation and to bless all the nations through them.

What other promises did God make to Jacob to encourage him? *(He would be with him, watch over him and never leave him. If you printed these promises, show them as the children answer.)* How did God keep these promises and help Jacob? *(He kept Jacob safe on his journey, helped him find his uncle and the girl he would marry, gave him many sons, increased his flocks and herds.)*

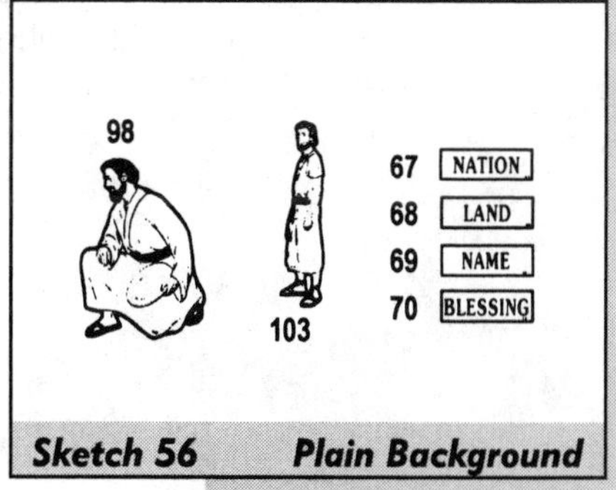

Sketch 56 **Plain Background**

God was taking care of Jacob, but stil he had some difficult times working for his uncle. But through all that happened Jacob learned to know God better and trust Him more. God helped Jacob and did not give up on him, for He had a special plan for Jacob's life.

Application

If you were Jacob, how would you have felt when your uncle deceived you? Would you have remembered how you deceived your family? Does Jacob's story make you think of times when you did things you know don't please God? Have you wondered what God thinks about you when you do these things?

God promises all who have trusted Jesus as their Savior that He will forgive us when we confess our sin to Him (1 John 1:9), and not give up on us. Let's say our verse again.

God wants us to become like the Lord Jesus and He will continue to work in our lives to make that happen. We must cooperate with Him by obeying what He says in His Word. God had a special plan for Jacob. He has a special plan for each one of us, too.

Response Activity

Pray, thanking God for loving us, His children, and for not giving up on us when we sin. Ask God to help us all to do what pleases Him this week.

Give each child a pencil and a ***"Statement of Purpose" response form*** *(see Materials to Gather). Challenge them to complete the sentence, "I trust You, God, to make me more like the Lord Jesus this week by helping me to________________________________" with some positive action (e.g., be kind to sister or brother, do dishes without being asked, come right away when mother calls, do homework before watching TV, etc.) rather than a sin they don't want to do. Have them take the paper home to remind them to pray for God's help each day.*

HELPS FOR YOUNGER CHILDREN

Introduction: Have Greg draw or build something suitable and interesting to their age group. Emphasize the importance and pleasure of finishing what we begin.

Memory Verse: Shorten the verse to "He which began a good work in you will perform it." Teach the remainder next week.

Jacob Learns God's Ways

Theme: God Calls Us — To Make Us Like Jesus

Lesson

12

Part Two: Jacob Becomes Israel

BEFORE YOU BEGIN...

Children easily identify with popular role models, from rock stars to sports figures to friends. They soon begin to dress and gesture like the ones they admire—even mimic their speech and behavior. They "transform" themselves by copying someone else. You can use this common experience as an illustration of what it means for believers to become "like Jesus Christ." Point them to Jesus as the greatest role model of all and teach them how they can become more like Him today, right where they live.

This lesson gives you practical guidelines for helping your children understand what it means to walk in the footsteps of faith and obedience. Help them see how they can please God in their daily circumstances and thus begin to become like Jesus. Teach them to think, when they are puzzled about what they should do, What would Jesus do in this situation? "And whatever you do, do it heartily, as to the Lord and not to men" (Colossians 3:23, NKJV).

☞ AIM:

That the children may

- Know that God wants to make His children like Jesus.
- Respond by choosing to trust and obey God each day so He can make them like Jesus.

SCRIPTURE: Genesis 31:1–33:16.

MEMORY VERSE: Philippians 1:6

He which hath begun a good work in you will perform it until the day of Jesus Christ.

MATERIALS TO GATHER

Visual for Philippians 1:6
Backgrounds: Review Chart, Plain, General Outdoor, River
Figures: R1-R12, 13, 45, 53, 54, 66, 74, 75, 77, 78, 83, 91, 92, 93, 99, 103, 104, 105, 106, 107
Special:

- ***For Bible Content 2:*** New word strips JACOB, ISRAEL.
- ***For Conclusion:*** A set of footprints for each child.
- ***For Options:*** Additional materials for any options you choose to use.
- ***Note:*** To make footprints, on posterboard trace around a small pair of shoes. Make a set for each child and cut out. Print BELIEVE on one of each pair and OBEY on the other. Or, see Option #2 on page 117.

REVIEW CHART

• *Display the Review Chart, having symbols R1-R5 in place. Briefly review symbols R6-R11, repeating the memory verses as you go. Put R12 in place as the class repeats the memory verse aloud together. Use the following questions to briefly review last week's lesson.*

1. Why did Jacob have to leave home? *(Because Esau had threatened to kill him.)*
2. What were some of the things Jacob "reaped" as the result of his wrong actions? *(Having to leave home alone; never seeing his mother again; being deceived by Laban.)*
3. What did Jacob see in his dream? *(A ladder reaching from earth to heaven; angels descending and ascending on it; the Lord standing at the top.)*
4. What promise did God give to Jacob and his descendants? *(I will give you this land; I will make you a great nation; through you all nations will be blessed.)*
5. How did God show He had not given up on Jacob because of the bad things he had done? *(He kept Jacob safe; He helped Jacob find his uncle and his future wife; He increased Jacob's flocks and his family.)*

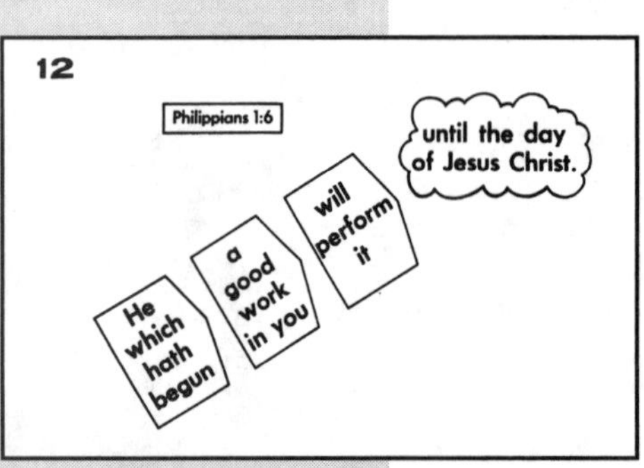

MEMORY VERSE

Use the verse visual to review and drill Philippians 1:6. Take time to review what the "good work" is and God's promise to never give up on us. ▲#1

BIBLE LESSON OUTLINE

Jacob Becomes Israel

Introduction

How can I be like Jesus?

Bible Content

1. Jacob starts his journey home.
2. Jacob becomes Israel, a prince.
3. Jacob is reunited with Esau.

Conclusion

Summary

Application

What "shoes" are you wearing?

Response Activity

Putting on the "believe" shoe by trusting Christ as Savior.
Putting on the "obey" shoe by writing what they need to do to obey God and praying for His help.

BIBLE LESSON

Introduction

How can I be like Jesus? ▲#2

Have you ever said or thought "I want to be like_____when I grow up"? What did you mean by that? *(If necessary, suggest "as pretty as" or "as tall as" or "able to do something like....")* ▲#3

Who is most like another person? One who looks like him (or her), or one who acts like him? *(Response)* Acting—or living—like the one we admire is really most important, isn't it? So, in order to be like that other person, what would you have to do? *(Response)* Yes, you would have to spend time with him (or her) to get to know him. Then you would need to work on those areas that you want to be like, such as playing an instrument, hitting a ball, or being kind.

We are learning that God wants to make each of His children like Jesus. Does that mean we should look like Jesus, or that we should act like Him? That's right, God wants us to act like Jesus. Choosing to trust God and obey Him each day helps us learn to act like Jesus. That's a pretty big assignment, isn't it? But remember, God has promised to help us and not give up on us.

In our Bible story let's look for the things God used in Jacob's life to make him a man of faith and obedience. Perhaps they will help us understand some ways God works in our lives to make us like Jesus.

▲ Option#1:

Reviewing the verse: Print words and reference on separate pieces of paper or cardboard. Distribute pieces in random order to the class.

At a given signal, have children with verse pieces arrange themselves in order, then say the verse as a group.

Repeat with a different group of children or have the same group repeat after redistributing the verse pieces.

▲ Option#2:

Provide pencils, markers, scissors and posterboard. As the children arrive, have them trace around their shoes on the posterboard, cut out the footprints, print BELIEVE on one and OBEY on the other, then write their names on the back of both. Collect and keep these until Response Activity time.

▲ Option#3:

Write "I want to be just like ________ when I grow up" on newsprint or chalkboard. Ask children "fill in the blank". Write their ideas under the statement as they give them.

■ Bible Content

1. Jacob starts his journey home. (Genesis 31; 32:1-8, 13-16)

(Rachel on camel 77, Jacob 103, Leah 107, servants 66, 78, flock 74, herd 75, Laban 106.)

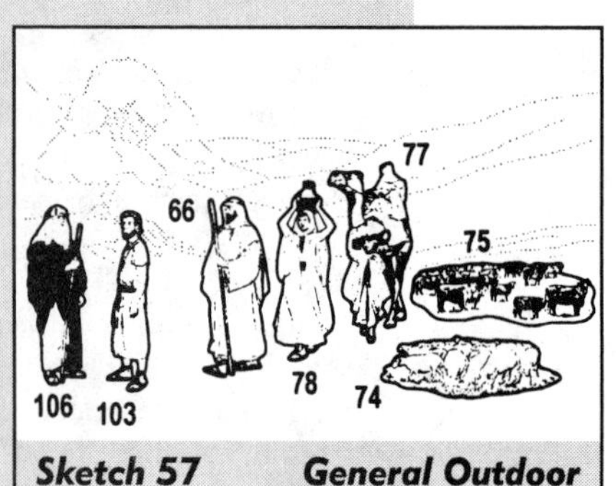

Sketch 57 **General Outdoor**

About 20 years after Jacob left home, God again spoke to him in a dream: "I have seen how Laban has been treating you. I am the God of Bethel where you poured oil on the pillar and made a solemn promise to Me. Leave this land now and go back to the land where your family is, and I will be with you."

Jacob knew that Laban was not happy with him, but he also knew that Laban would not want him and his family to leave. So they packed up and left when Laban was away from home.

They must have made a very long procession. There were servants to help care for the flocks and herds, and servants to care for the family. Jacob's wives and children rode on camels, but the rest walked. At night they stopped and pitched their tents.

When Laban learned that they had gone, he gathered some of his relatives and started after them. It took him seven days to catch up with them. Laban may have been very angry, but the night before he caught up with Jacob, God came to him in a dream and said, "Be careful what you say to Jacob."

So, when he caught up with them *(add 106)*, Laban said only, "Why did you take my family away secretly when I wasn't home? You should have told me you were going so I could have a farewell party for you." Then he kissed Leah and Rachel and his grandchildren good-by and went back to his own home *(remove 106)*.

Jacob and his family continued on their way to the land where his father Isaac lived. When they were getting close to home, Jacob sent messengers ahead to find his brother Esau and tell him they were coming. How would you have felt if you were Jacob about to meet the brother you had wronged? He must have felt very guilty and wondered if Esau were still angry enough to want to kill him.

The messengers returned with the news that they had found Esau, that he was coming to meet Jacob, and that he had 400 men with him. When Jacob heard that, he became very frightened and wondered what he should do. He didn't immediately remember God's promise to take care of him. Instead, he decided to divide all the people and all the animals that were with him into two groups. "Then," he thought, "if Esau attacks one group, the other will be able to escape."

▲ Option#4:

Copy Jacob's prayer on a card and give it to one of the children to read aloud when you come to this point in the story.

But then Jacob stopped to pray: ▲#4 "O God, You told me to go back to my land and You would take care of me. I did not deserve Your faithfulness to me all these years. I only had my walking stick when I left home. Since then You have given me a family and many animals and servants. Now I am afraid that Esau is coming to kill me and my family. You have said that You would make my descendants as the sand on the seashore. Save me from my brother; take care of us."

After that he decided to send Esau a gift. First he sent a servant driving 220 goats. A little way behind came another servant driving 220 sheep. Then came a third servant with 30 mother camels and their baby camels. A fourth servant followed with 40 cows and ten bulls. Finally came a servant with 30 donkeys. Jacob must have had many thousands of animals to be able to give such a large gift to Esau.

Note:

There is some uncertainty as to the exact meaning of Jacob's new name. The KJV suggests that Israel has the idea of a high ranking position bestowed by winning a contest, so includes the word *prince* in Genesis 32:28.

Most other translations reflect the actual etymology of the word and the struggle of the contest by suggesting the word to mean "contender with God."

Although Jacob never obtained royalty, he was greatly blessed by the Lord through his life-changing experience at Peniel.

2. Jacob becomes Israel, a prince. (Genesis 32:9-12, 16-32)

(Angel 83, Jacob 103, new word strips JACOB and ISRAEL.)

They were camped by a brook called Jabbok. That night Jacob sent his family and all his possessions across the stream. Then he was left alone. Eventually he would have to face Esau himself. Perhaps he wanted to be alone with God.

Suddenly a man appeared in the darkness. Jacob didn't know who he was and they began to wrestle. As morning began to dawn, Jacob realized that this was not an ordinary man; maybe he was an angel from the Lord. The angel grabbed Jacob's hip, putting it out of joint. Jacob was disabled and unable to continue wrestling. All that he could do was hold onto the angel and say, "I will not let you go unless you bless me."

Sketch 58 **River**

The angel replied, "You will have a new name now. Instead of being called Jacob, you will be called 'Israel,' which means *one who struggled with God." (Use new word strips here.)* After blessing Jacob, the angel left *(remove 83).*

Jacob said, "I have seen God face to face and my life has been spared." He named the place Peniel, which means the face of God.

As Jacob crossed the brook to meet his family he walked with a limp, but his face must have showed great joy for all that had happened between God and him. He was disabled for the rest of his life. Perhaps the limp became a reminder of what God had done for him.

3. Jacob is reunited with Esau. (Genesis 33:1-16)

(Jacob 103, Rachel 105, Leah 107, servants 92, Esau 91)

Sketch 59 **River**

Later that day Jacob saw Esau coming with his band of 400 men. When they got closer, Jacob saw that Esau was running to meet him. The brothers hugged each other and cried together. It had been more than 20 years since they had seen each other. God had taken away Esau's desire to kill Jacob. Esau had become so wealthy that perhaps he no longer cared about losing the blessing. God had answered Jacob's prayer by taking care of him even though he did not deserve it. God had begun a "good work" in Jacob's life and was working to finish it in order to make Jacob a man of faith.

■ Conclusion

Summary

(Esau 99, Jacob 103, boy 13, shoes BELIEVE 53, OBEY 54, word strip UNBELIEF 45.)

Place 53 and 54 on one side of the board. You or a child may then place them below each character as indicated in the text. ▲#5

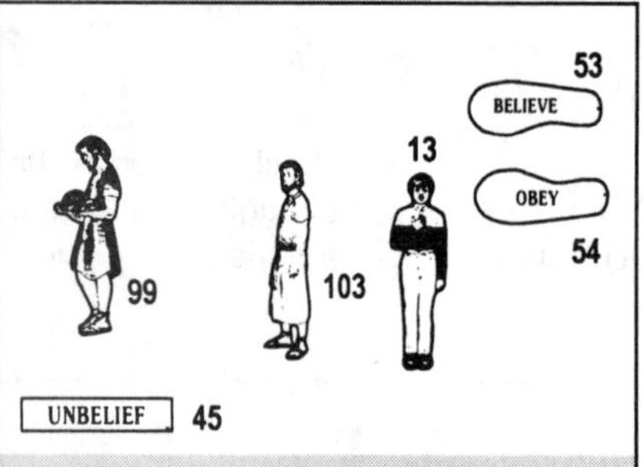

53 BELIEVE
13
OBEY
54
99
103
UNBELIEF 45

Sketch 60 **Plain Background**

Let's put these two figures on the board again to represent Esau and Jacob *(place 99 and 103 left and center)* and talk about how they "walked" before God. *(Encourage response throughout.)*

How did Esau walk? Did he BELIEVE God? No, he didn't. How do you know? *(He sold his birthright and married foreign women.)* Esau went his own way. So we can't put BELIEVE under him. If he didn't believe God, did he OBEY God? No, he didn't. *(Ask for a volunteer to remove both shoes and stand in stocking feet. Talk about how hard it would be to walk everywhere without any shoes.)* We will have to put UNBELIEF under Esau *(place 45 under 99)*. His unbelief separated Him from God.

Now let's think about how Jacob walked. What shoes will "fit" him? Yes, he finally learned to walk with both of them. First, he learned to BELIEVE God and not try and work everything out by himself *(place BELIEVE shoe under 103)*. Gradually he also learned to OBEY God. *(Place OBEY under 103; talk about how much easier it is to walk when wearing both shoes.)*

God kept working in Jacob's life because He wanted to teach Jacob to walk in His ways and become a man of faith. Let's list some things that happened to Jacob that God used to cause him to change. *(Discuss situation with Esau, being deceived by Laban, meeting the angel, etc.)* God never gave up on Jacob. He wanted Jacob to learn to trust or BELIEVE in Him *(place 53 under 103)* and then to OBEY Him *(add 54)*.

▲ Option#5:

Bring a pair of large shoes to class. Attach a card to each shoe—one labeled BELIEVE; the other, OBEY.

As you discuss the characters, have children take turns walking in whichever shoe is indicated in the text.

Application

These two words (BELIEVE and OBEY) are very important and remind us of what God wants us to do in order to be like the Lord Jesus. We must "walk" or live in God's ways. This boy *(place 13 on board)* represents you and me. Which shoes are you wearing in your life? Which shoes can we place under him? Are you wearing both shoes of BELIEVE and OBEY? Or are you like Esau with UNBELIEF in your life?

Our verse tells us it is God that does a good work in us. How does He do that? *(Encourage response.)* First, you must put on the BELIEVE shoe by receiving the Lord Jesus as your Savior *(place 53 under 13).* ▲#6 When you do that, God puts His life in you.

God then wants each of us to become like His Son the Lord Jesus by putting on the OBEY shoe *(place 54 under 13).* As we obey what God tells us in His Word, God works in us to make us more like Jesus in every area of our lives—our thoughts, actions, words and attitudes.

Let's make a list of some of the ways we can show we obey God and are becoming more like His Son. *(Write responses on newsprint or chalkboard for all to see. Some suggestions: forgiving someone who treats them unfairly, getting homework done on time, choosing not to use bad language, obeying parents or teacher, telling the truth, choosing good TV and videos to watch.)*

Because you have BELIEVED God and He lives in you, He promises He will help you to OBEY in these areas *(place 54 under 13).* As you trust Him and continue to obey His Word, He will make you more and more like the Lord Jesus.

Let's say our memory verse together to remind us that it is God who does the work and that He never gives up on us. *(Say verse aloud together.)*

▲ Option#6:

Again, have two children put on the real shoes as you talk.

Response Activity

Distribute the sets of BELIEVE and OBEY footprints you have made for the children (or the footprints the children made themselves if you used the Pre-session option) along with pencils.

Challenge those who have not put on the BELIEVE shoe by trusting Jesus as Savior to trust Him now and allow God to begin a good work in them. Give them opportunity to talk with teacher or helper immediately. Have those who make this decision sign their names and write the date on the back of their BELIEVE footprints.

Have those who say they have already trusted Jesus and are walking in the BELIEVE shoe write their names on back of their BELIEVE footprints. Then encourage them to decide to please God by walking in the OBEY shoe from now on.

Ask all the children who have trusted Jesus to think of an area where they need to start obeying God right now and write that on the back of their OBEY footprint. Then take time to pray that God will help each one obey this week.

Instruct the children to take the footprints home and put them where they will see them and be reminded to OBEY. Give opportunity next week to share what God has been doing in their lives.

Joseph — An Obedient Son

Theme: God Calls Us — To Do His Will

Lesson

13

BEFORE YOU BEGIN...

Does God make bad things happen to His children? Why do we sometimes get into trouble for doing the right thing? Why bother to obey God when people make fun of us as a result? Though we don't have all the answers for these troubling questions (and we can tell the children that), we can gain some insight through the life of Joseph. Favored by his father, hated and sold into slavery by his brothers, this teen-ager had no way of understanding what was happening or what the future held. Yet he always trusted God and honored Him.

Through Joseph we learn several things: that God doesn't always take away the hard things in our lives, but He will help us IN them. That our attitudes and reactions make a difference. That God wants us to obey Him and live so others can see that we are trusting Him. And that whatever happens, God will always bless us when we trust Him and obey. "And we know that all things work together for good to those who love God, to those who are the called according to His purpose" (Romans 8:28, NKJV).

AIM:

That the children may

- Know that God wants them to do His will.
- Respond by deciding to do God's will by obeying what He says in His Word.

SCRIPTURE: Genesis 35, 37.

MEMORY VERSE: Psalm 40:8

I delight to do thy will, O my God: yea, thy law is within my heart.

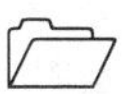

MATERIALS TO GATHER

Visual for Psalm 40:8
Backgrounds: Review Chart, Plain, General Outdoor, Plain with Tree
Figures: R1-R13, 5, 36, 51, 56, 79, 92, 93, 103, 104, 105, 108, 109, 110, 111, 112
Special:

- ***For Review Chart:*** Chalkboard & chalk or newsprint & markers or new word strips with Bible character names from review game printed on them.
- ***For Memory Verse:*** New word strips CHOOSE, TRUST, OBEY.
- ***For Introduction:*** New large card TEST TODAY.
- ***For Conclusion:*** New word strips for Joseph acrostic: -ESUS, -UTCAST, -OLD, -NVIED, -IT, -ATE (print words in a size proportionate to the JOSEPH letters); 3- x 5-inch cards, pencils.
- ***For Options:*** Additional materials for any options you choose to use.

Review Token:

REVIEW CHART

Display Review Chart with R1-R11 in place. Have R12 and R13 ready for use where indicated. Using the following Bible verses in any order, conduct a Bible drill to review the characters studied in previous lessons. Ask the children to locate the verse you give, find there the name of one character they have studied, then stand and say the name aloud. As they find the names, write them on chalkboard or newsprint or put up word strips you have made ahead of time. ▲#1

Genesis 2:23 - Adam
Genesis 16:4 - Hagar
Genesis 22:2 - Isaac
Genesis 4:1 - Eve
Genesis 24:51 - Rebekah
Genesis 7:1 - Noah
Genesis 25:25 - Esau
Genesis 12:1 - Abraham (Abram)
Genesis 25:31 - Jacob
Genesis 13:11 - Lot
Genesis 35:19 - Rachel

Place R12 on the chart as you review the theme and memory verse from Lesson 12. Introduce the new theme briefly as you add R13.

`The symbol we add to the telephone today tells us that God calls us to do His will. *(Add R13. Give a more complete explanation of the theme as you present the memory verse.)*

▲ Option#1:

Have the children tell about or pantomime a test each of these individuals had to face. When a child does a pantomime, have the class guess the character and what the test was.

Or, ask a different child to read each verse as the others listen. Let the first one who recognizes the character and stands place the word strip on the board.

Or, divide the class into small groups and give each group several verses. Have them find the name of the Bible character and write the test each had to face.

♥ MEMORY VERSE

Use verse visual from Bible Verses Visualized *to teach Psalm 40:8. Have word strips CHOOSE, TRUST, OBEY ready to use. Encourage response throughout.*

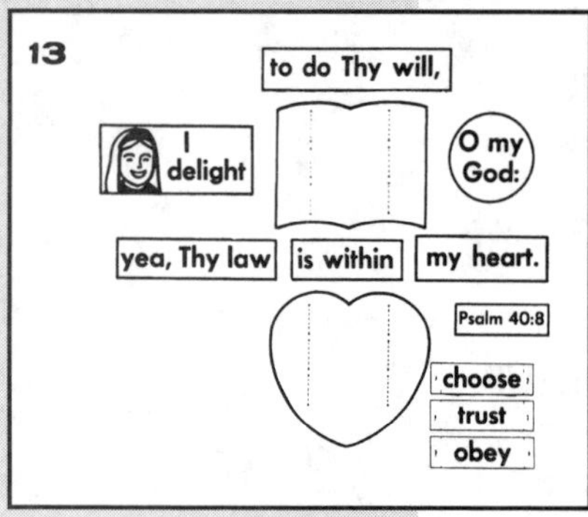

Our new memory verse tells us something that King David wrote about himself. *(Display the first half of verse visual and read it together.)* What does this part of the verse tell us David did? *(David delighted to do God's will.)* It means David was happy to do whatever God wanted him to do. ▲#2

In the last part of the verse David tells us something about God's law. *(Display the remainder of the verse visual and read it together.)* What is it? *(God's law was within his heart.)* David had learned God's commands—His law—and said that he was glad to do them. Even though David sometimes failed to obey, deep down in his heart he wanted to please God by doing what God said.

Many years later the Lord Jesus repeated these same words from Psalm 40 to express how He felt about God's will. Like David, He was delighted (or glad) to do what God wanted. Unlike David, He was always obedient.

Can we use these same words to tell how we feel about doing God's will? It is a good thing to want to do God's will, but how can we know what God's will is for us today?

To have God's Word in your heart means to learn about it, to love it and then to obey it. When we learn verses from God's Word, we are finding what God's will is for us. When we memorize them and put them into practice in our lives, we are hiding them in our hearts where nothing can ever take them away. God shows us His will through His Word, the Bible.

We have learned three important words in earlier memory verses: *choose* in Joshua 24:15, *trust* in Proverbs 3:5, and *obey* in Acts 5:29. *(Place word strips on verse visual as you mention each word.)* Each of these things is included in God's will for us. What are we to choose? *(Whom we will serve)* Who are we to trust? *(the Lord)* Who are we to obey? *(the Lord)* But they must be more than just words on a page in our Bibles *(lay word strips in your Bible)*. They must become a part of our lives so that we will naturally obey them. *(Move words from Bible to heart visual; work on drilling the verse and reviewing its meaning.)* ▲#3

▲ Option#2:

To help the children understand "God's will," review one or all of these memory verses: Acts 5:29, Proverbs 3:5, Joshua 24:15, Galatians 6:7, using visuals if necessary. Have them identify "God's will" for them from each verse.

▲ Option#3:

Learning the verse: Mix the verse visual pieces on a table. Have children each take a piece and place it on the board in correct order. As each piece goes up, allow a child to try to say the complete verse. When all pieces are on the board, have half the class say the first word, the other half, the second word, and so on back and forth. Then try to do it without the visual.

BIBLE LESSON OUTLINE

Joseph – an Obedient Son

■ Introduction

Taking tests.

Bible Content

1. Joseph learns from his father.
2. Joseph receives a special coat.
3. Joseph tells his dreams.
4. Joseph obeys his father.
5. Joseph is sold to the merchants.
6. Jacob sorrows for Joseph.

Conclusion

Summary

Application

God's test for us.

Response Activity

Choosing God's way of salvation.
Writing on a card how they will obey God's will this week.

BIBLE LESSON

Introduction

Taking tests.

Place the word card TEST TODAY in a visible place at the front of the room before the children arrive.

How did you feel when you saw this sign as you came in? *(Encourage children to express their reactions.)* What kinds of tests have you had to take? Do you realize that we all take tests every day of our lives, often without being aware of them? What are some of these tests? ▲#4

In school we take tests in different subjects. Our ability is tested when we try out for a sports team or a musical group. Why do we need tests? *(Wait for children to answer questions.)* They show us how much we have learned about a certain subject, or how much we have practiced in sports or music, or just how well we have listened.

We have learned that God often tests us who are His children to see if we are willing to trust Him, or how well we have learned what He has been teaching us. Sometimes He asks us to do things that are hard to understand or difficult to obey. We have met several people who were tested by God. Can you remember who they were? *(Have children name some—e.g., Abraham, Isaac, Jacob.)* Today we will meet another one. His name is Joseph. He had to face some very difficult tests in his lifetime. Let's see if we can identify some of his tests and how well he did in each of them.

▲ Option#4:

Use pictures of some of these examples to stimulate thinking about tests. Have children tell what test each picture shows.

■ Bible Content

1. Joseph learns from his father. (Genesis 34:1; 35:1-26)

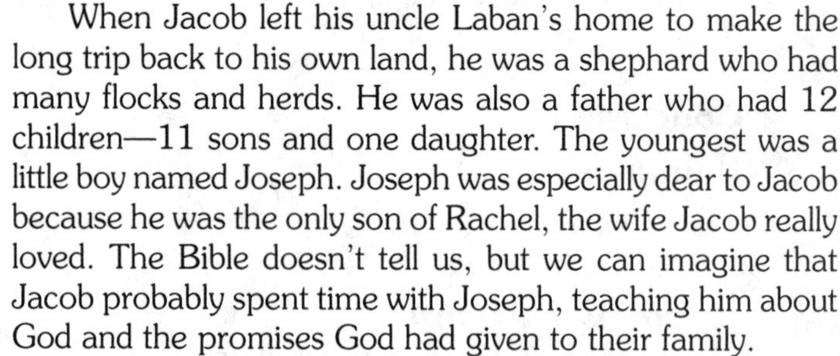

(Jacob 103, Rachel 105, Joseph 108, altar 36, offering 39.)

When Jacob left his uncle Laban's home to make the long trip back to his own land, he was a shephard who had many flocks and herds. He was also a father who had 12 children—11 sons and one daughter. The youngest was a little boy named Joseph. Joseph was especially dear to Jacob because he was the only son of Rachel, the wife Jacob really loved. The Bible doesn't tell us, but we can imagine that Jacob probably spent time with Joseph, teaching him about God and the promises God had given to their family.

Sketch 61 General Outdoor

As they traveled, they came one day to Bethel, the place where Jacob had dreamed of the ladder reaching from heaven to earth. He had wonderful memories of that place and all God had said to him there. Probably he thought about all the ways God had kept His promises and helped him during these 20 years. Perhaps Joseph watched as his father built an altar and worshiped God before they went on.

▲ Option#5:

Review the promises, placing word strips 67-70 on the board. Or, have the children recall each promise and review its meaning as a child places its word strip on the board.

After this God appeared to Jacob again, reminding him of the promises He had given to Abraham, then to Isaac, and now to Jacob and the nation of Israel, of which Jacob was now the leader. ▲#5

While they were still traveling, Rachel gave birth to another baby boy. Jacob and Joseph both must have been very happy with this little baby brother. Jacob named him Benjamin. But they were very sad, too, because Rachel died just after Benjamin was born *(remove 105)*. They buried her where they were, not far from what we know today as Bethlehem.

Finally the family reached the place Jacob had left so long ago. They found his father Isaac still living, but now an old man. He must have been very glad to see Jacob and meet his large family. And the children must have been happy to meet their grandfather. At last they could settle down!

Isaac lived to be 180 years old. When he died, Esau came home and the brothers together buried him.

2. Joseph receives a special coat. (Genesis 37:1-4)

Sketch 62 Plain with Tree

(Joseph 109, Jacob 111, tent 79, Joseph's brothers 51, 56, sheaf 110, star 5, sun 6, moon 7.)

Because Joseph was the son of Rachel, the wife Jacob truly loved, and because he had been born to Jacob in his old age, Jacob loved Joseph more than all his other children. You would think that Jacob would have known better after the problems they had in their home as he was growing up.

Favoritism by either parent in a family is wrong and always leads to trouble.

By the time Joseph was 17, he often worked in the fields with his older brothers caring for the sheep. It was hard work; sometimes they were gone from home for many days at a time. Joseph's brothers were not good men, and their father was afraid that their evil ways would give them a bad name throughout the countryside. He must have asked Joseph how they behaved when he was with them. Because Joseph told the truth about the wrong things they did, his brothers began to hate him.

Jacob showed his love for Joseph by making him a special coat *(place 111, 109 and 79 on board)*. It was a long, flowing robe with long sleeves, like those worn by princes or wealthy people. Whenever Joseph's brothers *(add 51, 56)* saw the coat, they were reminded that Joseph was their father's favorite. They hated Joseph and didn't say a kind word to him. *(Remove 111.)*

Note:

The Hebrew says literally that Joseph's coat was a tunic that went to the flat of the hands and feet; that is, a tailored long-sleeved undergarment that went down to the feet.

The Septuagint translation took the idea of variegated color from the tunic Tamar wore in 2 Samuel 13:18 and superimposed it on Joseph's coat, but there is no mention of color in this text. Joseph's tunic was probably off-white in color.

Tunics were made to be seen, but usually worn under something like a vest or short-sleeved coat.

3. Joseph tells his dreams. (Genesis 37:5-11)

In those days, God often spoke to people in dreams, just as He had to Jacob. One night Joseph had a very strange dream. He told it to his brothers the next day: "We were working in the fields binding up sheaves (or bundles) of grain. My sheaf stood up straight, but all your sheaves came and bowed down to mine." *(Place 110 at the top of the scene.)*

His brothers said to him, "Do you think you are going to rule over us?" And they hated him more than ever.

Then Joseph had another dream and he told it to his father *(replace 111)* as well as to his brothers: "This time the sun and the moon and eleven stars all bowed down to me." *(Add 5, 6, 7 to top of scene.)* Jacob didn't like Joseph's talking about this dream; it bothered him that it seemed to mean that he and all the family would someday bow down to Joseph. His brothers envied and hated Joseph even more.

4. Joseph obeys his father. (Genesis 34:30; 37:2, 12-17)

(Remove 5, 6, 7, 51, 56 and 110, leaving 111 and 109.)

One day Jacob called Joseph to him and said, "I want you to go to Shechem to see how your brothers are getting along with their flocks. Go and see them and then come and tell me how they are." Joseph went at once, even though he knew that his brothers hated him and might be unkind to him.

When Joseph came to Shechem, he found that his brothers had gone to a place called Dothan, ten or fifteen miles farther on. Joseph could have gone home and told his father he could not find his brothers at Shechem, but he knew that his father trusted him. So he kept on going. Finally, he saw them in the fields a long way off.

5. Joseph is sold to the merchants. (Genesis 37:18-35)

(Joseph 109, well 104, Reuben 56, brothers 51, 92, 93.) ▲#6

Sketch 63 **General Outdoor**

Joseph's ten brothers saw him coming and said to each other, "Look, here comes that dreamer! Let's kill him and throw his body into this pit (a cistern or dry well). Then we can say that an animal killed him."

The oldest brother Reuben said, "Let's not kill him; just throw him into this empty well and leave him." He thought he could come back later, rescue Joseph out of the well and take him back home.

When Joseph reached his brothers, they grabbed him roughly, tore off his special coat and threw him into the pit, which was so deep that he could not climb out. Joseph was very frightened and he pleaded with them not to let him die. But the brothers sat down to eat their dinner and paid no attention to his cries.

As they were eating, they saw a caravan of camels coming toward them. Traders were taking spices and other things to sell down to Egypt. Judah suggested, "What good will it do us if we kill our brother? Why don't we sell him to these men instead? After all, he is our brother."

▲ Option#6:

Use this section as a dramatic reading. Assign parts to children ahead of time. In class, read the section as a story for all to hear. Then read it again as the "actors" play their parts.

The brothers agreed to this, so they stopped the traders and told them they had a slave to sell. This was a terrible thing to do. God never intended for people to be bought and sold like animals or property. But it was a common practice in those days. Perhaps the merchants looked Joseph over carefully to see if he was strong and healthy and able to work hard. They bought Joseph from his brothers for twenty pieces of silver and took him to Egypt.

Joseph must have begged his brothers to let him return to his father, but they paid no attention (Genesis 42:21). Instead they watched the caravan go on its way, probably thinking that they were rid of Joseph and would never see him again.

Reuben was not with the others when the caravan came. When he returned, he hurried to the pit, thinking he would get Joseph out and take him home to their father. How terrible he felt when he saw that Joseph was missing! Because he was the oldest, Reuben felt responsible. He went to his brothers crying, "The boy is gone! What am I going to do?"

6. Jacob sorrows for Joseph. (Genesis 37:32-35)

(Reuben 56, Jacob 111, brothers 92.)

Sketch 64 **Plain with Tree**

To cover up the terrible thing they had done, the brothers planned how they would deceive their father. They killed a goat and dipped Joseph's coat in its blood. When they reached home, they took the coat to their father and said, "We have found this coat. Look and see if it is Joseph's."

Jacob recognized it immediately and said, "Yes, it is my son's coat. Joseph has been eaten by a wild animal!" Then he tore his clothing as people did in those days when they were in great sorrow over someone who had died. He mourned and wept for Joseph, thinking he was dead. His family tried to comfort him, but they could not help. I wonder how the brothers felt when they saw their father so sad.

The envy and hatred the brothers felt towards Joseph caused them to want to murder him. They did not actually kill him, but the Bible says that whoever hates his brother is a murderer in his heart (1John 3:15). That hatred also caused them to deceive their father and deeply hurt him and the rest of the family. God saw their hearts; they could not deceive Him. He knew exactly what they had done. He also knew all that was happening to Joseph.

■ Conclusion

Summary

(Joseph 109, letters 112 with acrostic word strips -ESUS, -UTCAST, -OLD, -NVIED, -IT, -ATE; word strips CHOOSE, TRUST, OBEY; 3 x 5 inch cards and pencils.)

Can you name some of the tests Joseph faced? *(Take children's responses before doing the acrostic.)* Let's see if we can match the tests with the letters of his name. *(Place 109 and the letters for JOSEPH on the board. As each test is named, place its word strip next to the corresponding letter.)* ▲#7

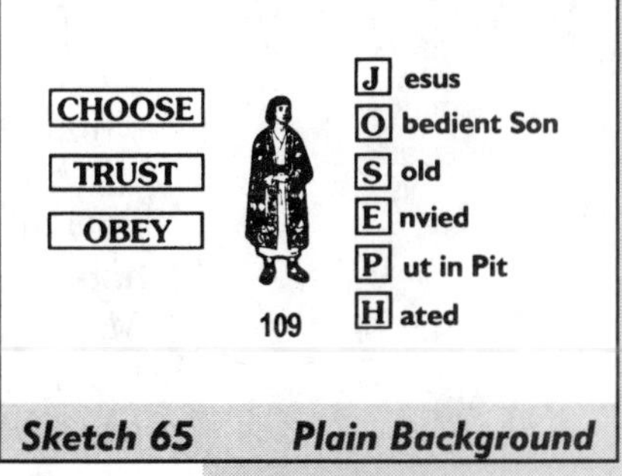

Sketch 65 **Plain Background**

The brothers *E-nvied* Joseph. To envy someone means to be angry with him or jealous because he has something you want. They envied—or were jealous of—Joseph because their father loved him best.

The brothers' envy grew until they began to *H-ate* Joseph. How difficult it must have been for Joseph to be hated by his own family when he had done nothing to deserve it.

Joseph was made an *O-utcast* by his brothers, for they did not even want him around. He was put into a *P-it* and finally *S-old* as a slave into a foreign country.

Why did God allow all this to happen to someone who had done nothing wrong? He was testing Joseph to see if he would trust God and do His will even when things seemed impossible and unfair. God had a plan in all this, although Joseph could not see or know it then.

Joseph reminds us of *J-ESUS* who went through many hard things on this earth, even though he never did anything wrong. He was always obedient to His Father God.

Did Joseph pass his tests? Yes, for he always remained obedient to God and to his father.

▲ Option#7:

Print the acrostic words on construction paper, one to a sheet, with the first letter of each word larger than the others. When a child mentions a test, give him (or her) its sheet to hold at the front of the room. Then have them arrange themselves to spell JOSEPH.

Application

Have you ever faced situations like the ones Joseph faced? *(Encourage children to share some of their own tests.)* Are you ever treated wrongly when you try to do what is right? Do others, even your own family, make fun of you when you live to please God? How does it make you feel? What can we do when that happens?

If we belong to God's family, then we can recognize these hard things as tests from Him. The question is, Am I willing to obey and do what God's Word says when it gets hard? We need to *choose* to do God's will, *trust* Him to help us and then *obey* what He says in His Word *(place wordstrips on board as you mention them).*

The Bible says we are to be kind to others, even when they are mean to us, just as Joseph was kind to his brothers who had mistreated him. That's hard! But when we "delight" (or are happy) to do it because God wants us to, He will give us His strength to help us. Let's say our verse together to remind us of what God wants us to do. *(Repeat memory verse together several times, each time emphasizing a different word: I, delight, do, will.)*

Response Activity

Follow up on the three words choose, trust and obey (which you emphasized when teaching the memory verse) and invite those who have never chosen God's way of salvation to do so.

Encourage the children who belong to God's family to decide how they will obey God's will for them this week. Have them think about the words choose, trust, obey and share their own ideas. Maybe some will need to choose to tell the truth or to act in a loving way toward a family member who is mean to them, or to trust God to supply a need, or to obey their parents.

Pass out the 3- x 5-inch cards and pencils. Give them time to write what they have decided. Take time to pray in class, asking God to help each one to delight to do God's will. If time permits, encourage the children to pray individually, asking God specifically for help in the choices they have made.

Tell the children to take their cards home and put them in a place where they will see them every day. Seeing the card will remind them of what they have decided to do for God. Suggest that they pray each time they see the card, asking God to help them do His will. Give them opportunity next week to tell whether they passed or failed the tests they faced.

HELPS FOR YOUNGER CHILDREN

Review (p.123): Read two or three key verses from the list given for the Bible drill. Have children listen to find the name of a familiar Bible character in each and then tell a test that person faced.

Joseph in a Prison and a Palace

Theme: God Calls Us — To Suffer for Him

Lesson

14

Part One: Joseph Suffers Unjustly

BEFORE YOU BEGIN...

Security and safety—important words for children, for all of us! Yet many of today's children lack both within their families, their neighborhoods and their schools. Every day we hear of boys or girls who are victims of abuse or violence. Whether we realize it or not, some of them sit in our classes crying out for a refuge, for someone to care, to make them feel safe in the midst of their suffering. Though they may not speak, their body language, their attitudes and their facial expressions reveal their need.

In this lesson help your children see Joseph trusting God in the midst of a difficult and unfair life situation because he knew that God was with him, that God was his refuge. Encourage your children to trust God to be their refuge and to depend on Him for help in their hard times. "God is our refuge and strength, a very present help in trouble. Therefore we will not fear..." (Psalm 46:1, NKJV).

AIM:

That the children may

- Know that God is always with His children, even when difficult things happen.
- Respond by claiming God as their refuge and calling upon Him to be their help in every situation.

SCRIPTURE: Genesis 39-40; Psalm 105:17-19

MEMORY VERSE: Psalm 46:1

God is our refuge and strength, a very present help in trouble.

MATERIALS TO GATHER

Visual for Psalm 46:1
Backgrounds: Review Chart, Plain, General Interior, Prison
Figures: R1-R14, 109, 113, 114, 115, 116, 117
Special:

- ***For Memory Verse:*** picture or drawing of a fortress or walled city;
- ***For Introduction and Conclusion:*** chalkboard & chalk or newsprint & markers.
- ***For Options:*** Additional materials for any options you choose to use.

REVIEW CHART

Review Token:

Display the Review Chart with R1-R12 in place. Have R13 and R14 ready to use where indicated. Use the following questions to conduct a brief review of Lesson 13.

Who Am I?

1. I worked for 14 years in order to marry Rachel. *(Jacob)*
2. My mother was Rachel and I was the youngest son. *(Benjamin)*
3. I gave Joseph a special coat. *(Jacob)*
4. My father loved me more than he loved my brothers. *(Joseph)*
5. I tried to keep my brothers from killing Joseph. *(Reuben)*
6. We bought a slave from the sons of Jacob. *(Traders)*
7. I was sold as a slave into the land of Egypt. *(Joseph)*

Have a child place R13 on the chart as you review the theme and verse. If you have time, do a brief review of earlier themes.

The words we place on the telephone today tell us something we don't like to think about: God calls us to suffer for Him *(place R14 on chart)*. What do we think of when we hear the word "suffer"? *(Encourage response.)* It doesn't sound very pleasant and may remind us of pain or of being hurt. But there are other ways people suffer. Have you ever had people make fun of you because you refused to go along with them in doing things you knew were wrong and sinful? That hurts on the inside. It also hurts when people are cruel to us, especially when we have done nothing to deserve it.

The Lord Jesus, God's Son, had the same things happen to Him. He suffered for doing what was right. People made fun of Him. They called Him names and even spit on Him! He was accused of committing crimes when He had done nothing wrong, and He was put on a cross to die. He went through all this suffering because He was obeying God and because He loved you and me so much. God was pleased when Jesus obeyed. Through His obedience and suffering Jesus made a way for us to come to God.

Note:

For Younger Children: Shorten the memory verse to "God is ... a very present help in trouble." Use the parts of the verse explanation that are suitable to them, including the concept of safety, even though the word "refuge" is omitted.

♥ MEMORY VERSE

Use a picture or drawing of a fortress or walled city along with the visual from Bible Verses Visualized *to teach Psalm 46:1.*

As we read our new verse together, look for three things it tells us about God. *(Display verse visual and read aloud with the group.)* What did you find? *(Allow time for children to respond to questions.)*

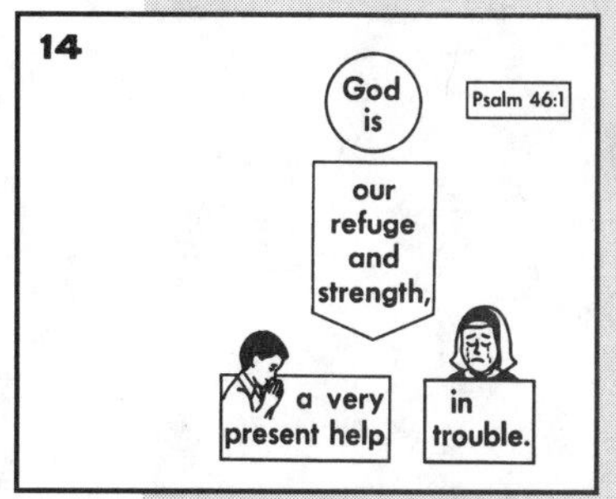

Our verse tells us that God is a refuge, a strength and a help. Who can tell us what these words mean? Why would the Bible describe God as these three things?

Have you ever needed a place of safety from danger? Long ago many people lived in small towns where they had no protection against attacks from their enemies. At one end of the town, or in its center, they would work together to build a structure of high, thick stone walls that had a big strong gate. This structure was called a fortress. (Show picture of fortress.) ▲#1

Someone would stand guard on the wall, and whenever he saw an enemy coming to attack the town, he would sound an alarm. Then the people of the town would run into the fortress and push the huge doors of the gate shut. In the fortress they were protected and safe. The fortress was a refuge, or a safe place, for the people. ▲#2

God does not look like this fortress, but for us He is a place of safety, a refuge from our enemy, Satan. Satan tries to get us to disobey God and to go our own way. If we do this, we often bring suffering and hurt to others and to ourselves. Sometimes we are hurt by the wrong things other people do. But when these things happen, we can run to God and trust Him to care for us and give us strength to obey Him.

Our verse also tells us that God is our help. What does it mean to help someone? (Allow response.) To help means to give someone assistance, to make things better for another. The fortress would do that for the people, but only if they chose to go inside it and close the gate. It is the same with us and God. We must choose to go to God and ask for His help. Then He will give us His help and strength.

Finally, our verse says that God is a "very present help," which means He will help us right now or at any time we ask. No matter what is happening to us, or how bad things seem, or how much we are suffering, we can go to God for help and safety right at that very moment. What a wonderful promise! (Work on drilling the verse and reviewing its meaning.) ▲#3

▲ Option#1:

If your class is large enough, have some of the children form a human fortress or wall; choose one to be a guard and others to be people from the town. Walk them through this description of a refuge.

▲ Option#2:

Definition word card: Refuge = a safe place.

▲ Option#3:

Learning the verse: Use motions with the verse:

"God" - *point upwards*;

"is our refuge" - *hug self*;

"and strength" - *clasp own hands firmly together*;

"a very present help" *point with index finger to palm of opposite hand, then hold both hands out in "palm up" giving position*;

"in trouble" - *cover face with hands*.

BIBLE LESSON OUTLINE

Joseph Suffers Unjustly

■ Introduction

More tests for Joseph

Bible Content

1. Joseph is sold as a slave in Egypt.
2. Joseph refuses to sin.
3. Joseph is sent to prison.
4. Joseph interprets dreams.

Conclusion

Summary

Application

Claiming God as our refuge.

Response Activity

Identifying a difficult problem and trusting God for help to deal with it.

BIBLE LESSON

Introduction

More tests for Joseph

(Newsprint and marker or chalkboard and chalk.)

Tests, tests, and more tests! Do you ever feel like that? Perhaps that's how Joseph felt when he found himself in the strange new land of Egypt. Everything was different. Instead of being a favored son, he was a slave in a country where he knew no one and probably couldn't even understand the language! He must have wondered why God was allowing all this to happen.

Though Joseph didn't know it then, God had a definite plan for his life, for his family and for his people. And to carry out His plan God needed a strong man in Egypt: someone He could trust to be faithful to Him and who would choose to do the right thing even when it would be difficult. God allowed tests in Joseph's life to show whether he was God's man or not. Would Joseph pass these new tests? How would he go through the difficult things God would ask of him?

▲ Option#4:

Print the four Genesis 39 verses on newsprint so all can see them.

Read them aloud as a group or have different children read each one. When they identify the key phrase, underline or highlight it.

Some Bible verses in the story of Joseph give us the answer. In our Bible search let's see if we can discover what helped Joseph and what can help us today. (*Use Genesis 39:2, 39:3, 39:21 and 39:23 to conduct a Bible search. Have the first child to find a verse read it aloud while the other children listen for the key phrase which is repeated in each verse. When they have identified the phrase, print it on the newsprint or chalkboard for all to see. Key phrase: The Lord was with Joseph [him].)* ▲#4

How could Joseph go through these hard tests? By remembering that God was with Him and trusting God to help him. Let's say the key phrase together: The Lord was with Joseph. Today we will discuss some situations where Joseph needed God's help. Let's find out how God was with Joseph and helped — in each one.

Bible Content

1. Joseph is sold as a slave in Egypt. (Genesis 39:1-6)

(Joseph 113, Potiphar 114, Potiphar's wife 115.)

Joseph traveled many days with the camel caravan across the desert until finally they reached Egypt. Everything must have seemed very strange and frightening to him: a foreign language, city streets and crowds of people instead of farm and pasture land, temples where the people worshiped idols, and a king called Pharaoh who ruled the land. He must have felt very lonely and homesick for his father and his home in Canaan.

Sketch 66 **General Interior**

There were many slaves in those days. They were people who had been captured or sold and were forced by their owners to work for no pay. Some worked in the fields and others acted as servants inside the homes of wealthy people. Joseph was sold as a slave to a man named Potiphar, who was the captain of the king's guard *(place 113, 114 on board)*. Joseph worked in Potiphar's house, along with many other servants.

How do you think Joseph felt when he was sold to Potiphar in this new land? *(Encourage response.)* But who did Joseph have with him all the time? Yes, the Lord was with Joseph *(have class repeat the phrase)*. As he worked day after day, he honored God. He was honest and truthful and did his work faithfully, even though it was not easy for him.

Potiphar soon saw that his new slave was different from the other slaves. He was a good worker and he did not worship their gods. Perhaps Joseph told Potiphar about the living God whom he worshiped. When Potiphar saw that the Lord was with Joseph and gave him success in everything he did, Potiphar made Joseph his special helper.

Potiphar did not believe in Joseph's God, but he soon realized that Joseph's God was blessing his household because Joseph was there. Soon Potiphar promoted Joseph again, putting him in charge of all the other servants and everything else he owned. Joseph became the manager of Potiphar's entire household *(remove 114, leaving 113)*.

2. Joseph refuses to sin. (Genesis 39:7-18)

Joseph was young and strong and handsome. Most important of all, he trusted in God and knew that God was with him. This was the reason he looked and acted differently from the other slaves.

Soon, another real test came to Joseph. Potiphar's wife was very attracted to him *(add 115)*, and one day she asked Joseph to make love to her. Joseph knew this was very wrong. He refused, saying, "My master, your husband, trusts me with everything in his house. He has not kept anything from me except you. You are his wife. How then could I do such a wicked thing and, most of all, sin against God?"

But Potiphar's wife did not give up. Day after day she tempted Joseph, and day after day he refused. He knew that if he did not do what she wanted, she could make trouble for him. But Joseph loved God and honored Him with his life. He hated sin and would not give in to her suggestion.

One day when she was tempting Joseph again, she grabbed him by his cloak. He pulled away from her, but as he did his cloak came off. He ran out of the room, leaving it in her hand. Then she became angry. When Potiphar came home, she lied to him, saying that Joseph had tried to attack her and left his cloak behind when she screamed.

3. Joseph is sent to prison. (Genesis 39:19-40:23; Psalm 105:17-19)

(Joseph 113, baker 116, cupbearer 117.)

Potiphar became very angry and put Joseph in the prison where the king's prisoners were kept *(place 113 on board)*. Joseph became a prisoner not because he had done wrong, but because he had obeyed God and done what was right. That doesn't seem fair, but the Bible tells us that while Joseph was there in the prison, the Lord was with him. God was watching over Joseph and working out His plan as Joseph went through this test.

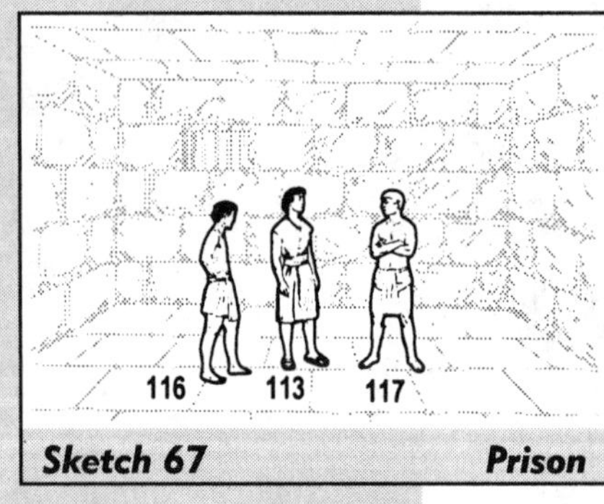

Sketch 67 **Prison**

Joseph was a young man in his twenties when he found himself in this filthy prison where there was probably no fresh air or sunshine. He was bound with heavy chains that hurt him when he moved. There were rough men all around him and the food was probably terrible. Maybe Satan tempted him to think, "God has forgotten me. I did the right thing; I obeyed God. But look at me now. I'll spend the rest of my life here. Is it worth it to obey God?"

But Joseph did not give in to that temptation either. He didn't complain or feel sorry for himself. He knew that God was with him and was taking care of him. The Bible says that the Lord was with Joseph and showed him kindness and gave him favor in the eyes of the prison warden.

Soon the warden noticed that Joseph was different. He didn't complain or fuss. He tried to help the people around him. And he could be trusted. So the warden put Joseph in charge of all the other prisoners. All this was part of God's plan for Joseph and his people, even though the situation must have seemed hopeless to Joseph at the time.

4. Joseph interprets dreams. (Genesis 40:1-23)

One morning Joseph noticed that two of the prisoners were looking very sad *(add 116, 117)*. They were both servants of the king, but the king had become angry with them and put them in prison. Joseph asked, "Why are you looking so sad this morning?" They told him that they each had had a dream the night before and no one could tell them what the dreams meant.

In those days, before God's Word was written down, God often spoke to people in dreams. Sometimes through the dream He would tell them what was going to happen in the future. Joseph said, "God knows what these dreams mean. Tell me what you saw."

One of the men had been Pharaoh's chief cupbearer. ⍓ He said, "In my dream I saw a grape vine that had three branches. It had buds, then blossoms and then ripe grapes. I squeezed the grapes into the king's cup and then gave him the juice to drink." ▲#5

Joseph said, "This is what your dream means. In three days Pharaoh will send for you. You will be his cupbearer again and serve him. But, when you are back in the palace, don't forget me. Ask the king to have me released from this prison. I was brought into Egypt from the land of the Hebrews (Canaan) and I have done nothing wrong."

The other man had been the chief baker in the palace. He said, "In my dream, there were three white baskets on my head. The top one was filled with all kinds of baked goods for the king, but the birds came and ate them out of the basket." ▲#6

Joseph said, "This is what your dream means. In three days Pharaoh will send for you. You will be hanged on a tree and the birds will come and eat your flesh."

Three days later Pharaoh had a birthday and he sent to the prison for his two servants. Their dreams came true, just as Joseph had said. The chief baker was hanged. The chief cupbearer again served the king as he had done before, but he forgot all about Joseph.

And so Joseph remained in prison. This must have been very disappointing, but next week we'll see what God did for him.

■ Conclusion

Summary

(Newsprint and marker or chalkboard and chalk)

Let's identify the things that happened to Joseph after he arrived in Egypt and how God was with him. *(List answers as given on newsprint or chalkboard or print them ahead of time on flash cards or word strips.)* What happened to Joseph? *(He was sold as a slave. Potiphar became his master. He became manager of all Potiphar's household and servants.)* Why did Joseph get such a good job? *(The Lord was with him and he honored God.)*

⍓ Note:

The Hebrew word for *butler* in the KJV is the word for *cupbearer* and was so tranlated elsewhere in the Old Testament.

In Eastern countries, the cupbearer was a highly respected official who poured drink into the cup, tasted it and gave it to the king. He had to be a person of high moral character so the king could trust him not to take a bribe to poison his drink.

▲ Option#5:

Take to class a real grape vine with three branches, three bunches of grapes, a cup of grape juice.

▲ Option#6:

Take to class three baskets, stacked, with bread rolls in the top one.

Then Potiphar put Joseph in prison. Why? *(Potiphar's wife lied, saying Joseph had attacked her.)* When Joseph found himself in prison even though he had done nothing wrong, who was with him? *(God was.)* Let's look at Genesis 39:21; it tells us that the Lord was with Joseph, even in prison. Joseph did not know what would happen to him. He was forgotten by those he had trusted. But he knew God was with him, he knew God was in control, and he trusted God to help him, to be his refuge. *(With the class, read aloud the list you have made, emphasizing "The Lord was with him.")*

Application

Sometimes hard or bad things happen to us too. Can you think of some hard things that could happen to you and cause you to need God as your refuge? *(List responses on chalkboard or newsprint. Use some of the following to stimulate thinking: parent gets sick or loses a job; a brother is hurt in an accident; a house burns down; kids at school tease us or call us names; we get a failing grade.)* What can we learn from Joseph that will help us in our hard experiences? *(Discuss)*

Let's say our memory verse together again, using the motions. *("God is our refuge and strength, a very present help in trouble.")* How can you make God your refuge when something hard or bad is happening to you? *(Encourage answers to see if children understand.)* By remembering this verse—that God is your help in trouble—and asking Him to give you strength to honor Him by how you live in that hard place. Then trust Him to do what He promised and obey what He tells you to do in His Word.

Response Activity

Is there some difficult problem in your life right now? Someplace where you need God's help or safety? *(Allow children to share or think of their problem quietly.)* First, let's thank God for loving us and promising to be with us even in trouble. *(Have several children thank God aloud for this.)*

Next, let's each ask God to help us right now with our problem. *(Allow children to pray silently or aloud, naming their problem to God.)*

Finally, let's thank God for the help He will give and then ask Him to help us continue to trust Him in the problem. *(Allow children to do this silently or ask several to lead in a prayer of thanks.)*

Close by saying the memory verse aloud as a group several times, each time emphasizing a different word: refuge, strength, very present help, trouble.

Joseph in a Prison and a Palace

Theme: God Calls Us — To Suffer for Him

Lesson

14

Part Two: Joseph is Promoted to the Palace

BEFORE YOU BEGIN...

Can God really bring good out of terrible and hurtful circumstances? Can I really obey Him when I'm in trouble? More tough questions, but we find some answers as we watch God's plan for Joseph's life unfold.

Joseph chose to honor God and obey Him—even when he couldn't see an end to his suffering or any good in it. And God brought good to Joseph as well as to those around him: Potiphar, those in prison, the people of Egypt and, finally, his own family. Our children often live in similarly difficult situations. We must guide them to see that God can work in their circumstances if they will honor Him by the way they live, even if it means suffering for doing right. "Oh, love the Lord, all you His saints! For the Lord preserves the faithful... Be of good courage, and He shall strengthen your heart, all you who hope in the Lord" (Psalm 31:23, 24, NKJV).

AIM:

That the children may

- Know that God uses suffering in our lives to accomplish His higher purposes.
- Respond by continuing to live to please God, knowing He is working out His plan.

SCRIPTURE: Genesis 41

MEMORY VERSE: Psalm 46:1

God is our refuge and strength, a very present help in trouble.

MATERIALS TO GATHER

Visual for Psalm 46:1
Backgrounds: Review Chart, Plain, Prison, Palace
Figures: R1-R14, 109, 113, 117, 118, 119, 120, 121, 122
Special:

- ***For Memory Verse:*** Picture or drawing of a fortress or walled city.
- ***For Conclusion:*** New word strips: PIT, POTIPHAR, PRISON, PALACE; "Fortress" reminders.
- ***For Options:*** Additional materials for any options you choose to use.
- ***Note:*** To make "Fortress" reminders, use a copy machine to duplicate pattern R-11 found on page 163.

▲ Option#1:

Provide crayons or markers and newsprint. Have the children review the dreams by drawing pictures of them. Or, have two children be the butler and the baker and use the grapes and basket visuals from last week's lesson to act out their dreams.

REVIEW CHART

Display the Review Chart. Briefly review all the memory verses by reciting them as a group and placing the symbols on the Chart.

To review last week's lesson have several children tell the dreams of the cupbearer and baker and what happened to them. ▲#1

Review Token:

♥ MEMORY VERSE

Use the verse visual from Bible Verses Visualized *to review Psalm 46:1 and its meaning.* ▲#2

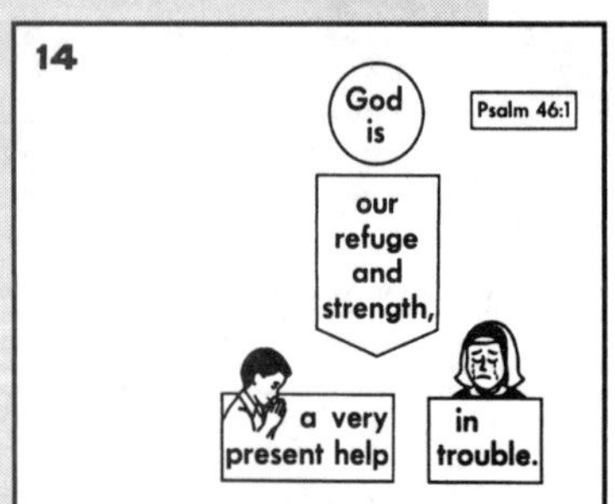

BIBLE LESSON OUTLINE

Joseph Is Promoted to the Palace

■ Introduction

More tests!!

■ Bible Content

1. Joseph is forgotten in prison.
2. Joseph is called before Pharaoh.
3. Joseph interprets Pharaoh's dreams.
4. Joseph is made a ruler.

■ Conclusion

Summary

Application

Joseph's secret of success can be ours.

Response Activity

Using "fortress" reminders to record tests they face this week.

BIBLE LESSON

Introduction

More tests!

(Newsprint and marker or chalkboard and chalk.)

Can you remember a time when you felt forgotten or when no one cared for you? Maybe that is how Joseph felt as he sat in prison. Last week we learned that God put him through some difficult tests. Where did Joseph find his help? *(On newsprint or chalkboard prepare a fill-in-the-blank game to review the phrase "The Lord was with Joseph." For example: T_ _/_ _ _D/_a_/_ _th/_o_ _ _ _. When the children have completed the puzzle, repeat the sentence together.)*

Sometimes in school, especially in the higher grades, you have to take many tests in one week in order to be promoted to a higher grade. It seems hard at the time, but if you pass you soon forget all about the tests. You just look forward to being promoted to the next grade. Like Joseph, we can say "The Lord is with me!" Let's say it together. *(Do so.)* Now let's say it one more time, but this time put your own name in place of me. *(Do so.)*

God wanted to promote Joseph to a high position. He allowed even more tests to come to Joseph to see if he could be trusted to walk in the footsteps of believing and obeying. We will see today if he passed them all and how God continued to show Joseph He was with him.

Option#2:

Reviewing the verse: Verse relay: Before class, print verse and reference on a sheet of paper. Make as many copies as you will have teams in your class (2-4). Cut words and reference apart. Put each set of pieces in an envelope.

In class, divide group equally into teams and designate one on each team who can say the verse to be "verse checker." Line up teams. Have verse checker with envelope at the far end of the room. *Explain the rules.* At the signal, the first person on each team runs to their checker, takes the envelope, empties it and puts the pieces in correct order. The checker OKs it if correct and mixes the pieces and puts them back in the envelope while the first child runs back to tag the second child who repeats the action. The first team to get all their people through and say the verse as a group wins.

For a smaller class, prepare one envelope and have each person play against the clock. Give each one a second turn to improve his time.

Bible Content

1. Joseph is forgotten in prison. (Genesis 40:23; 41:1)

(Joseph 113.)

Last week we left Joseph in prison, forgotten by the chief cupbearer. *(Encourage the children to help you bring the story up to date.)* Maybe he woke up each morning hoping that the cupbearer had remembered to tell the king about him and that someone would come and take him out of prison. If that is what he thought, he was disappointed. Two long years passed and he was still a prisoner.

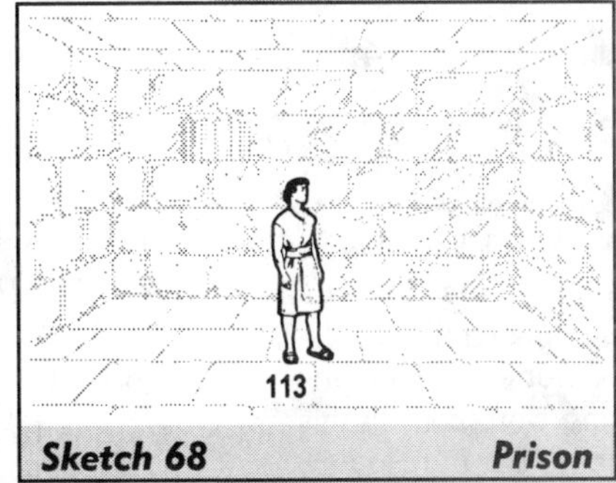

Sketch 68 **Prison**

The waiting must have been a hard test, but Joseph was learning that God was his refuge, his strength and his help in trouble. As he looked to God for help—not to the king or the chief cupbearer—God kept him strong and peaceful. He went on doing his work faithfully every day, not knowing what God would do or if he would ever be free.

2. Joseph is called before Pharaoh. (Genesis 41:1-24)

(Pharaoh 118, cupbearer 117, cow 119, cornstalk 120, Joseph 113.)

Sketch 69 Palace

One morning there was great excitement in the palace. Pharaoh had dreamed a strange dream the night before and he was very troubled by it *(place 118 on scene)*. He had called all the wise men and magicians and told them the dream, but no one could tell him its meaning.

In his dream the king saw seven fat, healthy cows come up out of the Nile River and begin to eat grass in a field *(add 119)*.Then he saw seven very thin and sickly- looking cows come up out of the river and swallow up the healthy cows. Then he woke up. ▲#3

Pharaoh slept and dreamed again. This time he saw seven good healthy heads of grain growing on a single stalk *(add 120)*. After them seven thin heads of grain, scorched by the sun, grew on another stalk. The thin heads of grain ate up the full heads. ▲#4

The chief cupbearer *(add 117)* was serving the king while the king was telling his dreams to the wise men. Suddenly he remembered Joseph. He said to the king, "Now I remember something I had totally forgotten! I was in prison two years ago with the chief baker. We both had dreams that troubled us. There was a young Hebrew prisoner there. We told him our dreams and he told us their meaning. They both came true, just as he said."

Immediately Pharaoh sent for Joseph. The messenger arrived at the prison in a great hurry. Quickly, Joseph shaved himself and put on clean clothing. Then he and the messenger hurried to the palace.

The king said to Joseph *(add 113)*, "I have had a dream no one can explain, but I've heard that you can tell the meaning of dreams."

▲ Option#3:

Have children role play the seven good and seven sickly cows. Give each player a sign (good cow, sick cow) to hold or hang around his or her neck. As the lesson progresses, have the seven "good cows" sit down.
Or, make a drawing of the cows on newsprint and cross out or cover up the good ones as you tell the story.

▲ Option#4:

Get some real grain stalks from a farm or a craft store to show the class.
Or, show a picture of grain stalks or a drawing you make on newsprint.
Note: Some translations use the word corn in this passage, but the Hebrew means grains. What we call corn today is a New World food and was not known in ancient Egypt. Wheat or barley were commonly grown in Egypt and Canaan.

3. Joseph interprets Pharaoh's dreams. (Genesis 41:25-36)

Joseph spoke boldly about his God, even though he knew the king worshiped the idols of Egypt. "I cannot do it," he said, "but God can give you the answer you want."

Pharaoh told Joseph the dream. When he had finished, Joseph said, "God is showing Pharaoh what He is going to do. The dream means that there will be seven years of great plenty throughout the land, when everything will grow in abundance. Then there will be seven years of famine when nothing will grow. Just as the seven thin cows ate up the fat cows, and as the seven thin heads of grain ate up the good heads, so the seven years of famine will use up all the grain of the seven good years. The reason you dreamed the same thing twice is that God will surely cause it to happen very soon."

Joseph spoke clearly and strongly to the king, for he knew that God was with him and this gave him courage. He told Pharaoh what h to do to prepare for the famine. "Let the king find a wise man to take charge of gathering up and storing part of the food during the good years. Then there will be food for all during the years of famine."

Pharaoh and his officials agreed that this was a good plan, and Pharaoh said, "Where can we find another man for this job, one in whom is the spirit of God?"

4. Joseph is promoted to the palace. (Genesis 41:39-57; Psalm 75:6, 7)

(Joseph 121.)

Pharaoh said to Joseph, "Since God has made all this known to you, and no one else is as wise as you, you shall be in charge of my palace and all my servants will obey your orders. You shall also be in charge of the whole land of Egypt."

Pharaoh took a ring from his own hand and put it on Joseph's finger *(replace 113 with 121)*. With this ring Joseph could seal official papers and orders with the king's own seal. They dressed Joseph in beautiful robes instead of his poor prison clothing. They put a heavy gold chain around his neck and gave him the second-best chariot in Egypt, drawn by splendid horses. When Joseph drove out in his chariot, servants went running ahead to cry out to the people, "Make way!"

Because Joseph had walked with God and trusted Him through many years, he was ready for this promotion. It was all part of God's plan. Because he had said no to temptation and because he had trusted God in all the suffering and difficult places, God could now trust him to stand up for Him in this country that worshipped idols. If Joseph had not trusted God in the prison, he would not have gotten to the palace. God honored Joseph because he trusted Him and obeyed Him.

Pharaoh also gave Joseph an Egyptian girl named Asenath to be his wife, and after a while two little boys were born into their family.

■ Conclusion

Summary

(Large letter P 122, Joseph 109, 113, 121; new word strips PIT, POTIPHAR, PRISON, PALACE; "Fortress" reminders.)

What tests did God allow to come to Joseph? *(Encourage response.)* Did he pass them? Did he get a reward? This letter P stands for the word PASSED. *(Place P on board.)* It also reminds us of the major tests Joseph faced: ▲#5

The PIT — Joseph's first big test was being thrown into the pit and then sold by his brothers. *(Place PIT word strip under 109.)* How did he get through that one? Did he pass?

POTIPHAR — His second big test came when he was sold to Potiphar and became a slave. *(Place POTIPHAR word strip under 109.)* How did he pass this one?

PRISON — *(Place word strip under 113.)* Why was

▲ Option#5:

Allow children to put the words on the board and tell how Joseph passed each test.

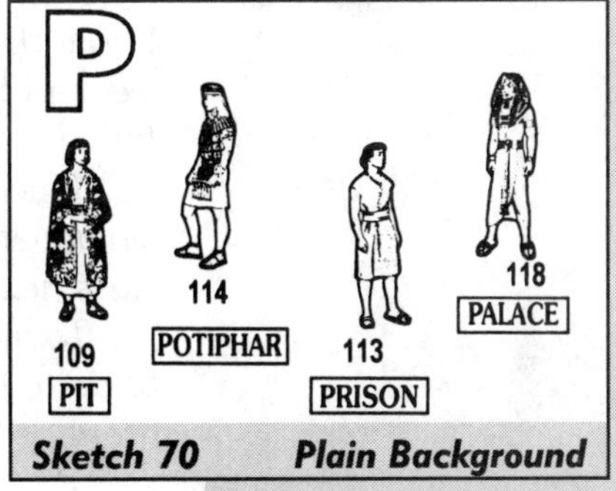

Sketch 70 Plain Background

Joseph put in prison? How was he tested there? Did he pass?

PALACE — Why was Joseph promoted to the king's palace? *(Place word strip under 121.)* Because he had trusted and obeyed God for 13 years. He had passed all his tests. What was his reward? *(He lived in the king's palace and became second in command in Egypt and the means for saving the civilized world.)*

Application

How was Joseph able to pass these tests? He knew that "the Lord was with him." *(Use the visual from the introductory game; read the words together.)* Joseph could stand alone for God and even suffer for Him, because God was with him and was ready to be his help and refuge. *(Say memory verse aloud together.)*

God is ready to do the same for you and me today. Some of you may have to suffer this week because of some "test." How will you face it? Will you complain or give in and fail? Or will you remember that God is your refuge and strength and promises to help you in every situation? Will you ask God to help you so you can pass the test and please Him in it?

God has a plan for your life, just as He did for Joseph's. He will work it out as you pass the tests He allows to come into your life. We can each be like Joseph. We too can stand for God in difficult places, as we trust Him to be our refuge and help every day.

Response Activity

Challenge your boys and girls to be sure they know the Lord Jesus as their Savior. They cannot ask God for His help in the tests they face unless they first belong to Him.

Ask the children to give examples of the kinds of tests they might have to face in the coming week. ▲#6 *If you need to, begin the discussion with suggestions chosen from the following list: Being made fun of for doing right, obeying right away, not using swear words with their friends, allowing only good and kind words to come from their mouths, dealing with a difficult home situation with only one parent, saying no to drugs, or actual written school tests on subjects that are difficult for them.*

▲ Option#6:

Have pairs of children act out some of the following test situations and how they would respond to show they trust in God as their refuge.

Pass out the ***"Fortress" reminders*** *(see Materials to Gather). Show the children how to write some of the tests they face this week in the space provided and then check whether they passed or failed.*

Teach them to pray specifically, asking God to help them in whatever tests they might face each day. Give them opportunity in class next week to share what happened.

To help any who failed to pass a test, talk about what we have to do to improve and then to "pass" the test in the future. Remind them of God's promises in the memory verse, Psalm 46:1.

Joseph Forgives His Brothers

Theme: God Calls Us — To Forgive Others

Lesson

15

BEFORE YOU BEGIN...

What does it mean to forgive? Joseph teaches us by example. Rather than become bitter over what his brothers had done to him, he chose to focus on God who was "with" him. And he learned a magnificent lesson: Though his brothers "meant evil against [him],...God meant it for good" (Genesis 50:20). So he forgave.

Encourage your children to follow Joseph's example, to focus on God who loves them and is always with them, if they have trusted Jesus as their Savior. Teach them how important it is to forgive others and how God says to do it. And talk with them again about whether they have been born into God's family and experienced His forgiveness. Remind them of how they can walk with God by reading His Word, obeying what it says, confessing when they do wrong and experiencing His daily forgiveness. "Therefore,...holy and beloved, put on tender mercies,... bearing with one another, and forgiving one another,... even as Christ forgave you, so you also must do" (Colossians 3:12, 13, NKJV).

AIM:

That the children may

- Know that God wants them to forgive others as He forgave them for Jesus' sake.
- Respond by choosing to forgive those who have wronged them.

SCRIPTURE: Genesis 41:46; 50:26

MEMORY VERSE: Ephesians 4:32

Be ye kind one to another, tenderhearted, forgiving one another, even as God, for Christ's sake, hath forgiven you.

MATERIALS TO GATHER

Visual for Ephesians 4:32
Backgrounds: Review Chart, Plain, Courtyard, Plain with Tree, Palace, General Outdoor
Figures: R1-R15, 1, 13, 51, 55, 56, 66, 79, 82, 83, 92, 93, 106, 111, 121, 123, 124, 125
Special:
- ***For Conclusion:*** Pencils and Heart reminders.
- ***For Options:*** Additional materials for any options you choose to use.
- ***Note:*** To make Heart reminders, use a copy machine to duplicate pattern R-9 found on page 161.

REVIEW CHART

Display the Review Chart. Have selected children put symbols R1-R14 on the chart as individuals or the class repeat the themes and verses. Have R15 ready to use when called for. Use the following "Complete the statement" quiz to review Lesson 14.

Review Token:

1. Joseph's brothers sold him because ... *(they were jealous of him).*
2. Potiphar made Joseph manager of his household because ... *(Joseph obeyed and honored God and God blessed Potiphar's family).*
3. Potiphar put Joseph into prison because ... *(his wife lied about Joseph).*
4. Joseph was put in charge of the prisoners because ... *(the warden trusted him).*
5. Joseph was able to interpret dreams because ... *(God gave him special ability).*
6. Joseph was made a ruler in Egypt because ... *(God gave him wisdom and Joseph lived an honest life).*
7. Joseph was able to pass God's tests because ... *(Joseph obeyed God and trusted Him completely and God was with him).*

▲ Option#1:

Definition word card:
Forgive = cancel the wrong.

Today we place the last symbol on our telephone. It is a command God gives to each one of us who belong to Him. God calls us—to forgive others. What does it actually mean to forgive a person? *(Encourage children to answer your questions.)* To forgive someone means to cancel or erase the wrong they have done and promise never to mention it again, to stop being angry about it. ▲#1

Do you find it difficult to forgive people who treat you unfairly or cruelly? *(Allow response to questions.)* That is pretty hard, isn't it? Usually we don't want to forgive others for hurting us. What do we want to do instead? Yes, we want to get even with them and hurt them. But God wants us to forgive. Our memory verse and Bible lesson will show us how we can do this.

♥ MEMORY VERSE

Use the verse visual from Bible Verses Visualized *to teach Ephesians 4:32.*

Our new memory verse is Ephesians 4:32. *(Display verse visual as you talk and have the group read verse aloud in unison.)*

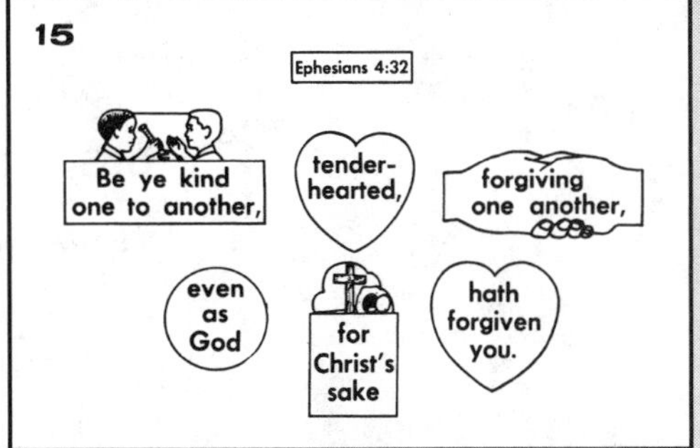

These words are written to Christians. They tell us how we should treat other people. Who can find the three things God wants us to do? *(Encourage the children to identify the three commands and read them aloud.)* That's right. We are to be kind, tenderhearted and forgiving.

To be kind is to be friendly and generous. To be tenderhearted is to be loving and caring toward other people. We have already learned what forgive means. Who can tell me? *(To cancel the wrong others do to us and never mention it again.)* This verse is a command, not a suggestion, which means that if we are to obey God, we must do these things.

Why should we be kind and tender- hearted and forgiving? Because God is kind and tenderhearted and forgiving toward us. Does He forgive us because we deserve to be forgiven? No. Then why does He forgive us? He does it "for Christ's sake." God can forgive us only because Jesus took the punishment for our sins when He died on the cross. Jesus is our example. On the cross He even prayed for those who crucified Him, "Father, forgive them for they know not what they do" (Luke 23:34).

It is not easy to forgive people who hurt or wrong us, but God promises to help us do it because of what the Lord Jesus did for us. *(Drill the verse and review its meaning together.)* ▲#2

▲ Option#2:

Learning the verse: Print the verse reference and each of the words on separate pieces of paper, place them in a bag or basket and shake.

Allow the children a minute to study the verse visual on the board; then remove it.

Have the children take turns drawing a word from the bag or basket and telling the word that follows the one they drew.

Variation: Have them say the word that precedes the one they drew, or the two words that follow it.

Time the game, or declare it over when all the pieces have been drawn. Have the class say the verse together when the game is complete.

BIBLE LESSON OUTLINE

Joseph Forgives His Brothers

■ Introduction

Billy gets angry at his brother.

■ Bible Content

1. Joseph rules in Egypt.
2. Joseph's brothers arrive in Egypt.
3. Joseph's brothers return to their father.
4. Joseph forgives his brothers.
    a. The brothers are invited to dinner.
    b. Benjamin is accused of stealing.
    c. Judah pleads for Benjamin.
5. Joseph's brothers confess to their father and bring the family to Egypt.

Conclusion

Summary

Application

Learning how to forgive others.

Response Activity

Planning to forgive or be kind to a specific person.

BIBLE LESSON

Introduction

Billy gets angry at his brother.

Billy was really upset! He would never, ever loan his brother anything again! Billy's brother had "borrowed" Billy's favorite video game without asking. Then he let some of his friends borrow it and they ruined it! And the worst part was that the game was not available anymore! Billy was already planning how to get even with his brother. He would never, ever forgive him! ▲#3

Joseph found himself in a similar situation with his brothers. They had sold him to be a slave and sent him away to a foreign country! Now he was about to meet them again. What would he do? Let's listen to our last Bible story to see how he reacted.

▲ Option#3:

Ask two children to role play the Billy story, using their own words.

Bible Content

1. Joseph rules in Egypt. (Genesis 41:46-57; 47:13-26)

(Joseph 121, people 55, 82, 83, 106)

Pharaoh's dreams came true, just as God said they would. First, there were seven years of good harvests. Joseph worked hard, organizing and supervising the people who stored the extra grain in warehouses all over Egypt. Finally there was so much that they could not even measure it.

Sketch 71 **Courtyard**

Then the seven years of famine began. Seed planted in the fields didn't grow and finally people had no more food. Then Joseph opened the storehouses and began selling grain.

When the people had spent all their money to buy food, Joseph sold them food in exchange for their cattle. When they had sold all their animals, Joseph sold them food in exchange for their land. In the end, Pharaoh owned all the animals and all the land, and the people rented their farms from him. But they were grateful to Joseph because they knew that he had saved their lives. Joseph had gained great honor and power in Egypt and everyone respected him.

2. Joseph's brothers arrive in Egypt. (Genesis 42:1-26)

(Joseph 121; brothers 51, 56, 92, 93, 123, 124)

The famine was in other countries, too, including Canaan. Word spread that there was food in Egypt and people traveled great distances to buy grain from Joseph who was in charge of the market.

One day Joseph saw ten men dressed like shepherds from the land of Canaan in the crowd. He knew at once that they were his brothers, even though he had not seen them for more than 20 years. They did not know him, because he was dressed as an Egyptian ruler and everyone was bowing before him.

Sketch 72 **Courtyard**

When it was the brothers' turn to approach Joseph, they also bowed down. And Joseph remembered how his brothers' sheaves had bowed down to his in the dream he had so many years before.

Joseph didn't want them to know he understood them, so he spoke to them in the Egyptian language and an interpreter told them what he said. "Where do you come from?" he demanded.

"We've come from the land of Canaan," they answered, "to buy food."

Joseph accused them: "You are spies!"

"No, my lord," they said. "We have come to buy food for our old father and younger brother and our families in Canaan."

But Joseph accused them again! "You are spies!" And he put them in prison. They must have been very frightened of this powerful man.

After three days, Joseph said to them, "To prove that you are honest men, one of you must stay here in prison. The rest of you may take food back to your families. But you must bring your youngest brother with you when you come again or I will not sell you any more grain." Joseph wanted to find out if his brothers had changed or if they were still as cruel as they had been when they sold him. He also wanted to find out if they had mistreated Benjamin when he was gone.

The brothers said to each other, "This is our punishment because of the way we treated Joseph." When Joseph heard them say this, his eyes filled with tears and he had to turn away.

But to be sure they had really changed, he had Simeon tied up and put in prison. Then he told his servants to secretly put the money the brothers had paid into the sacks of grain they had bought. He also gave them extra food to eat on the way home. How do you think they were feeling when they finally started out on their long jouney home without one brother?

3. Joseph's brothers return to their father. (Genesis 42:27-43:15)

(Jacob 111, tent 79; Judah 51, brothers 56, 92, 93, 125.)

Jacob was very old now and still grieving for Joseph. His sons had been gone a long time. He had no way of knowing what was happening. How relieved he was when he saw them coming down the road with the long line of donkeys carrying the loads of grain.

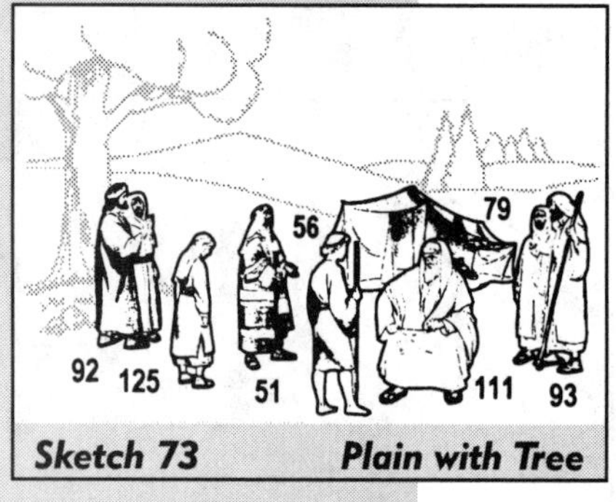

Sketch 73 *Plain with Tree*

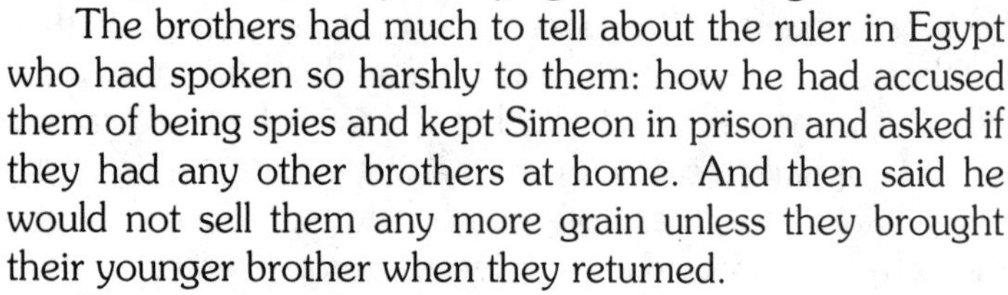

The brothers had much to tell about the ruler in Egypt who had spoken so harshly to them: how he had accused them of being spies and kept Simeon in prison and asked if they had any other brothers at home. And then said he would not sell them any more grain unless they brought their younger brother when they returned.

They were opening their grain sacks as they talked when they found their money inside. They all were frightened! They could not understand the strange things that had happened on this trip to Egypt.

Jacob was afraid, too. He said, "Joseph is gone. Now Simeon is gone. You cannot take Benjamin. If anything happened to him, I would surely die!"

Months later they began to run out of food. Jacob said, "You must go back to Egypt and buy more grain."

His sons said, "We cannot go unless Benjamin goes with us." But Jacob was still afraid.

Then Judah said to his father, "Let Benjamin go with me. I will be responsible for him and promise to bring him back safely."

Finally Jacob agreed, since it was the only way to get food for their families. They prepared a gift of honey, spices, and nuts to take to the ruler and started off on the long trip again. Soon they were back in Egypt.

4. Joseph forgives his brothers

a. The brothers are invited to dinner. (Genesis 43:15-34)

(Brothers 51, 56, 92, 93, 123, 124, 125; Joseph 121.)

When Joseph saw that his brothers had returned and had Benjamin with them, he said to his servant, "Take these men to my house and prepare a meal. They are to eat with me at noon." So the servant took the brothers to Joseph's house.

Sketch 74 *Palace*

They were frightened. "Why are we here?" they wondered. "Is it because he thinks we stole the money that was put back in our sacks the first time?" But the servant treated them kindly and brought Simeon from prison to join them.

When Joseph came in *(add 121)*, they gave him the gift they had brought. He asked if their father was still living, all the while looking for Benjamin, who had been just a little boy when Joseph was sold into Egypt. He was so glad to see him that his eyes filled with tears and he quickly left the room so no one would see him cry.

The brothers were surprised to find themselves seated around the table in order of their ages, from oldest to youngest. How could these people know? they wondered. And why did Joseph send five times as much food from his table to Benjamin as he did to the rest of them?

b. Benjamin is accused of stealing. (Genesis 44:1-17)

As the brothers were getting ready to go home again, Joseph said to his servant,"Fill their sacks with grain and put their money in the top. Then put my silver cup in the sack of the youngest."

When the brothers had gone only a short way, Joseph sent his servant after them. "Why have you taken my master's silver cup?" he demanded. "We treated you well. Why would you steal from us?"

The brothers said, "We have not stolen anything. Search our bags! If you find the cup, the one who has it will die and the rest of us will become your master's slaves."

The servant searched every sack. When he got to Benjamin's, he found the silver cup. The brothers tore their clothing, the way people in those days did to show sorrow and sadness. Then they loaded their donkeys and returned to Joseph.

c. Judah pleads for Benjamin. (Genesis 44:18-45:15)

(Joseph 121, brothers 56, 92, 93, 123, 124, 125; place Judah 51 before Joseph.)

Joseph said to them, "Why would you do such a thing? Didn't you think I would find out? The one who had my cup in his sack will stay and be my servant. The rest of you may go home to your father."

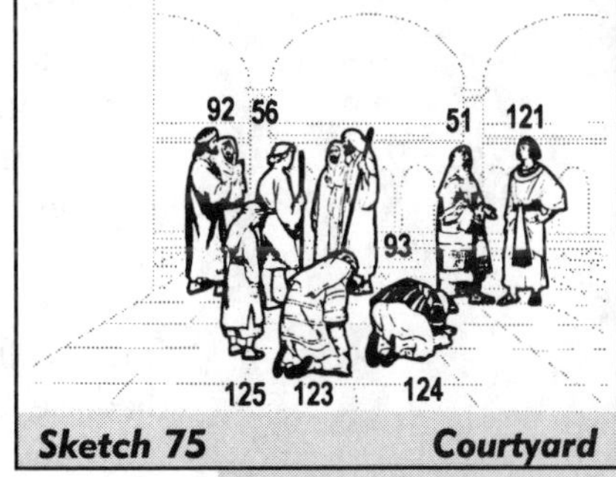

Sketch 75 **Courtyard**

Judah, who had promised he would bring Benjamin safely home, begged Joseph to allow him to stay in Benjamin's place. The brothers were afraid their father would die of grief if Benjamin did not come home.

When Joseph saw how concerned they were for their father and for Benjamin, he knew they had really changed. His heart was so full that he could hardly speak. Quickly, he sent all the servants out of the room so that he was alone with his brothers. Then he began to weep so loudly that the Egyptians in the other rooms could hear him. When he was able to speak, he said, "I am Joseph; is my father still alive?"

The brothers were so terrified that they could not speak. Would Joseph treat them as they had treated him? But Joseph spoke kindly and said, "It was God who allowed you to sell me as a slave, for now

He has given me the power to take care of you and our father. There are still five more years of famine. You must bring our father and your families to Egypt where I can take care of you."

Then Joseph put his arms around Benjamin and kissed him. He did the same with all his brothers and they sat and talked together. Joseph forgave them for the wrong they had done to him.

Joseph gave each of them a new suit of clothes. To Benjamin he gave five suits and 300 pieces of silver. And he said to them, "Take this food and these wagons and go home. Bring our father and all your families back with you. The king says he will give you some of the best land in Egypt to be your home. And please don't quarrel on the way!"

5. Joseph's brothers confess to Jacob and bring the family to Egypt (Genesis 45:16-47:12).

(Jacob 111, Joseph 121, brothers 51, 56, 92, 93, 125.)

Jacob must have watched for them every day. When they finally came, what a story they had to tell! "Joseph is alive!" they said. "He is the ruler of Egypt and wants you to come to him. He has sent these wagons and all this food for you."

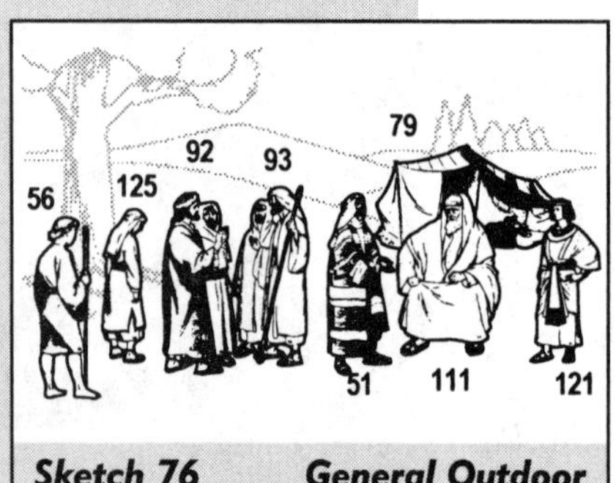

Sketch 76 **General Outdoor**

Jacob could not believe what he was hearing! Joseph was alive! And his sons had been deceiving him all these years! It must have been hard for them to tell what they had done. It is always difficult to confess the sins and wrongdoing we have hidden from others. But they were probably relieved when their father finally knew the truth.

A long procession made that trip to Egypt: Jacob and his 11 sons with all their wives and children, flocks, herds and servants. On the way they stopped at a place where Abraham had worshiped so Jacob could build an altar and offer a sacrifice. That night God spoke to him again: "Jacob, I am the God of your father Isaac and your grandfather Abraham. Do not be afraid to go down into Egypt. I will make you a great nation there."

One brother went ahead to tell Joseph they were coming. Immediately Joseph got into his chariot and went to meet his father. What a happy meeting that was! *(Place 111, 121, 51, 56, 92, 93, 125 on board.)* Jacob said to Joseph, "Now I am ready to die, since I have seen your face again."

The whole family with all their flocks and herds settled in a part of Egypt called Goshen. Jacob lived 17 more years in Egypt. Before he died, he talked to his sons about what would happen in the future and gave each of them a blessing. Then he said, "When I die, take me back to Canaan and bury me in the cave where my father Isaac and my grandfather Abraham are buried." They did as he asked. *(Remove figures.)*

When they came back to Egypt from burying Jacob in Canaan, the brothers became afraid again. They said to each other, "What if Joseph is still holding a grudge against us and decides to get even for all the wrong things we did to him, now that our father is dead?" So they all went and bowed before Joseph again saying, "We are your slaves." *(Replace 121, 56; add 123, 124.)*

But Joseph spoke kindly to them: "Don't be afraid. You meant to harm me by what you did, but God used it to bring about good. He brought me here to save many lives. I will take care of you and your families."

Joseph lived for many years after that. Before he died, he said to his family, "God will lead you out of Egypt some day, back to the land He has promised to give us. When you go, take my bones and bury them in that land." The Bible says he did this by faith (Hebrews 11:22). He knew that God would keep His Word to give the Jewish people a special land of their own and many blessings—just as He had promised Abraham, Isaac and Jacob.

■ Conclusion

Summary

(Memory verse visual, Joseph 121; brothers 51, 56, 92, 93, 125; cross 1, boy 13)

What did Joseph choose to do for his brothers? Yes, he chose to forgive them. Who can remember what it means to forgive someone? *(Response)* It means to cancel the wrong and never bring it up again. ▲#4 Did Joseph show this kind of forgiveness to his brothers? Did his brothers deserve to be forgiven? No, they didn't. But Joseph chose to forgive them.

How did Joseph demonstrate what our memory verse tells us? *(Place verse on board beside Joseph and brothers.)* Yes, he showed kindness. How? He showed he was tenderhearted. How? He showed forgiveness to them. How did he do this? *(Discuss what Joseph did for his family.)* ▲#5

Application

This story of how Joseph forgave his brothers reminds us of someone who forgave us. Let's say our memory verse together. *(Recite Ephesians 4:32 aloud together.)* Who has forgiven us? *(God)* Did we deserve to be forgiven? No, we didn't. Then why has God forgiven us? *(For Christ's sake)* What does that mean? *(That God forgives us because of what Jesus did on the cross)* When we trust Jesus as Savior, God forgives us because Jesus took the punishment for our sin when He died on the cross in our place. And then each day when we do wrong things and confess them to God (or tell God what we did), God cleanses us for Jesus' sake.

This cross *(place ✝ and 13 on the opposite side of board)* reminds us that Jesus died for us even though we did not deserve it and that when we confess our sin God forgives us for Jesus' sake, because He took the punishment for our sin.

▲ Option#4:

Use the definition word card to review "forgive."

▲ Option#5:

Write responses on chalkboard or newsprint as children give them.

This cross also reminds us that God wants us to forgive others just as He has forgiven us, even when they don't deserve it!

Let's go back to Billy and his brother. It would be really hard for him to forgive his brother. What should Billy do, especially since he is a Christian? How could Billy demonstrate our verse? *(Have class discuss choices or role play them.)* Instead of getting angry and trying to get even with his brother, he needs to forgive and be kind, even though he has been wronged.

What about you? Are you like Billy? Is there someone who has done something to you that you can't seem to forgive? Our verse says we are to forgive and be kind to them. But how can we do it? First, by asking God to help us be willing to forgive that person. Maybe you need to tell God you don't feel like forgiving and that you need His help to change your attitude so you can obey what He says.

Response Activity

Invite any who have not done so to talk with you or a helper about receiving Christ as Savior.

Challenge Christians who have just asked God to forgive them for disobeying the commands in Ephesians 4:32 to ask God for help in obeying them instead.

Give each one a pencil and a ***Heart reminder*** *(see Materials to Gather). Encourage the children to think of one person they need to forgive or show kindness to in some way. Have them print that person's name under the words KIND, TENDERHEARTED, FORGIVING and then circle the word that tells what they must do towards that person in the coming week. Lead in prayer or give the children opportunity to pray sentence prayers asking God to help them be kind, tenderhearted and forgiving for Jesus' sake.*

HELPS FOR YOUNGER CHILDREN

Memory Verse: Shorten the verse to "Be ye kind one to another, tenderhearted, forgiving one another...." Explain the idea of the whole verse.

RESOURCE SECTION

Use the materials in this section to help your children incorporate the Bible truths they are learning into their daily lives in a practical way.

Transfer the place locations on the old testament map (R-1) to the flannel background map you use when teaching.

Reproduce the remaining patterns as hand-outs for the specific lessons where they are recommended.

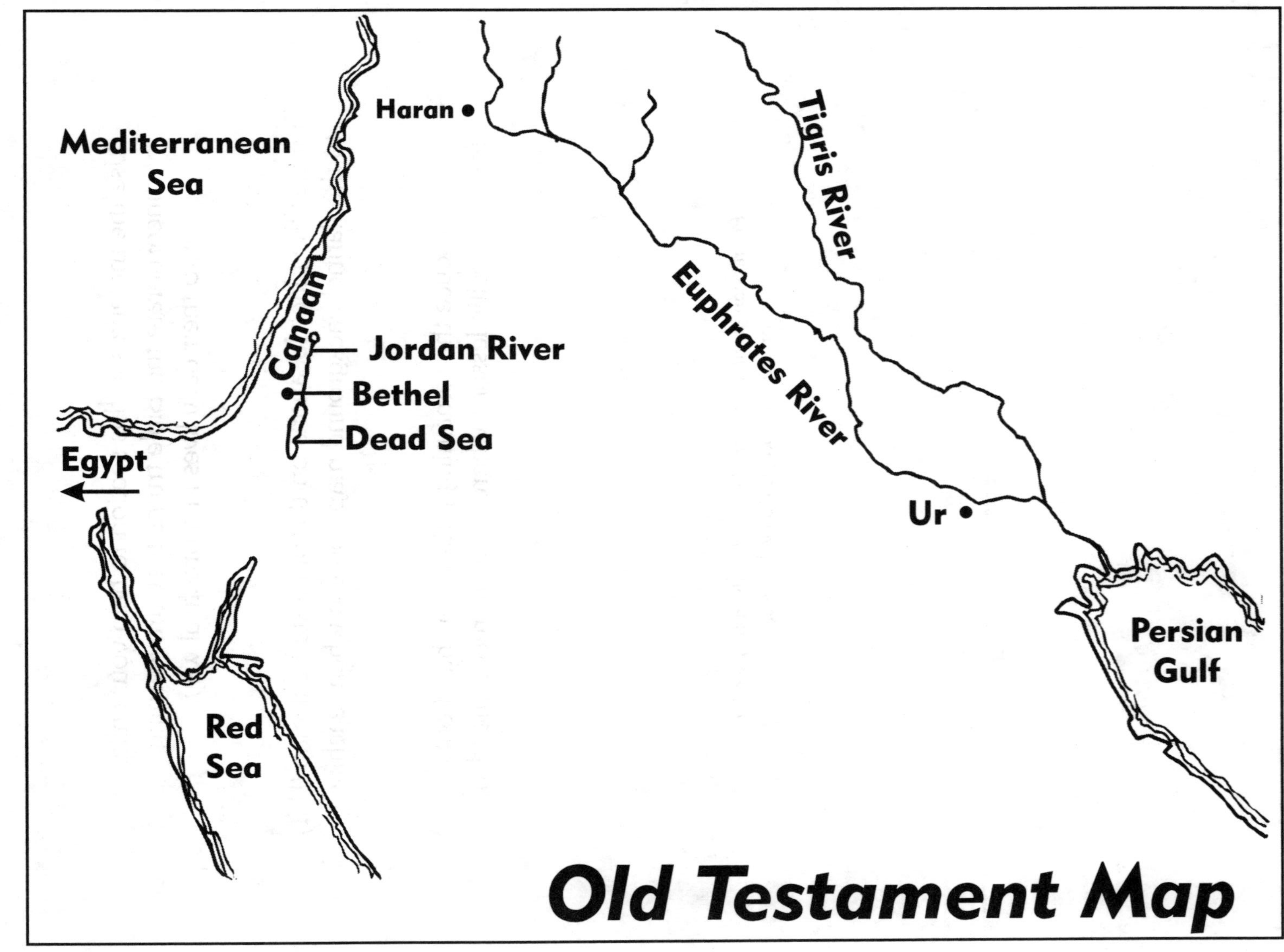
Mediterranean Sea
Haran
Tigris River
Euphrates River
Canaan
Jordan River
Bethel
Dead Sea
Egypt
Ur
Persian Gulf
Red Sea
Old Testament Map

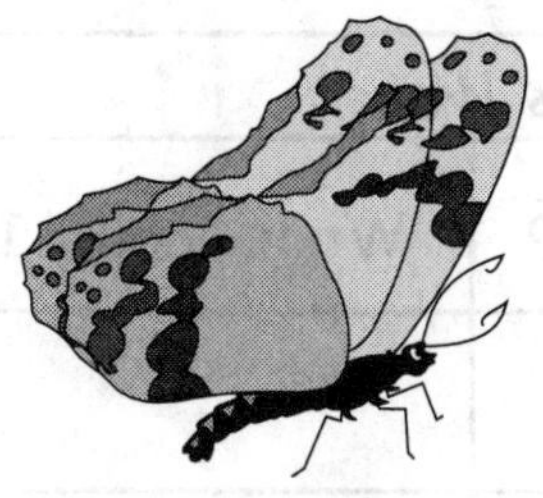

Dear God,

I choose to believe that You created the world and everything in it, no matter what anyone else may say. Thank you for doing such a great job!

Amen.

R–2

Dear God,

Thank you for making such a wonderful world for me to enjoy. Thank you for loving me. I choose to accept the way You made me. I trust You and believe You will always love me and do what is best for me.

Love,

R–3

God Speaks to Me from His Word!		
Bible Verse	What Does God Say?	What should I do?
Ephesians 4:32		
Ephesians 6:1		
Exodus 20:15		
Colossians 3:9a		

R–4

A Choice Between—	I Chose to—	I asked for God's help		The result of my choice
		Yes	No	

"Choose you this day whom you will serve" Joshua 24:15

R–5

"Be not deceived; God is not mocked;
whatsoever a man soweth,
that shall he also reap."

WE REAP WHAT WE SOW!

This week I will trust God to help me sow the "good seed" of ____________________ in my life.

Signed ___________________________________

R–6

Statement of Purpose

I trust You, God, to make me more like the Lord Jesus this week by helping me to _______________

____.

R–7

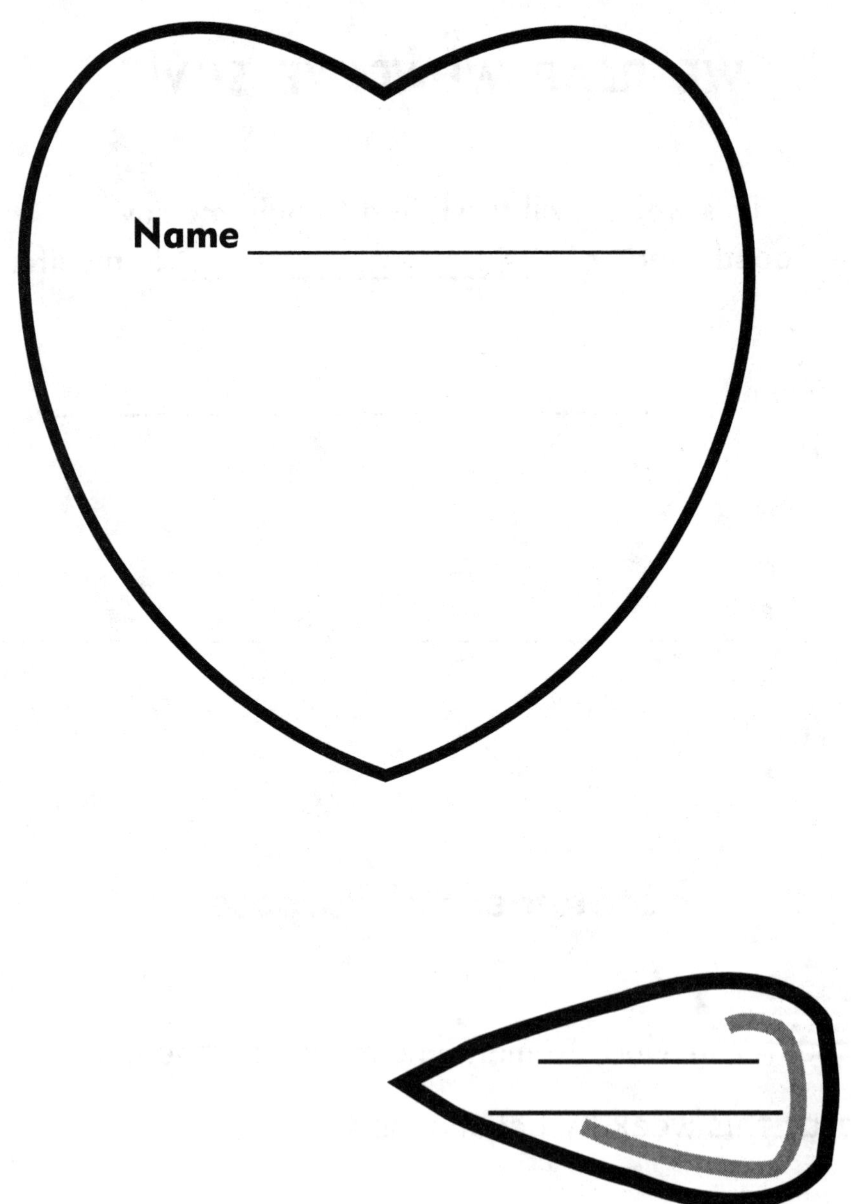

R–8

R–9

R–10

R–11

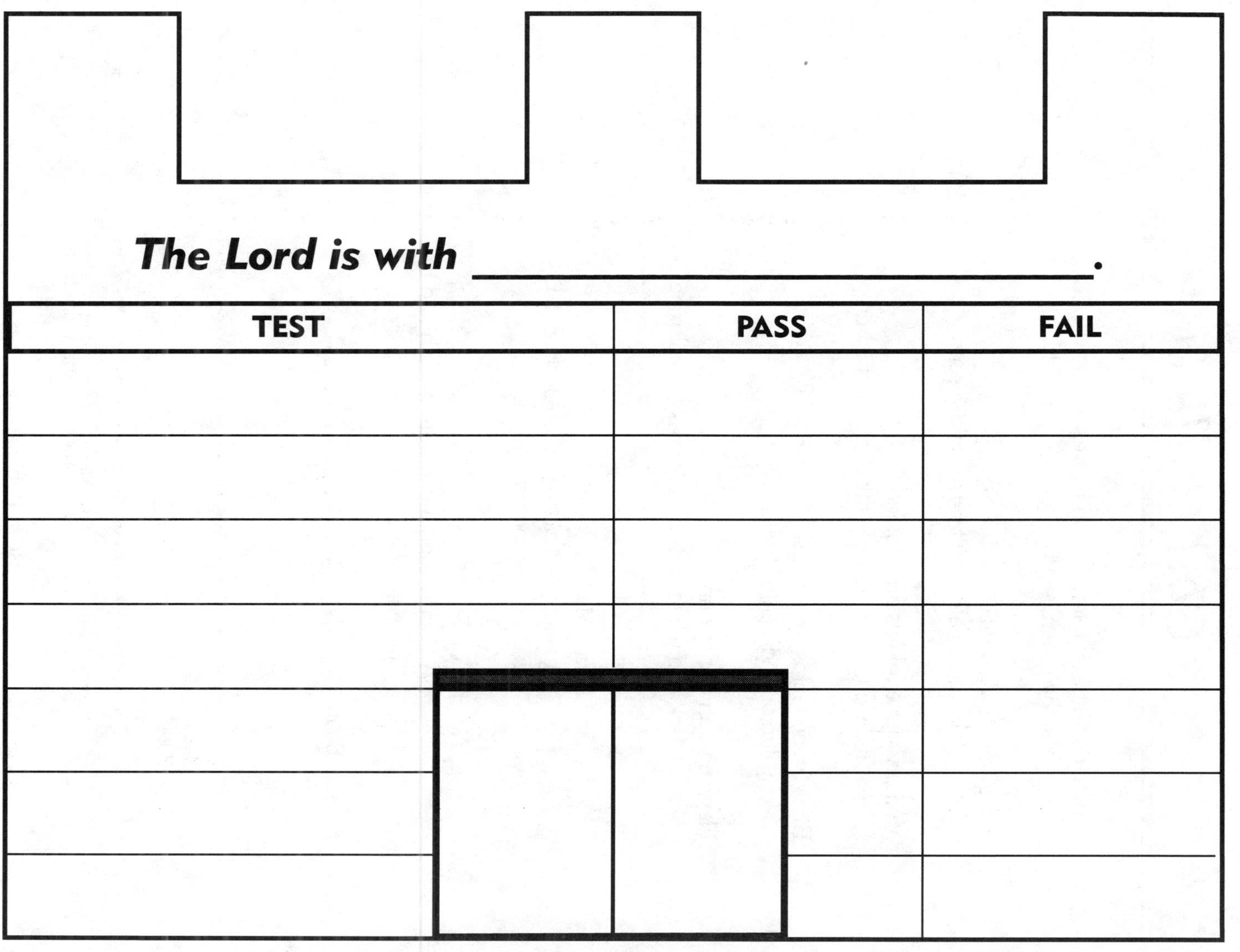

Teaching Materials and Supplies
available for
God Calls Us

Teacher's text and flannelgraph figures packet
May be purchased in a kit or separately.

Bible Verses Visualized *
Colorful visuals for all verses in the series.

Memory verse tokens and holders *
Individual take-home reminders for children.

Bible Study Helps for Genesis
Junior and Senior levels.

Flannelgraph backgrounds
Black and white with instructions for coloring.

Tracts
"God Loves Me"
A salvation tract based on John 3:16.
Use with younger children.

"A Child of God"
A tract presenting salvation truth and basic truths for Christians. Use with older children.

Flannel board

Easel

* Request information about available translations.

To request a catalog or order materials, contact:

BCM Publications
237 Fairfield Avenue
Upper Darby, PA 19082-2299
Phone: (610)352-7177 FAX: (610)352-5561
E-mail: BCMintl@compuserve.com

or a National Office listed on page xi.